More Praise for *Living by the Gun in Chad*

'A welcome contribution, providing a wealth of data and rare detail, resulting in new scholarly insights whose significance goes far beyond Chad's borders.'

Mats Utas, Uppsala University

'A compelling and deeply-informed account of the militarisation of politics and society in Chad. Rather than leading to chaos, it convincingly shows how armed violence produces political order and is a crucial part of daily practices of dominance.'

Koen Vlassenroot, Conflict Research Group,
University of Ghent

About the author

Marielle Debos is an associate professor in political science at the University Paris Ouest Nanterre and a researcher at the Institute for Social Sciences of Politics (ISP).

LIVING BY THE GUN IN CHAD

COMBATANTS, IMPUNITY AND STATE FORMATION

MARIELLE DEBOS

Translated by

ANDREW BROWN

ZED
Zed Books
London

Living by the Gun in Chad: Combatants, Impunity and State Formation was originally published in French under the title *Le métier des armes au Tchad: le gouvernement de l'entre-guerres* in 2013 by Editions Karthala, 22–24 Boulevard Arago, 75013 Paris, France.

www.karthala.com

This edition published in 2016 by Zed Books Ltd,
The Foundry, 17 Oval Way, London SE11 5RR, UK.

www.zedbooks.net

Marielle Debos, *Le metier des armes au Tchad: le gouvernement de l'entre-guerres* © Editions Karthala, Paris, 2013
English language translation © Andrew Brown, 2016, with the collaboration of Benn Williams

The right of Marielle Debos to be identified as the author of this work has been asserted by her in accordance with the Copyright, Designs and Patents Act 1988.

Typeset in Sabon by Swales & Willis Ltd, Exeter, Devon
Index by Ed Emery
Cover design by www.stevenmarsden.com
Cover photo © Espen Rasmussen/Panos

A catalogue record for this book is available from the British Library.

ISBN 978-1-78360-533-0 hb
ISBN 978-1-78360-532-3 pb
ISBN 978-1-78360-534-7 pdf
ISBN 978-1-78360-535-4 epub
ISBN 978-1-78360-536-1 mobi

MIX
Paper from
responsible sources
FSC
www.fsc.org
FSC® C013604

Printed and bound by CPI Group (UK) Ltd, Croydon, CR0 4YY

CONTENTS

. . . .

ACKNOWLEDGEMENTS

The translation of this book was supported by the Centre National du Livre, the Institute for Social Sciences of Politics (ISP-CNRS), and the Marie Curie Alumni Association.

Fieldwork was supported by the ISP as well as by the research programme 'No war, no peace: the interweaving of violence and law in the formation and transformation of political orders', coordinated by Dominique Linhardt and Cédric Moreau de Bellaing and funded by the French National Agency for Research (ANR).

This book is a testimony to the innumerable debts that I have accumulated over the years, starting with my debt to all the people in Chad who honoured me with their trust and shared their insights and stories. For their own safety, they have to remain anonymous. Over the course of fieldwork, three of my informants were victims of forced disappearances: Khamis Doukoun, Abakar Gawi and Ibni Oumar Mahamat Saleh. They should not be forgotten.

Since the publication of *Le Métier des armes* in 2013, a large number of colleagues have provided me with valuable comments and have helped me write a better book. Thanks to their contributions, this book is much more than just an updated version of the first one. I particularly wish to thank Richard Banégas, Gilles Bataillon, Jean-François Bayart, Morten Bøås, Magali Chelpi-Den Hamer, Mirjam de Bruijn, Guillaume Devin, Mariane Ferme, Vincent Foucher, Laurent Gayer, Remadji Hoinaty, Milena Jakšić, Louisa

Lombard, Kelma Manatouma, Roland Marchal and Johanna Siméant.

A special note of thanks to Andrew Brown, who translated the manuscript from French and did a wonderful job with some particularly puzzling translation issues. Justine Brabant was finally an inspiring reader and a wonderful support throughout the many rewritings of the text.

FOREWORD

. . . .

This book is an extensively revised and updated version of a book published in 2013 by Editions Karthala in Paris. It covers the 'inter-war' of Chad: namely, those spaces and times on the margins of war and where war seems emergent. Much has changed since my first fieldwork in Chad, twelve years ago. The combatants I mention in this book have mostly abandoned armed struggle. Some have joined the regular forces, others live by the gun in a militarised economy. Most, however, have returned to civilian life and resumed their lives as farmers or pastoralists.

By contrast, Idriss Déby and his allies now 'live by the gun' on the regional and international scenes. Déby has acquired a new status thanks to Chad's military activism in the region, and the war waged by the army against the rebels is now mostly aimed at elements outside the country. The Chadian army is mobilised on several fronts in Mali and in the Lake Chad Basin. Chad, which hosts the base of the French anti terrorist operation Barkhane, has become a key partner of France and the United States in the 'war on terror'. The need to preserve the supposed 'stability' of Chad encourages its allies to ignore the violence and undemocratic practices there, including the re-election of Idriss Déby in a contested election.[1] Déby knows that his survival depends as much on external support as on internal legitimacy.

As this book goes to press, 'peace' has become a much debated issue. During the campaign for the April 2016 presidential election,

President Idriss Déby, standing for a fifth term, promised on the large posters visible on every street corner in the capital a 'guaranteed social peace'. In response, opposition supporters and civil society activists denounced the way in which 'peace' was being used as a form of 'blackmail'. In an attempt to delegitimise the protests, the ruling party said that these protests constituted threats to the peace and stability of the country. A few months earlier, when civil society organisations created their platform of demands with the slogan 'enough is enough' (*'trop c'est trop'*), pro-government civil society responded by creating its own version, 'hands off my achievements' (*'touche pas à mes acquis'*). In the spirit of the creators of this latter platform, the 'achievements' in question were peace and stability. Activists of the former platform did not fail to point out the ambiguity of the formula: the 'achievements' could just as well be understood as profits from the oil industry, profits monopolised by a small class of political and economic entrepreneurs close to the presidency.

If the main rebel movements have now surrendered, war remains close at hand. Since NATO's intervention in 2011, the south of Libya is a grey area conducive to all sorts of political and military adventures and every kind of trafficking. Veterans of the Chadian rebellion have congregated there. If we take their statements at face value, they are preparing for the next uprising – but the initial combats have been between the different factions claiming to represent the Chadian opposition. The other borders of Chad are also crisis areas. The jihadist armed group Boko Haram has expanded its area of operations to western Chad, northern Cameroon and south-east Niger. While relations between Chad and Sudan are now good, this rapprochement has come at the cost of N'Djamena abandoning its former allies in Darfur. As for relations with the Central African Republic (CAR), they have improved since the election of Faustin-Archange Touadéra in February 2016, but the question of Chadian influence on some elements of the former Séléka in the CAR is undecided.

For civilians, the end of war does not mean the end of violence. The problem is not (or not only) the number of troops or weapons in circulation. The problem lies in the mode of government. If the state resorts less and less often to physical violence, the government by arms referred to in this book has not been fundamentally challenged.

The war continues in the positions of power and the impunity granted to those close to the presidency and the ruling party.

Women have to cope with both a militarised and a male-dominated political and social order. In February 2016, for the first time in the history of the country, women spoke out and denounced the impunity of the 'big men' and its gendered cost. The rape of a teenage girl by the sons of some of the President's closest associates (sons of army officers and one of the sons of the Foreign Minister) triggered an unprecedented wave of protest, in a country where the discussion of sexual violence has long remained taboo. Demonstrations were organised in all regions of Chad and involved a new generation of young men and women.

In the silences of the inter-war, when combatants have abandoned their arms, insidious forms of violence become visible. They assume the form of naked violence less and less often, and increasingly appear as a threat to those who would dare collectively to claim their rights and criticise the routine way in which injustice operates. It is difficult to say whether Chad has moved from an inter-war situation to a situation of peace: the government itself cannot make up its mind, since it continues to recruit for its security apparatus, far in excess of what is required by a response to the threat posed by Boko Haram and the uncertainty in southern Libya. What is certain, however, is that the country is still marked by the practices of a state built on violence, an economy that leaves a large part of the population in poverty, and a society dominated by 'untouchables' who are all connected to this history of war. These forms of violence also have a high human cost. In addition to documenting a little-known country, this book will be an invitation to reflect on the forms of domination rooted in violence that become a permanent feature of political and social orders, as well as on the forms of resistance that oppose these unjust orders.

Marielle Debos
May 2016

INTRODUCTION

It is necessary to learn to keep company with war and peace simultaneously, to convince oneself to go from one to the other as one goes from one room to another in a castle. One thereby has the means of understanding from which catastrophic sludge our humanity is drawn.[1]

November 2005 on the outskirts of N'Djamena. I was with Ganda, a demobilised soldier, waiting for a taxi that would take us to the home of a former combatant of the southern rebellions of the 1990s. We were in the Walia neighbourhood, close to the Cameroon border, approximately 900 kilometres (560 miles) from the camps for refugees and displaced persons in eastern Chad,[2] and equally far from the rebels' rear base in Darfur. The zone was situated between two wars: soldiers, ex-rebels and combatants awaiting re-mobilisation intermingled, collaborated and competed. They tried to get good deals near the Ngueli Bridge abutting Kousseri, Cameroon. On the side of the road, merchants awaited their customers, men in uniform, the next war. Everyone watched a funeral procession: minibuses, cars and motorcycles proceeded towards the nearby cemetery. Women sang. Suddenly, a pickup arrived at full speed with armed, turbaned men in fatigues standing in the back. Astonishingly, it did not roll over while taking the curve. Ganda explained to me: 'Those are *bogobogos*; they are likely pursuing a vehicle carrying smuggled goods.' He smiled: 'Or they are escorting the smugglers.' The *bogobogos* act as customs officers; some are ex-rebels. They are coyly called 'volunteer customs officers' because they are not officially integrated into the customs service. They are also called 'crooks disguised as customs officers'.[3]

We stepped into a 'taxi' – a minibus in a deplorable state. While I tried to make Ganda's daughter laugh, a seven-year-old too wise for her years, the taxi was stopped by armed, turbaned men in combat uniforms, posted by the side of the road. The travellers fell silent and strained to listen to the conversation between one of the men and the driver. I quietly asked Ganda:

He's one of the bogobogos *that we were just talking about?*

Yes. He is asking the driver to get everyone out to check our IDs. The women with us have *koros*[4] of sugar and *pagnes* from Kousseri [merchandise imported from Cameroon]. But we're going to leave. The driver refused.

The driver refused? But how is that possible?

The driver ... knows well-seated people [well-off, benefiting from good connections]. If the customs officer doesn't let us pass by peacefully, he's going to talk to his relatives and it won't go well.

And if the bogobogo *had well-seated relatives, too?*

In that case, they would have negotiated.

So, we have less to worry about in taxis driven by well-seated people.

People know that with certain drivers, they're cool.

Who were these individuals who worked in the confusion of Ngueli between two wars? A preliminary question relates to the *bogobogo*'s stopping of the taxi: have untimely stops and racketeering developed in an anarchic context? Or is this an institutionalised practice governed by rules? Next, the identity and the role of the taxi driver: why could he refuse the 'customs stop'? What kind of connections do people need to benefit from Ngueli's apparent chaos? Why didn't my friend, a demobilised career soldier, give a moment's thought about intervening on behalf of the female merchants, the other passengers or the *bogobogo*? Chadians knew the answers to these questions and understood the situation. The only thing they could not grasp was what a Frenchwoman was doing in a taxi without brakes in the afternoon heat.

This book attempts to make sense of what happened that day in Ngueli, by asking a set of questions. How have arms become an everyday form of political protest and a way of life? Why are arms so pervasive in Chad, including when there is no war? Because the country has experienced a succession of wars? Because the state and the economy are governed by violence? Despite the apparent anarchy, how have well-understood rules, borders and hierarchies emerged? What are they?

The goal of this book is to explain how people wage war and how they use arms (and uniforms) when war is suspended. I do not list the causes of successive conflicts in Chadian history, nor do I isolate the factors that render war more or less likely. Rather, I intend to explain a process that cannot be reduced to war: that is, how one part of the male population has specialised in the handling of arms. I conceive of the use of arms as a practical occupation or a *métier* – a word that, in French, indicates a non-institutionalised profession, a mundane or ordinary job. This practical occupation refers to the activities of those who have lived by the gun for years, being alternately or simultaneously soldiers, rebels and road bandits. My aim is to write their (hi)story and to describe their *métier*. To do this, I explore the historical, political and social trajectories of the various protagonists of the Ngueli taxi anecdote, all of whom are connected, in one way or another, to the realm of arms. Their physical and social positions in and around the taxi are not uniquely the result of chance. The anecdote reveals as much about the banality of the *bogobogos'* extortion practices as the social and political hierarchies inscribed in Chadian history.

The violence of the inter-war

The uncertain boundaries between war and peace

If we are to produce a grounded analysis of the handling of arms as a practical occupation, we first need to investigate the frontiers between war and peace.[5] It is true that war marks a major break. War displaces boundaries: crimes become political acts; certain types of violent discourse and practice that are otherwise illicit become licit. However, the start of a conflict does not represent a dive into the Hobbesian war of all against all; the practices and representations of the pre-war period do not disappear overnight. War is not a pathology; it produces neither chaos nor anomie.[6] Violence in civil wars can be rational.[7] Even when alliances are fluid, and acts of interpersonal violence apparently take precedence over political struggle, there are still norms.[8] For certain individuals and groups, life at war can become a 'social project'[9] that can be studied with the most classic tools of the social sciences. If we are to understand the ordinary dimension of violence, we need to consider the social underpinnings of violence.[10] We also need to rid ourselves of the idea that peace and non-violence are a default social condition or situation.[11] As Laurent Gayer writes, we also need to 'move away from a long tradition, whether in sociology or political science, equating social order with the control of violence and its gradual monopolization by the state'.[12]

The forms of violence that are at work in the most ordinary procedures are not entirely different from the violence of war. Quite the opposite: they are crucial for understanding how the most spectacular violence can explode.[13] Structural and political violence is linked to ordinary violence.[14] Violence may be pervasive in ordinary social spaces. With reference to the Lake Chad Basin,[15] Janet Roitman insists that the historicity of raiding practices is essential for an understanding of the contemporary problematisations of violent modes of accumulation.[16] She shows how spoils become illegal but licit forms of wealth. In Chad, violence is not just part of 'economic regulation' but also part of politics.

In this book, I focus on the (dis)continuities between war and peace without postulating a radical break between them. Such a perspective allows us to make sense of the contexts in which war is part of the modern, day-to-day framework of politics. If we are to understand the use of arms as a practical occupation, we need to rid ourselves of a widespread opinion according to which a violent action occurs as an accident that befalls the normal order of things. From this point of view, it is the breakout of violence as an exceptional phenomenon that needs to be explained. But combatants are often socialised into violence long before they join a rebellion. One former rebel who had experienced extremely difficult conditions while living in the *maquis* on the border between Chad and the Central African Republic (CAR) told me: 'We suffered when we were in hiding, but there's suffering at home, too.'[17] So, going into hiding needs to be seen in context – the context of a country (indeed, a whole region) where violence and threats belong to the instruments of power, and where civilian life is often difficult.

In Chad, armed violence is one of several modes of intervention in the political field. From the point of view of those who resort to such actions, engaging in politics by force of arms is neither more nor less commonplace than engaging in politics without arms, even if the results are not the same. This does not mean that Chadians are satisfied with the ubiquitous nature of violence or that they seem 'not to recognize it anymore',[18] but simply that violence no longer surprises them. Violence has become a defining mode of political sociability, one that is linked to the praise of masculinity and virility. My informants did not justify the use of violence when they talked about their life experiences – even when they talked to a female, foreign researcher – for the very reason that a recourse to violence was anything but exceptional. By contrast, those who belonged to a rebel group without having experienced armed struggle themselves wanted to justify the fact that they had never gone into the 'field'. Rebels had a peculiar relationship to the 'field': it was at the core of their *métier* and it determined to a large extent their career in the politico-military sphere. Those who had not fought with arms (political leaders who stayed at a safe distance from the battleground or spokesmen who lived in exile) were said to 'eat cold': they were accused of enjoying the political and economic benefits gained by – and in – war without taking the associated risks.

War as a 'situation'

However, by questioning the boundary between war and peace, I am not equating all forms of violence with a state of war. Nor am I claiming that war dissolves into acts of random violence. The fact that violence is diffuse, and that the logic of war leaves its mark on the times and spaces in which fighting is suspended, does not imply that war has ceased to exist. While it is right to analyse its continuing impact and to envisage situations in which the logics of war and peace overlap, it is still true that war can refer to precise situations that involve specific rules. What does war actually mean in the context of Chad? How do combatants and civilians define the spatial, temporal, social and political borders between war and peace?

The militarisation of politics does not imply that men in arms are permanently mobilised or that the whole country is constantly under fire. Rebellions are limited in time and experiences of warfare are intermittent. Between 2005 and 2009, there were only about twenty major rebel attacks. Rebels based in Darfur crossed the border to launch an attack and then retreated to their camps. Furthermore, warfare is seasonally determined: war is waged only during the dry season. The daily life of both soldiers and rebels implies long periods of waiting. War is also a localised phenomenon that may be perceived differently from one village to another.[19] This is especially true in a country such as Chad where rebellions have broken out successively in every region. The gulf between different local perceptions of the same political situation is highly significant. In September 2006, armed groups were active in the east of the country when I was in Goré, a small town in the south. The inhabitants of Goré said little or nothing about the troop movements in the east, even though they were aware of them via the radio. I soon realised that they would start to follow the rebels' movements and attacks only when the latter started heading for the capital.

Contrary to a deep-rooted misconception, armed violence and war are *not* the mechanical results of hate. Chadians who took up arms did not necessarily hate the people they had to fight. One must refrain from psychologising the supposed 'hatred' between armed factions and combatants. This simplifying discourse obscures more than it clarifies. In Chad, war was thought of as a 'situation'. This 'situation' implied and justified the recourse to arms and the (tragic but unavoidable) possibility of a violent encounter with a friend or relative who had been recruited to a competing faction. War was not fought in a context of hatred or ideological polarisation; rather, it was characterised by a coexistence of enmity and amity. As Henrik Vigh argues, wars in Guinea-Bissau are 'brotherly' when combatants fight an enemy who is not a radical Other: 'aggression becomes, as such, related to the situation that demanded it, rather than to the other that enacted it. It is seen as specific to periods of actual combat during the war, rather than as a characteristic of the relationship between the two parties in general.'[20] In Chad as well, there were no ideological disagreements between the ones who were 'in' and the ones who were 'out'. There was a sense among soldiers and rebels that they were divided by circumstances and divergent tactical choices rather than by irreconcilable identities or political stances. Dialogue and negotiations between warring parties were only interrupted during actual fighting. Faction leaders had friendly relations when they met at the negotiation table. A rebel leader explained this pattern thus: 'The social and affective sides of things, the alliances among tribes are crucial. But when the war is on, you have to be ready to fight. When there is no fighting, we are brothers. That's the way it is.'[21] My informants were as proud of their ability to reconcile when they were not 'in a situation' as they were of their braveness in combat. In Chadian wars, perhaps even more than in others, combatants fraternised outside the actual time of fighting. Chadian wars were 'brotherly' for another reason: they often opposed brothers and cousins. Combatants often had close ties with more than one faction. Kin-based social networks were not destroyed overnight with the beginning of the war, and men in arms often helped relatives who happened to be on a different side of the war. Thus, war belongs to politics and violence derives from the situation rather than from radical enmity. War is not waged because there are enemies; there are enemies because a war is waged.

My analysis of war as a situation does not imply that I overlook its political dimensions. The first rebellions in Chad that developed during the Cold War were socialist and anti-imperialist. Some factions were inspired by Gaddafi's *Green Book*. Post-Cold War conflicts have been less obviously ideological, but politics has not vanished. In the 1990s and 2000s, Chadian political entrepreneurs did not cease being connected to regional and global players, but the latter also modified their political discourse.[22] In addition to the political discourses and programmes of those involved, interpretations of the conflicts have also changed. In the media, the dominant discourses on conflicts in Africa tend to depoliticise them. These conflicts are treated either as security issues ('we need to take an interest in them because they pose a threat beyond the continent') or as humanitarian issues ('we need to take an interest in them so we can go and save the Africans') – and much more rarely as primarily political issues. The key question is not whether today's rebellions are less or more 'political' than before, but rather how political agendas are formulated in times of ideological paucity. Rebel leaders of the 1990s and 2000s in Chad did not articulate sophisticated political agendas, but the wars they waged were fuelled by highly political issues such as state-sponsored violence, impunity and the capture of resources by political and economic entrepreneurs connected to the global economy.

The inter-war

If war refers to specific situations, what term can be used to refer to spaces and periods of time when there is no direct fighting? In countries such as Chad, there is no such thing as the 'normalcy' of the pre-conflict. 'Peace' is a project rather than a lived experience. For this reason, I do not use the categories of 'war' and 'peace'. Instead, I refer to 'war' and 'inter-war'. The inter-war refers to the spaces and times that are affected by violence even if there is no direct fighting between rebel and governmental forces. In my use of the term, I do not mean that a war is mechanically and automatically followed by another one, nor do I mean that Chad is condemned to be affected by a succession of conflicts. I choose to refer to inter-war rather than the binary opposition of war and peace in order to portray a situation in which war is always emergent. So the term 'inter-war' does not describe an implacable logic that gives the population no respite other than unstable and violent periods between wars; instead, it depicts a situation in which people claiming to be 'just under a suspended sentence of death because of the recurrent insecurity'[23] live in expectation of the next war, while hoping that it will not break out.

In this work, I have decided to document and analyse what happens in the times and spaces in which war seems to be suspended. The violence of the past is invisible in the public space; its traces have been wiped away. The deaths of those who are 'victims of forced disappearances' are never announced, and their bodies, by definition, are never found. The state shows its dominance by killing and then spiriting the bodies away. 'Here, people have been killed and buried when the fighting between the army and the rebels resumed,' an inhabitant of Moundou told me one day, as we were walking down a street that was indistinguishable from any other.[24]

In the inter-war, physical violence remains the exception rather than the rule. It is the threat of violence, rather than violence itself, that marks everyday life, as in the 2010 film *Un homme qui crie* (*A Screaming Man*) by the Chadian director Mahamat Saleh Haroun, in which the sounds of war can be heard at regular intervals (planes flying over the town, news about the battles broadcast on radio and television, and so on), while the war itself never appears on screen. In this film, as in the book, the off-screen sounds enable us to understand that the violence of war is inseparable from the more insidious violence of the state and the market.[25] The film's main character, Adam, is powerless in the face of the state and the war that tear his son away from him, and in the face, too, of the rules of neoliberal management that deprive him of his job and humiliate him, just as the women traders and the bus passengers I discussed in the first pages of my introduction have to put up daily with the impunity granted to certain individuals by virtue of the fact that they are close to state power. This approach comes with a certain risk – that of relegating the violence of war to the background. It does, however, have the merit of highlighting the way in which war is prosecuted by other means, outside the battleground – and outside our field of vision, at a time when the production of expert reports has declined as a result of the apparent fading of the 'crisis'.[26]

So this book asks the following questions. How well can we understand war when we study it in and through its margins? How well can we understand a violent mode of government when we, together with the people whose lives we are investigating, cross the borders between war and peace? For what is at stake here, theoretically speaking, is an attempt to think in terms of non-linear, interwoven processes that lie outside the framework of the transition between war and peace. We need to study what is happening in times and spaces that are no longer at war, but in which violence has become a matter of routine and war has granted death a central place.[27] The notion of inter-war is key to understanding the breaks comprised by the starting or ending of a conflict, but also to grasping the crucial processes that straddle the boundaries of war and peace. As I shall explain below, the violence of the inter-war cannot be reduced to the pursuit of the *imaginaires* of war, or of a habitus of war, that obstinately continue to hold sway. This violence, rather, is the product of a specific mode of government and a specific economy.

Living by the gun

Arms as a practical occupation

While my work here draws on contemporary studies of conflicts, it does not constitute an analysis of conflicts or armed movements in Chad, but of the handling of arms as a practical occupation. It aims to take a new look at how people wage war and also how they use arms when they are not mobilised by war, and how they regard the use of arms in these different situations. Neither of the two angles – conflict, or arms as practical occupation – is in itself more relevant or more heuristic than the other. They both simply shed light on different perspectives. Studying how people use arms when they are not fighting helps us grasp structural characteristics of the conflicts that would remain hidden if we focused solely on actual wartime. To put it another way, the questions 'Why do rebels and soldiers wage war on one another?' and 'How has the use of arms become a practical occupation?' should not be confused, but the answer to the second sheds light on the first.

If the professionalisation of violence is at once a cause and a consequence of wars, it cannot be reduced to either of these dimensions. It is certain that voluntary and enforced recruitments speed up in times of war and that the professionalisation of violence would not have developed as it has without the conflicts that have marked the history of Chad. It is also certain that when a proportion of the masculine population specialises in the handling of arms, this facilitates recruitment activities and makes wars more dangerous. However, our analysis cannot remain content with simply pointing out that the professionalisation of violence leads to war, which in turn leads to the professionalisation of violence. One of the hypotheses that I put forward here is that the use of arms has become a practical occupation because it is linked not only to war but also to a specific economy and to a mode of government. The question of the violence of, and in, the economy has been discussed by Stephen Reyna (in connection with the empire of Baguirmi) and by Janet Roitman and Saibou Issa (with regard to the Lake Chad Basin).[28] My own focus is on the mode of government that is the product of Chad's unique historical trajectory (albeit not an exceptional one). However, I am also interested in violent modes of accumulation, and I bring out the political logics that shape them.

Violence is work, and not just a symptom or a strategy, as the anthropologist Danny Hoffman has emphasised in connection to the Mano River war.[29] Hoffman shows that this work fits into the pattern of other economic activities carried out by a young male workforce that can be deployed on different sites to wage war or to work the diamond mines. The issue of the exploitation and consumption of a cheap workforce by political and economic entrepreneurs is also central to the situation in Chad. I aim to show how this workforce is used in different spaces of war and inter-war, both in Chad and in the neighbouring countries. However, Chad is not the Mano River region, and the ways of waging war and of thinking about the use of violence are not the same. In Chad, resorting to arms, as a mode of political protest and as a way of life, is routine. The trajectories of the combatants are marked by episodes of rebellion and reintegration into the regular forces with periods spent undertaking economic activities performed with or without arms, often in the margins of the state. Men in arms can live by the gun for years without actually firing a shot. As Louisa Lombard shows in her study of rebellions in the CAR, threat itself – rather than threatened violence – may be a political technique.[30]

I call the individuals who carry out this activity 'men in arms'. This expression refers to the set of individuals who live by the gun, not just rebels. The number of individuals involved varies from one historical period to another. At the end of the 1970s and during the civil war, a large section of the male population took up arms, while the recent rebellions (2005–09) comprised just a few thousand combatants. One example: the last significant attack launched by the rebel coalition in May 2009 involved between 3,000 and 4,000 combatants. There are some tens of thousands of men in arms active in the regular forces, while the number of those who work for themselves is difficult to assess. However, it is not only the number of men in arms that is important: what counts is the centrality of their activities in economic, social and political life.

This is a work about men in arms, not women. This does not mean that the history of wars in Chad is exclusively a male affair. Women are both victims of and participants in war. Admittedly, the vast majority of army recruits are male – and Chad is no exception. The army began to admit women in 1970, but they did not fight alongside men. As far as rebellions are concerned, the first rebellion of Chad, known as the Frolinat, did not enrol women as combatants, although there were a few exceptions. In the 1980s, the armed groups in the south relied on the work of the women who lived in the bush with the male combatants, but few women actually bore arms. As for more recent rebellions, few women were enlisted as combatants.

Women are, however, active participants even when they do not wield a rifle. Many women lived in the rear bases of the rebellions or hid out in the bush and shared the daily lives of the fighters. They could then provide food, care, and information on enemy troop movements. Some of them were sexually exploited.[31] In Chad, as in many other contexts, there is a 'sexual division of revolutionary labour'.[32] The tasks assigned to women are undervalued; their role is rendered invisible.[33] While men in arms are dependent on women both inside and outside the military, the contribution of women has not been acknowledged. Moreover, the participation of women in the rebellion is often stigmatised. In the post-war period, they win scant reward for the part they played in the war. Armed violence is a practical occupation that is not just carried out by men; it is also viewed as essentially masculine.

More broadly, politics and the conduct of state affairs are considered to be men-only activities. Access to the public sphere and to the political field is gendered. A small group of female activists are well known for their involvement in women's rights, human rights, justice and peace issues. They are, however, exceptions. All major political parties and all rebel groups have male leaders. Less than 15 per cent of members of parliament are female. Women are also under-represented in state administration. The exclusion of women from politics is part of a continuum of social structures that perpetuate gender inequalities and forms of domination, and which is compounded by the very functioning of the political field. While women's under-representation is not specific to Chad (or to Africa), the militarisation of politics and the associated militarised masculinity make it even more difficult for women to participate in politics, to fight gender-based violence, and to promote their rights.

I wish that this work on men in arms could have been accompanied by more in-depth research into the place and role of women in rebel movements. Such an investigation, unfortunately, was not possible, and my study will not do justice to their contribution. For one thing, shortly before my 2010 fieldwork on the former members of the United Front for Change (the only armed group in recent history to have recruited women – women who played a direct part in the fighting), a female commandant was assassinated in N'Djamena. While it is not certain that her assassination was linked to her rebel past, it encouraged women ex-combatants to keep a low profile. Their safety was my main concern. For another thing, once I had entered the men's arena, it became difficult to talk to women who had been members of, or close to, an armed movement without the men interfering. Moreover, in contrast to the men, who were often proud of their rebel past (even when they admitted that this had been a hard time), many women did not want to talk about this experience, which had often been difficult and traumatic. Many of them still face stigma because they crossed the social and moral boundaries of what is considered acceptable for women. On the other hand, I spent time and conducted interviews with female civilians, especially with women traders and smugglers who had to cope on a daily basis with men in arms, army recruits and other *bogobogos*. In this sense, my book owes as much to the women of Chad as it does to the men.

The ordinary use of arms

People do not take up arms for no reason. While some of my interviewees talked about the violence in their region, or the need to defend their relatives and friends, by way of explaining how it was that they eventually took up arms, others mentioned the desire to renegotiate their status within the regular forces or their hope of rising up the social scale. Understanding how arms and war have become one repertoire of action pretty much like any other, a relatively ordinary way of solving a problem – such is the aim of my book.

My work tackles the use of arms in times of war (both in the government army and its militias and in the rebel forces), but it focuses essentially on its exercise in the inter-war periods. I have paid particular attention to the use of arms over and above physical violence. Arms are used to wound and to kill, but also to intimidate, to inspire fear, to arouse admiration and, more generally, to enable a person to dominate in any interaction with others. When engaged in extortion, for example, it is recommended (though not entirely necessary) that you wear a uniform and carry a weapon, but it is still unusual to resort to violence. The use of arms may be symbolic. The driver in Ngueli who refuses to be checked by the *bogobogo* is linked to networks of ex-combatants even if he is not necessarily an ex-combatant himself. He does not need (or no longer needs) to be armed in order to dominate a routine interaction with customs officials and *bogobogos*. Indeed, one hypothesis that should be considered is that a man in arms can be seen as having reached the pinnacle of his career when he can do without them.

However, handling arms is not an occupation like any other. Men in arms move in an unstable environment: they do not make career plans. They 'navigate' in and through their society.[34] Apart from the risk of death, they need to be aware of the dramatic shifts in alliances that can ruin their upward social mobility in less time than it takes to strip down and reassemble a weapon. This practical occupation is characterised by the complex trajectories of individuals and the fungibility of different statuses: soldier, rebel and road bandit. Does this mean that the world of arms is anomic or chaotic? Is it ruled solely by violence? As opposed to the notion that violence is produced by a collapse of political order and of forms of social control, I formulate the hypothesis that armed violence is governed by rules and structured by boundaries. The fluidities that characterise violence should not be seen as merely a case of the war of all against all. Nor should they be confused with a strictly economic rationality of the quest for profit: activities linked to arms may be lucrative, but men in arms are not mere predators and the reasons why they take up arms cannot be reduced to their supposed 'greed'.[35] State violence, huge socio-economic inequalities, and a belief in the opportunities associated with violence all go to explain the twists and turns of these men's careers.

While the boundaries between soldiers, rebels and bandits have been blurred, the milieu of arms is strongly hierarchised. There is little selection on entry but few individuals find themselves in a position to rise up the social ladder. Within regular forces, the men in the troops with their faded uniforms and their old sandals have little in common with the powerful officers who parade in their pickup trucks. Rebel movements, too, are extremely hierarchical: elements of the combatant workforce do not become commanders simply by doing 'good work'. The social trajectories of men in arms do not depend solely on their skill in handling a Kalashnikov; they also, indeed especially, rely on political power relations. The realities are far removed from the romantic vision of armed struggle as social vengeance. In the following pages, I inquire into these specific forms of integration and differentiation experienced by those who take part in armed violence.

Last but not least, armed violence should not be thought of as a strictly Chadian problem. Studying how combatants live by the gun requires attention to be paid to these networks that involve not just Chadians but also external actors. Professionals of violence in Chad are connected to major global actors: governments, international organisations, aid agencies, private companies and military establishments. Politico-military leaders who need support and material sponsorship to wage war tap into regional and global resources. Despite the changing identities of protagonists and their allies, the interference of regional[36] and global actors forms a structural pattern of conflicts in Chad. Over the last fifty years, the main actors were France[37] and Libya, and to a lesser extent the US and Sudan. France has used Chad as a training ground for its own military for decades. The US offered strong support to Chad under Habré. Chad also has been a core partner of the US for over a decade in its counter-terrorism policy. In addition, China has played a key role in the oil sector since 2006, the year Chad recognised China instead of Taiwan.

The global capital of an unstable 'island of stability'

To what can we compare Chad, that vast and isolated country with a population of 13 million, about a half of whom are Muslim and the other half Christian and animist? A popular joke clearly illustrates the way in which many Chadians view their own country: 'We're all going to heaven as we've already experienced hell on earth.' While Chad is not exactly hell, it is a country where the population has lived from one armed conflict to the next for several decades. Chad regularly comes towards the bottom in international ratings on human development, access to health and education, or the number of girls able to attend school, while it heads the lists when it comes to corruption.[38] Chad ranks 185 out of 188 countries on the 2015 UN Human Development Index. According to the World Bank, one in seven children dies before the age of five. Life expectancy at birth is fifty-one.

Chad has changed a great deal since my first fieldwork in 2004. Over the past twelve years, the country has gone through a new episode of war with the reconstitution of a rebel coalition, two attacks on the capital, and the reintegration of most of the rebels after the signing of the agreement between Chad and Sudan in January 2010. The renovation of the city centre of N'Djamena is emblematic of the efforts made to cover up the past violence and celebrate the country's entry into oil-fuelled capitalism in 2003. There is no longer any trace of the combat of February 2008 when the rebel coalition faced the government forces. Nowadays, it is building sites and new constructions that mark the urban landscape. A few years ago, the inhabitants of N'Djamena could not cross the Place de l'Indépendance without feeling nervous. It was forbidden to stop or turn round in front of the President's palace: the guards could beat anyone who was acting in an incautious way, and could even use their weapons. The ban has now been lifted and you can stroll in the entirely reshaped square. The Camp des Martyrs, the soldiers' barracks facing the palace, and the buildings around it have been razed (the soldiers are now confined to the outskirts of N'Djamena, or to Moussoro, a hundred kilometres or so to the north of the city). On the new square there is a host of symbols celebrating the country's independence and glorifying the nation. Children and young men play football; a large poster announces that Idriss Déby, the former warlord and now President, is a 'man of peace and tolerance'.

The people out strolling in the Place de l'Indépendance know that the renovation of the city centre is also a way of ensuring the security of the President's palace, in a context where the threat of coups d'état is taken very seriously. The asphalt that has replaced the sand and mud on certain roads of the capital and of the country also arouses lively debates: 'How long is it going to last? When are we going to see the first holes?' The scepticism about the solidity of the asphalt, whose quality is in inverse proportion to the extent of corruption, echoes a deeper uncertainty: 'How long is the regime going to maintain its new appearance?' For readers who are discovering the Chad of the 2010s, this book is an invitation to note the presence of arms, camouflaged behind the new asphalt.

In a few years, and with a certain amount of political cunning, Chad has also changed its status on the international scene. The old crisis-ridden country has become a key ally of France and the Western powers within the framework of the 'war on terror'. It is now viewed as an 'island of stability in a crisis-ridden Sahel–Sahara area', as the President of the Commission of National Defence and Armed Forces of the French Assembly put it in 2014. International actors are perfectly ready to ignore the misdemeanours of such a useful partner. Déby has worked to project an image of Chad as a regional powerbroker and valuable player in the fight against jihadist armed groups throughout West and Central Africa. In January 2013, the Chadian army moved decisively to support France's military intervention in Mali. The arrest and intimidation of opponents who were wrongly accused of a coup in May 2013 aroused only very measured reactions on the part of Western countries. Two months later, a detachment of the Chadian army was invited to take part in the Bastille Day military parade in Paris. In March 2015, Chad, along with other countries bordering Lake Chad, launched military operations against Boko Haram.

Operation Barkhane, the French anti-terrorist operation, settled into a new base in N'Djamena in August 2014.[39] By basing troops for this operation in the capital of Chad, France shows its ongoing commitment to and reliance on the country. In addition, Chad serves as a base for recent US support to Nigeria in combating Boko Haram. While international actors praise Chad for its military interventions, we may ponder the possible effects of the global political capital (or diplomatic rent) being offered to Chad and the other states in the region.

Investigating the inter-war

During my first stay in Chad, in 2004, I was immediately struck by the massive presence of men in uniform on the streets of the capital and on the country's roads. The main anxiety among civilians at that time was not about the possibility of a rebel attack, but the ordinary practices of elements in the regular forces. Although I thought it was a matter of importance and urgency to investigate this phenomenon by looking beyond the notion that it was all due to the opportunism of men in arms, the advent of a culture of war or a symptom of state failure, I was embarking on research that risked throwing up various difficulties. It required a set of improvisations and tactics, doubts and reassessments, and methodological and ethical questions. I had to adapt to political circumstances, constantly re-evaluate the risks (for my interviewees and myself) of a journey, a meeting or an interview, and adopt a flexible research method.[40] One of my main concerns was to manage the possibilities and assess the respective doses of audacity and caution that each new day was going to need.

Carrying out research on Chad means having to cope with a paucity of written sources[41] and a restricted secondary literature.

In Chad, an 'old fallow land for research'[42] and an 'anthropological gap',[43] we also have to deal with data that are vague. Statistics on the military and the security forces are unreliable, and this lack of information on the numbers involved is part of a political and strategic rationale. As for figures relating to the rebellions, they have to be viewed with considerable caution. The rebels tend to inflate numbers that, in any case, vary with the desertions, reintegration and intermittent activities of the combatants. These uncertainties are not (or not only) an obstacle to inquiry: they are its very subject.

It is precisely because it has become commonplace to resort to arms that fieldwork, despite bearing on a sensitive issue, was ultimately possible. In some *départements* in eastern Chad, especially Dar Tama, which I visited in 2010, a huge number of men were recruited into the rebellion. Every family saw young (and not so young) men signing up. With the collapse of the Tama rebellion and the fighters returning to their homes, armed mobilisation is no longer taboo. Ex-rebels are known as such, and their past is a secret neither to the local inhabitants nor to the authorities. Furthermore, Chad is a country marked by a violent mode of government, but one that does not aim to control every little aspect of the lives of individuals. People dare to speak out and criticise the government or the army. Scathing remarks on the government and on the country's military are regularly heard on radio and published in the press. However, I did sometimes encounter refusals, and on several occasions I set up interviews with people who had agreed to meet me solely to find out who I was and what I wanted. Refusals, mistrust and misunderstandings are unpleasant, but they are all part of fieldwork and are themselves events that need to be interpreted. The loquacity or the silence of interviewees is, after all, not just the product of their bravery or cowardice, but needs to be understood in its political context. The mode of government rewards loyalty and punishes defections without bothering about the things people might say. Thus, the civilians and military personnel closest to the President are not necessarily great defenders of the President or of the government. Indeed, they often assume very critical positions in private, and are happy to share information and opinions on the most sensitive issues. At the other end of the social scale, those who have little to lose, but who do have frustrations and bitterness to share, can greet a foreign researcher with enthusiasm. The most cautious interviewees are those individuals whose positions are threatened or who are waiting to be appointed to an important post.

My work deals with the inter-war and not with conflicts. This means that my fieldwork was never dangerous – at least, no more so than is everyday life for a foreign woman who does not live in padlocked houses and does not travel in air-conditioned 4x4s. My research does not focus on the battlefield, but on the routine forms of violence in the inter-war. As Michel Taussig has noted, even in the most violent areas, 'it looks so normal most of the time'.[44] In the inter-war, violence appears in the practices of the military or the police forces. One morning, in N'Djamena, I came across a friend who was in a dreadful state, having been beaten by policemen and chained to a tree for the whole night. But there are also wounds that leave no scars. When in a small town in eastern Chad I saw an exhausted woman faint – she had lived alone since her husband had gone into exile and she had just lost her daughter in a domestic accident that might have been avoided if she had been less poor – I realised that the violence of the inter-war was also an intimate experience. 'Militarization creeps into ordinary daily routines', as the feminist writer Cynthia Enloe explains.[45] Militarisation is not only a question of 'high politics', it also affects people's daily life. When men join the army or a rebellion, women are mobilised on the home front. In times of war, the life of those confined to unpaid domestic labour becomes even more difficult. In the inter-war, women pay the price of the impunity granted to men in arms and powerful men.

The main sites of fieldwork were N'Djamena; Mongo in the centre; Abéché and Guéréda in the east; and Moundou, Goré and Sarh in the south. This allowed me to see that the trajectory of rebellion–reintegration–desertion is commonplace in every region, contrary to the common perception that the 'southerners' are more 'peaceful' than their compatriots in the north. But while all the regions of Chad have had their men in arms, armed violence has a different history and varies from one region to another.

I could hardly arrive in a town or village announcing to all and sundry that I was there to do research on men in arms. My contact with men in arms (or people close to that milieu) was frequently established by those I had already interviewed. Ex-combatants who had come together in associations of demobilised soldiers, for example, opened the doors to the world of their sons and nephews, younger men who were still active men in arms. In this way, I met several groups that formed networks of acquaintances. Some of them were linked by kinship, or by the common experience of a rebellion, or by a period spent in the same army regiment, while others met after the war. These different groups helped me to understand the many varied trajectories of the combatants, but also what they have in common: living in a country marked by protracted conflicts, the violence of the mode of government and the commonplace nature of violent forms of appropriation. I also learned a great deal from chance encounters with taxi drivers, traders, peasants and farmers who turned out to be former combatants or soldiers sometimes claiming to still be 'active' (*en situation*).

The men in arms whose trajectories I describe have one point in common: for their own reasons, each one agreed to talk to me about their lives. There are many potential pitfalls. The first, and the most significant, is the ease with which one can be taken in by the narratives of the most garrulous people while failing to pick up on the important signs – so difficult to interpret – of those who do not speak so readily. Some of them told their life story as a long river – with nothing tranquil about it – while others allowed only dribs and drabs of information to build up over the days. Whereas 'Western man has become a confessing animal',[46] the Chadians are rarely asked to provide an autobiographical narrative. Telling one's life story is a procedure less familiar in Chad that it is in Europe or North America. The fact that forms of self-presentation are not institutionalised makes discussion easier: interviewees do not produce a discourse shaped by the habit of talking to their psychoanalyst or their adviser at the employment agency. On the other hand, one has to find the right words to explain to them a procedure with which they are not familiar.

What did I represent to those with whom I spoke? I was a foreign woman and, what is more, a *nassara* (a term meaning 'Christian' in Chadian Arabic, used to refer to whites). On the one hand, I certainly did not have access to certain social spaces that are forbidden to foreigners; on the other, I was not considered a threat. As the Chadian anthropologist Djimet Seli explains, Chadian researchers have an in-depth knowledge of their own society but they face a specific challenge: they raise suspicions and are sometimes considered to be informers, especially when they do fieldwork in rural areas.[47] By contrast, I got a sense that interviewees opened up more easily to a person who belonged to no region, ethnic group, or political movement in the country. Meeting a foreign woman also gives added value to the stories of interviewees, something that is particularly important in the eyes of those who are now marginalised or stigmatised.[48]

While I was not at all rich according to European standards, in the opinion of most people in Chad I belonged to the privileged class of white foreigners. The fact of being French in Chad matters. Officers, some of them trained in France, told me of their admiration for General de Gaulle and the supposed professionalism of the French army. But France has a bad reputation and I often had to explain that I do not support my home country's foreign policy and that I am aware of the history of French involvement in Chad and in Africa. I should point out here that foreign women are seen as having an ambivalent status in terms of gender. Although they are over-sexualised through images of the white woman as being 'easy', foreign women are allowed to frequent places both where men and where women gather. In all the regions of Chad, men and women eat from different plates and sometimes in separate rooms. I was always invited to sit with men and to share their meal.[49] However, I could also visit women in the spaces reserved for them.

Plan of the book

As Howard Becker writes, 'our business' in academia is 'to arrange ideas in so rational an order that another person can make sense of them'.[50] Explaining that the handling of arms have not become a practical occupation in Chad just by chance, and that this occupation is not merely chaotic, is the aim of my book. I still needed to find an orderly way of explaining how the apparent disorder and violence of the inter-war is governed by rules. While writing the book, I constantly hesitated between two objectives that are difficult to reconcile. On the one hand, I wanted to produce a manuscript that would be readable by anyone not familiar with the complex history of conflicts in Chad. On the other, I wanted to convey the complexity of this practical occupation, not to flatten out the effects of contingency, and to allow the men in arms their uncertainties. Nobody joins a rebellion or the army with a very precise idea in their minds and a manual in their hands. Furthermore, it would be absurd and deceptive to impose a docile shape on the trajectories of men in arms, making them appear straightforward, linear and simple, as if their routes obeyed some implacable logic. The fact remains that presenting the reader with all the complexities of the subject of my inquiry would force me to give to a piece of academic research something of the appearance of an experimental novel. Hence the following compromise. After a historical first part, the work covers two key elements: the complex trajectories of rebel leaders and men in arms, and then their places and roles in the mode of government that has come to dominate Chad.

The aim of this first, historical part of the book is to analyse the social, economic and political institutions that are the root causes of armed violence and to explain how one section of the male population has specialised in the use of arms. To make sense of this process, I put armed violence in its colonial and postcolonial context. I study how the French governed with arms and how the colonial order fuelled local tensions. I then show the role played by the French in the postcolonial period. Since independence, there have been very few periods in that geographical space when French forces have not been there. Seen from Chad, France has a violent and conflict-ridden history too.

The second part is devoted to an analysis of the spatial, social and political careers of men in arms. How do they move from one rebel faction to another, and from the army to rebellion? From war to inter-war, and back to war? This part shows that fluidity is not a synonym for anarchy and that armed violence as a practical occupation does not emerge from a collapse of the state or from a society that has become bogged down in a culture of violence. The careers of men in arms are part of a political context: they are linked to armed factionalism and to the post-war reproduction of the conditions that led to war. I also stress the gap between globalised politico-military entrepreneurs and the cheap combatant labour force.

The third and final part is an analysis of the government[51] by arms. This mode of government needs to be understood, first, as the government of the world of arms (structures aimed at controlling combatants, soldiers and *bogobogos*) and, second, as the government of the state and society by men in arms. Government by arms is a form of 'private indirect government';[52] I call it, taking up an emic expression, a 'decree without a number'. This problematisation sheds light on a paradox: how can men in arms be at the centre of the exercise of power even though they partly evade state bureaucracy?

PART I
ARMED VIOLENCE:
A (POST)COLONIAL HISTORY

In this first part on the historicity of armed violence, I will study the militarisation of the economy and of politics – taking account of the different forms it has assumed in the precolonial, colonial and postcolonial periods – that has produced generations of men in arms. I aim to bring out various continuities and discontinuities. Recurrences, here, are understood not as the product of fate, or of some culture, but as historical trajectories. The long-term persistence of conflicts does not imply that they are engendered in some automatic and inevitable fashion. There is no repetition, no mechanical reproduction of past practices. The history of armed violence is complex, uneven, full of peaks and troughs. In this part, I set out to untangle some of the processes involved in the reinvention of the multiple uses of arms since the precolonial period, thereby revealing the 'objective connections'[1] between the different moments of the trajectories followed by men in arms.

Men in arms may have remained central social figures – though continuously changing in nature – since the period of precolonial empires, but this is not because of some culture of bellicosity. Revealing the lines of continuity between certain social practices does not mean that we see them as evidence of some national atavism. Economic, social and political institutions lie behind the development of a specialised occupation involving the handling of arms. First, the different forms of violence are linked to a political economy of predation that is inseparable from state formation, and has been since the precolonial period. Second, politics is marked by violence: state violence, and the violence of rebels against those in power. War has become part and parcel of the everyday operation of the political field. Third, the repeated outbreaks of war and violence in Chad are not just part of the history of Chad; they are also the product of a regional and (post-)colonial history. The former colonial power has never ceased to play a key political and military role in Chad. Chad has become a key area in the African sphere of French influence, and one in which the military dimension is paramount.

CHAPTER 1

· ·

Colonial wars and inter-wars

This chapter highlights the main processes of the precolonial and colonial periods that produced generations of men in arms. While the colonial period lasted for only sixty years or so, it constituted a definite break. In this chapter, we shall be seeing how the colonial state maintained a form of permanent inter-war in the colony, which was left in the hands of a small number of military commanders. French colonisers used the men in arms who were already active in the Sahel and I also focus on how they subsequently recruited and deployed combatants inside and outside the country during the two World Wars. Chadians, as well as other inhabitants of the colonies in French Equatorial Africa (*Afrique Equatoriale Française* or AEF), played a key role during the Second World War, even though their contribution to the French Liberation has still to be recognised.

The warriors of predation

The Sahel empires and their border territories

The region of Central Sudan, in which the borders of Chad currently lie, is characterised by a fragmented geography. It has always been a meeting point for caravans of traders, for nomads and sedentary peoples alike. There were several poles of power and groups belonging to numerous overlapping spaces at the same time: spaces that could be political, cultural, religious or mercantile. The different identities never excluded one another; the notion of an individual with a fixed, unique identity had no meaning before it was introduced by the colonial power.

More or less centralised political organisations were formed and confronted one another from the ninth century onwards. States with strongly hierarchical political structures began to emerge: in the ninth century, Kanem to the north-east of Lake Chad (seven centuries later it would become Kanem-Bornu[1]); in the sixteenth century, Baguirmi on the River Chari and Wadai to the east. These three states spread across the region currently known as north Chad, but at the peak of their power they also included Bornu (Nigeria), Darfur (Sudan), Borku-Ennedi-Tibesti (far north of Chad) and several regions south of the River Chari. In the seventeenth century, the Wadai empire was locked in conflict with its eastern rival, the empire of Darfur (now in Sudan). Political influence and the control of territory and commercial routes were at stake. This region also included other, less powerful, sultanates concentrated in the interior and on the edges of the empires concerned: Dar Massalit (on the Sudanese side of the current border), Dar Sila,[2] Dar Fongoro and Dar Sinyar. The populations in this zone, which corresponds to the present border between Chad and Sudan, swore allegiance to their powerful neighbours.

Islam spread under the influence of Muslim scholars, and Arabic became a common language. Trans-Saharan trade developed and became a factor in significant social transformations: caravans brought ivory, ostrich feathers and skins as well as slaves to Libya, Sudan and Egypt. They returned with fabrics, religious manuals and weapons. Arabo-Muslim countries had a powerful influence on the empires of Chad, although the political independence of the latter was never threatened.[3] Thus Chadian empires, like other African societies, were always deeply involved in trading activities with the trans-Saharan and Mediterranean worlds. In the nineteenth century, the Chadian empires became border territories of the Muslim economies of the northern Sahara, which were themselves border territories of Europe.[4] These relations with the non-African world were constitutive of the political organisation of those societies.

In the margins of these empires, towards the south, there were societies whose political organisation was not centralised. Described as 'anarchic' by colonial administrators whose historical skills were rapidly improvised,[5] these societies were often deprived of any state organisation. According to Mario Azevedo, states were in the process of being formed at the time of the colonial conquest, at the end of the nineteenth century,[6] with the training of militias in the service of traditional chiefs.

Wars and raids

While war played a major role in the construction of the state in Europe,[7] it also encouraged the emergence and reinforcement of the empire states of the Sahel. In the region of Central Sudan, war and trade went hand in hand. According to Stephen Reyna, 'states … warred to trade and traded to war'.[8] States embarked on offensive wars in order to take part in trans-Saharan trade. In return, long-distance trade made it possible to acquire 'goods' that were necessary for the development and maintenance of the state bureaucracy, as well as the means of organised violence: horses and firearms.[9] 'Wars without end'[10] were inseparable from 'predatory accumulation'.[11] The organisation of those empires that lived on predation was turned towards war. The armed forces of Baguirmi were managed in an efficient and decentralised way. Troops were organised with an eye to military objectives: the number and origin of the men involved depended on the nature of the war that had to be waged. This flexibility was a response to the need to adapt to the constantly changing threats that hung over the empire. As for the police, this was a permanent structure that intervened in regions near the capital. According to Reyna's estimates, the army of Baguirmi could comprise as many as 3,000 or 4,000 cavalry. At the end of the nineteenth century, the army of Wadai was the most powerful: observers claim a figure of 7,000 or between 10,000 and 11,000 cavalry.[12] The military institutions of these empires were hierarchical, and we need to distinguish between the warrior aristocracy and the ordinary soldiers who were often their slaves. Military practices depended on technological developments but also on the way in which these were envisaged. The horse, an indispensable element in any raid, became a highly envied possession and a symbol of nobility. When firearms developed in the nineteenth century, they were reserved for the troops.[13]

Renegotiating their fluid borders was a crucial issue for these empires. According to Stephen Reyna, who adopted and refined an earlier theory put forward by Jacques Le Cornec,[14] the political geography of Baguirmi can be represented as three concentric circles. The first, 'the centre', was the heart of political power; the second comprised 'tributary regions' subject to a form of indirect government; and the third corresponded to the 'zone of predation' where the laws of Massenya, the capital of Baguirmi, did not apply. The centre payed taxes, the tributary regions payed tribute, and the zones of predation provided merchandise and slaves. The empire of Wadai operated on the same model. The territories of the different empires overlapped: the zones of predation of one could be tributary zones of another.

We can distinguish between two types of military expeditions: raids and wars. Raids, most often carried out in stateless societies in non-Islamic territories, were aimed at pillage and capturing slaves. Wars followed a different logic: they were waged against another empire and involved greater numbers of troops, over longer periods of time. In wartime, empires deployed a majority of their soldiers. The objective was not just pillaging, but the defeat of the enemy army and the confiscation of the revenue and treasure of the vanquished empire. Baguirmi and Wadai clashed in the nineteenth century in the equivalent of a Hundred Years' War that ended with the arrival of the French.[15]

Predatory violence comes with a military ethos: men are subjected to a permanent military socialisation. Raids are means of accumulation: they are also, for the nobility in the slave-owning empires, opportunities to prove their heroism. The songs of the Kanem-Bornu empire also emphasise the norms and codes of honour in force at that time: they praise those who are able to take 'the best [slaves] as the first fruits of battle', separating children from their mothers and women from their husbands and sending them to 'lands far removed from one another'.[16]

The increasingly commonplace nature of raids as a mode of accumulation also involved the development of new representations of the definition and source of wealth. As Janet Roitman explains, when the slave becomes a category of capital (in exchange), labour (in agriculture), a condition (servility) and even a mode of being (the 'slave', an ontological category), the distinction between individuals who are free and the rest tends to become fixed.[17] These representations are especially important for the history of the region because the opposition between free people and slaves relates to other oppositions formulated in religious (Muslims/'infidels') or ethnic terms. In this way, slaves were at the heart of the processes of constructing identities and the reshaping of social relations in the empire states of present-day Chad as well as in the rest of the Lake Chad Basin.

Thus, the societies in the south of the country were drawn into the political economy of their northern neighbours, as reservoirs of resources. Thousands of people were captured in the south every year.[18] The resistance put up by the Sara[19] triggered reprisals on the part of their assailants. Some chiefs preferred to reach an agreement with the slave drivers: villages were obliged to provide a certain number of slaves in exchange for protection. The best alternative for avoiding raids was still, however, to take flight or to emigrate (*hijra*) from the territory of the infidels (*dar al-Harb*) to the territory of the believers (*dar al-Islam*) – the frontier between the two worlds being subject to constant negotiation.

Traders and religious figures in arms at the dawn of colonisation

The sultans of the empires were not the only people who took part in raids. The regional economy was controlled by the Awlad Sulayman, Arabs from what is now Libya who migrated to the north of Lake Chad around the middle of the nineteenth century. Thanks to a combined use of camels, horses and firearms, these outstanding horsemen (in the admiring view of the explorer Nachtigal) launched rapid and repeated long-distance military expeditions. They were thus able to engage in battles and diplomatic negotiations with empires in the region, such as the sultanate of Wadai.[20] At the end of the nineteenth century, the Awlad Sulayman were faced with other armed traders who gave a religious dimension to their enterprise: the Sanusi, who also came from Libya.

The Muslim brotherhood of Sanusiyyah, a military theocracy, established itself in 1899 in Goura, a palm grove located on the eastern edge of Tibesti. The Sanusi set up *zawiya* (centres that were simultaneously warehouses for goods and arms and buildings for worship and religious education) at Ain Galaka (Borku) and Bir Alali (Kanem).[21] When the French attempted to conquer their territory, the brotherhood organised the resistance. Although they were allied to the empire of Wadai, the Sanusi were defeated. Rabah Fadlallah is another key figure. A slave trader from Sudan, he commanded a number of solid, seasoned troops. He acquired modern arms thanks to the sale of ivory and slaves. He took control of Bornu in 1893 and planned to conquer the empire of Wadai, which had inflicted an initial defeat on his troops in 1887. However, his advance was halted in 1900 by the French colonisers. Both a slave trader and a warrior opposed to the conqueror, Rabah has remained an ambiguous historical figure in Chad.

The colonial period: commanders, auxiliaries and tirailleurs[22] (1900–60)

The 'Chad of the commanders'[23]

Colonisation was not an attempt to 'pacify' a territory ravaged by wars and raids: instead, it imposed new forms of violence. The army of the empire of Wadai was beaten by the French in 1909. The cousin of the defeated Sultan Doudmourrah (Muhammad Da'ud Murra ibn Yusuf), who had sworn allegiance to the French, was enthroned. Sultan Doudmourrah and the military chiefs who had stayed faithful to him rebelled, but were forced to surrender in 1911. Jean Ferrandi's narrative of the entry of the vanquished Sultan into the city of Abéché reveals the fascination the conquerors felt for the conquered. Doudmourrah was compared to a 'sort of hero from a *chanson de geste* of the kind known in France at the time of Bertrand de Born'.[24] The last empires to be conquered were Darfur, taken by the British in 1916 (the frontier between Chad and Sudan more or less respects the areas of influence of Dar Wadai and Darfur), and Dar Sila, conquered by the French in the same year. The successive outbreaks of resistance were followed by bloody episodes of colonisation.[25]

The disruption to economic life brought about by the French conquest caused even more deaths than the actual fighting. The impacts of the military campaigns in the north of Chad were disastrous: livestock was largely decimated and cultivation inter-rupted. Traditional trade circuits were progressively dislocated. Three consecutive years of drought and the arrival of locusts in 1915 added to the disaster: the populations of Wadai and Borku-Ennedi-Tibesti suffered food shortages, famine and epidemics.[26] General Hilaire estimated that the population of Wadai declined from 700,000 inhabitants in 1912 to 400,000 in 1914. Moreover, people had to endure a brutal mode of government. In 1917, a French commander ordered colonial troops to assassinate dig-nitaries of Wadai.[27] This event, known as the 'cut-cut massacre' ('*massacre au coupe-coupe*'), resulted in more than 100 deaths and prompted the intellectuals of Wadai to leave for Sudan or Egypt. Villages emptied, with their populations fleeing to Sudan, and the teaching of Arabic was severely affected. Hostility towards the French increased. For this massacre, Commandant Gérard was merely obliged to take early retirement.

The decree of 17 March 1920 made Chad a colony directly attached to the General Government of French Equatorial Africa. Regarded as an unprofitable zone, the colony was left in the hands of the military and of colonial administrators who were often novices and adventurers. Being sent to this poor country, with its harsh climate, was often synonymous with punishment.[28] Chad's administrative districts were understaffed. Military administration was maintained until the 1930s in most of the country; the governance of the extreme north – the Borku, Ennedi and Tibesti region known as BET – returned to civilian administrators only in 1964, four years after independence.

From the sultanate to the colony: the winding path of an auxiliary in arms

The French soldiers who undertook the conquest of the territories of the Sahel were few in number and poorly equipped. Furthermore, they were unfamiliar with the terrain. The existing political authorities – chiefs and sultans – and their territorial structures were thus often considered ideal intermediaries who could ensure that domination was successfully imposed. During the conquest, and in the period of colonial occupation, the French resorted to using 'native auxiliaries', 'often unscrupulous intermediaries whom they viewed as a necessary evil'.[29] These included interpreters and transporters, but also combatants. One example: the 'French' troops who attacked the Sanusi *zâwiya* of Bir Alali in January 1902 were composed of *tirailleurs* and former supporters of Rabah. As for the Sanusi, they too utilised auxiliaries: Zuaya and Tuareg who had fled the military territory of Zinder.[30]

The *faki* (religious instructor) Naïm was one of these men in arms who adapted to the new times, had exciting careers, and enjoyed a rise in social status through the use of arms. His trajectory is also very similar to that of the combatants who, many decades later, would excel in the profession. The *faki* Naïm was the hero of a fantastic, epic adventure related by a French soldier, Lieutenant Georges Joubert, in a scientific bulletin.[31] Naïm was born in 1863 in the small village of Kérémanka, near Massenya in present-day Chad. His name means 'son of poor people'. As a boy, Naïm attended the Qur'anic school and became a *faki*. After several adventures, Naïm was engaged as a *faki* by the Sultan Gaourang. However, relations between the Sultan and his *faki* soon worsened. After being expelled from Baguirmi, Naïm offered his services to the Sultan's most bitter enemy: Rabah. He then played a key role, as a warrior and an intelligence agent, in the wars between the slave dealer from Sudan and the sultans of Baguirmi and Wadai. When Rabah was killed by the French, Naïm went over to the victors. He started his career as a 'native auxiliary' by taking part in the construction of the fort that was to become the country's capital: Fort-Lamy. But he soon resumed his activities as a warlord, a spy, a messenger and a righter of wrongs in the service of the colonial administration. As France's interests in this zone were limited, the aim was to carry out colonial policies as cheaply as possible. The French opted, de facto, for a policy of indirect government (although there was no unanimity about this among the administrators). They used the prestige of the local chiefs, while gradually destroying their authority: in 1917, the sovereign of the Baguirmi empire, for instance, became merely the head of a canton and an auxiliary on the payroll of the administration.[32]

Furthermore, the colonial state did not hesitate to delegate to men in arms missions to collect taxes and maintain order. Thus, the *faki* Naïm enjoyed a successful career in the service of the administrators: he accompanied soldiers in their 'pacifying' operations, he robbed, pillaged and raided. Complaints about his behaviour flooded into Fort-Lamy. His pride irritated the French commanders, who clapped him in jail on several occasions. He always emerged and embarked on new missions: in Bol, he took over from a native sergeant who had been assassinated with his men; in Melfi, he brought the captain in command of the station the order relieving him of his command; and in Kanem he was an intelligence agent. Like the *bogobogos* in contemporary Chad, he was a state auxiliary who availed himself of his wages from the population. In Bornu, where he was sent as a tax collector, 'he acquitted himself of his task very well, and did not neglect his own personal profit'.[33] When Naïm took up his post in Moussoro, he handed the head of the battalion in charge of the district of Kanem an official note that stated:

> Given the current circumstances, in view of the reduction in the numbers of staff, a reduction that may increase, and the urgent need to submit the nomads of Bahr-El-Ghazal to our demands, the *faki* Naïm is hereby dispatched to Moussoro as an agent.

> He will have no more than the number of men (with their families) authorised by the leader of the district; he will live off the land, under the control of the commander of the subdivision, and what he has to collect in these conditions will be considered to be a permanent collective fine inflicted on the nomads of Bahr-El-Ghazal. These nomads will have only themselves to blame for the extra tax they will need to pay as a result of their state of permanent rebelliousness. Faki Naïm ... will be particularly employed in the quest for brigands and thieves, and in carrying out seizures, and will be in a position to do great service in this respect.[34]

As extortion was authorised by the colonial bureaucracy, the *faki* Naïm did not hesitate to rob and pillage. At the beginning of the 1920s, when the French administrators decided that the nomads of Bahr-El-Ghazal were in a state of 'semi-rebelliousness', a debate started on the need to adopt 'procedures that drew on more regular and conventional methods'.[35] The best way to bureaucratise Naïm seemed, in the eyes of the administrators, to 'exchange his role as a jack-of-all-trades gendarme for that of a canton leader who respects our administrative methods'.[36]

Naïm was then gradually incorporated into the colonial administrative apparatus. In 1922, the Lieutenant Governor of Chad decided to pay him from 'political funds' for various specific missions and so his income no longer depended solely on extortion – even if the products of his plunder were still to be found in the markets of Moussoro. The Gorans in the region frequently rebelled against the authority of Naïm, who was still, in the view of the French, 'the only effective means of dealing with intransigent and elusive people'.[37] After long years of service, when he was now an old man, the *faki* Naïm was awarded the cross of a Chevalier de la Légion d'honneur and was given a pension. In 1934, he was ordered to leave Bahr-El-Ghazal and live in N'Djamena. In the words of a Kreda chief reported by Lieutenant Joubert: 'He had worn himself out in the service of the Whites.'[38]

The career of *faki* Naïm highlights the relations between the colonised and the colonisers. The latter endorsed native institutions and relied on local chiefs and auxiliaries. Lines of continuity between the precolonial, colonial and postcolonial periods emerge; the use of men in arms with fluid loyalties and the recourse to auxiliaries who live off local populations have been characteristics of Chadian political societies from the nineteenth century to the present day. This does not mean that nothing has changed since that time, but it does show the extent to which certain political and economic processes are historically rooted.

From forced labour to the enlistment of tirailleurs

Under colonisation, the left bank of the Chari, which provided empires situated further north with most of their slaves, became a reservoir of manpower for the French, who described this region as 'useful Chad'. Colonial administrators spoke of the Sara as a 'fine race', with reference to their supposed strength and robustness; they emphasised the apparently 'docile' character of the Sara and their great 'usefulness' as a labour force.[39] This brings us to the very heart of the question of violence in the colony. As Achille Mbembe notes, 'the colonized could only be envisaged as the property and thing of power':[40] the relation to the colonised is a relation of violence, servitude and domination, which goes hand in hand with a relation of domestication. Thus, violence was carried out on a daily basis, in the very ways in which the body of the colonised was used.

The cultivation of cotton was initially an economic as well as a political business. Introduced in 1928[41] and imposed by coercion, it met with resistance. Cotton was not very profitable for the Chadians due to the low prices paid to producers; it also took the peasants away from food production, which was more useful.[42] Furthermore, cotton was at the heart of the colonial project of 'civilisation' and 'domestication': cultivating this inedible plant, which requires a significant labour force, on rectangular fields that ignored local habits (cultivating various crops on irregularly shaped fields) was deemed to stimulate forms of behaviour that the colonisers viewed as rational and economically viable. Growing cotton, finally, was meant to allow the colonial administration to raise capitation taxes on the income from its cultivation – as the colony had no resources other than its own budget from taxes and duties.

Indeed, the peasants of the south had to put up with direct duties higher than those paid by the herders of the north:[43] the latter refused to pay duties on livestock and the French found it very difficult to control the export of cattle. But taxation, which relies on a fixed population that can be subjected to census, was not just a source of income for the French but also a proof of submission. The dream of the colonial administrator was a colonised subject who was immobile physically (i.e. did not move from one place to another) and conceptually (i.e. belonged to a clearly defined ethnic and religious group).[44] The colonial administrators never did manage to control the 'floating population', however.[45]

In addition to the imposition of cotton cultivation and taxation, people had to endure forced labour. There was a massive amount of compulsory conscription for porterage and the construction of the

Congo–Brazzaville railway (better known by the name of Congo–Ocean). The construction of this railway, which was intended to link the port of Pointe-Noire to Brazzaville in order to open up Chad and Oubangui (today's Central African Republic), began in 1921. Between 1924 and 1934, more than 120,000 people were forcibly recruited in AEF. Among them, at least 20,000 came from Chad;[46] 90 per cent of the workers recruited in Chad were Sara. André Gide, a French writer who travelled in the region in 1926 and 1927, talked about a 'horrifying consumer of human lives'.[47] Because working and living conditions were extremely bad, the mortality rate was dreadful: 15,000 to 30,000 dead among the Africans. According to Mario Azevedo, the number of dead among the Sara was nearly 10,000, or half of those recruited from Moyen-Chari.

The south was also a major source of recruits for the colonial army. In December 1915, a decree of the Governor General extended to AEF the recruiting system in force in French West Africa. The contingent was fixed at 1,500 men; in 1916, the number of 'volunteers' exceeded the number anticipated by the administration. At that time, the army was a means of evading forced labour. In 1920, an order was made that recruitment should be limited to the Sara, Baya, Yakoma and Banda (groups from the south of Chad and Oubangui-Chari).[48]

With the outbreak of the Second World War, the continent was seen as a huge reservoir of manpower. Chad, like the majority of African colonies, was much more obviously affected by the course of the war than it had been during the First World War. In the years 1940–45, Chad participated on the side of the Free French, and, in 1940, the governor of Chad, Félix Eboué,[49] a Black French Guiana-born colonial administrator, offered his support to the resistance. He defied the collaborationist Vichy government and rallied to the government-in-exile led by Charles de Gaulle – indigenous populations had no say in determining resistance or loyalty. As Eric Jennings demonstrates, French Equatorial Africa and French Cameroon played a critical role in the early Fighting French movement: his estimate is that there were about 27,000 men from AEF and Cameroon in the Free French forces.[50] Contrary to standard accounts, the heart of Free France between 1940 and 1943 was not located in London but in a territory that spanned from the Libyan border to the Congo River. Chad became a vital supply base for the Allies and the launching point for the extended war in the Libyan desert. Chad, like many African colonies, endured an increase in forced labour and coerced recruitment. In this respect, both men and women supported the war effort. The famous Leclerc Column, which set out from the Sahara to reach Berchtesgaden in Germany, was made up of 3,000 men, of whom only fifty-two were French.[51] There were many Chadians among the colonial troops who died during the Battle of Bir Hakeim in June 1942.

In Chad, as in other French colonies,[52] the status of combatants in the French army changed with the post-war reform of the colonial system. They now benefited from material and symbolic rewards. According to the evidence of Captain Aerts of the Colonial Infantry, in 1954, the number of volunteers after the opening of hostilities in Indochina was greater than the number of places needing to be filled. Town and city dwellers now volunteered to serve with the colonial troops. Joining up became a way of rising up the social ladder. Veterans who returned to Chad after their contracts ran out (the period of service was shortened from fifteen to five years) were monitored by the colonial authorities – witness the anxieties of Captain Aerts, who recommended longer service times in the army: 'Five years, in the current environment, is enough to awaken the vanity that sets ex-soldiers apart from their usual contexts, but hardly enough to shape patriotic and military reflexes.'[53]

The complex and ambiguous relations between the veterans and the French comprised a structuring element in the history of this social group. In spite of the experiences of violence endured by the veterans, and to a lesser degree by the civilian populations that had to participate in the war effort and submit to redoubled efforts of coercion, in the south of Chad and in most other French colonies that fought alongside the Free French, the Second World War gave birth to a new heroic figure: General de Gaulle. Former combatants gave their children 'de Gaulle' as a first name, or an often mangled variant of it: D'Gol, Dagol or Dogol.[54] Other children had first names referring to experiences in the colonial troops: Larmé (*l'armée*, i.e. the army), Sarwous (*service*), Létnan (*lieutenant*), Captaine (*capitaine*) and Drapeau (French for 'flag').[55] Apart from the appropriation of the figure of General de Gaulle, veterans constituted a group that carried forward a specific military ethos. The veterans were the first professional soldiers in independent Chad.

The ethnicisation of men in arms' careers

During colonisation, the formation of men in arms (especially armed auxiliaries who were paid from the fruits of their plunder and the *tirailleurs* who had a salaried profession) was not a process isolated from other forces that were impacting on the societies of Chad. Previously fluid ethnic and religious identities now hardened. The careers of men in arms were part of a landscape whose lines and features were growing ever more evident. The colonial period fostered the crystallisation of so-called 'northern' and 'southern' identities. Colonial policies and the different local responses to them in the north and the south lay behind a process whereby the complexity of ethnic identities was gradually reduced to an opposition between 'north' and 'south'.

The polarisation of identities was inseparable from a reversal in relations of domination between the societies of the empire states and the stateless societies. Indeed, colonial policies had a paradoxical effect on Chad's societies: while these policies transformed the populations of the south into a labour force, they promoted the value of the cotton-growing zone and gradually enabled a 'southern' elite to rise. In the 1940s, the Muslim elites who had resisted colonisation and had refused en masse to have their children educated in 'French schools'[56] became aware of the high status achieved by a section of Chadians from the south of the country. At that time, French was the only official language, and these elites were worried that they might be socially and politically marginalised if the 'southerners' led the country to independence.

From 1946 onwards,[57] electoral competition widened social and political divisions that were mainly based on regional and ethnic identifications. The Parti Progressiste Tchadien (PPT) established itself in the south; this was dominated by Gabriel Lisette, a French colonial administrator born in Guadeloupe who became a fierce opponent of the French administration. A section of the Rassemblement Démocratique Africain (RDA), the PPT-RDA, soon organised workers' mobilisation in the factories of Cotonfran (the cotton company) as well as resistance to the administration and traditional chiefs. Two women were in charge of mobilising women: Hadje Halime in the north, and Kaltouma Djembang in the south. As for the other major party, the Union Démocratique Tchadienne (UDT), it emerged as the party of the French colonial administration. UDT members were mostly recruited among Muslims in the north. A third party should be mentioned here: the Mouvement Socialiste Africain (MSA), created by Ahmed Koulamallah in 1952. While the marginalisation of the elites in the north fostered the growth of a 'northern' and Muslim identity, the politicisation of the 'southern' identity was reinforced by the discrimination and violence to which the members and sympathisers of the PPT, which was then considered to be the party of subversion, were subjected. Inter-community tensions developed against a background of political rivalry from the end of the 1940s onwards. Armed clashes between PPT and UDT supporters broke out at Fort-Lamy (N'Djamena) and Fort-Archambault (Sarh) in 1946 and 1947: houses and shops were pillaged and torched, and revenge attacks turned into pitched battles.[58]

The 1958 referendum on the constitution of the Fifth Republic gave birth to the Republic of Chad.[59] François Tombalbaye, a former schoolteacher from Moyen-Chari, became Prime Minister in 1959. He took advantage of Lisette's absence on an overseas visit to seize power.[60] He led the country to independence, which was proclaimed on 11 August 1960: François Tombalbaye and André Malraux (the latter representing France at the ceremony) had to decipher their speeches in the light of a torch, on the first floor of the modest Palace of Governors.

What was Chad in 1960? A landlocked country whose territory was defined by European imperialists at the end of the nineteenth century. A country with hardly any paved roads. A country with few schools: there were only three high schools in Chad at the time of independence – and of its 3.5 million inhabitants only a few thousand were literate. A country that had not only inherited a state apparatus conceived in order to maintain a permanent inter-war state, but also saw its regional and ethnic identities hardening. A country that was still dependent on the former colonial power: the French were still very much in evidence in the management of the country even after independence (for example, the last French General Attorney left his post only in 1973).[61]

The colonial period had a dramatic impact on the practices and rules governing the world of arms: at the time of the conquest, the auxiliaries in arms of the sultans and the slave trader Rabah managed to accommodate the 'decentralized despotism'[62] of the French in the north of the country, while the *tirailleurs* from the south, initially victims of forced recruitment, enjoyed a gradual rise up the social ladder. The divergent careers of men in arms contribute to the formation of distinct professional identities and of groups that can recognise themselves in different ethnic and religious identities.

So the history of men in arms is never solely Chadian. As we shall see in the next chapter, the French army never really left Chad after the colonial conquest. Their relationship to the colonisers still marks the political *imaginaires* of men in arms, while the experience of Chad – that of the desert and its nomads, images and snapshots (however clichéd these may be) brought back to France by meharists (camel corps made up of colonial armed forces), as well as the experience of resistance and the Leclerc Column – has left its mark on the memory of the French army.

CHAPTER 2

. . . .

The professionalisation of
armed violence

For foreign observers with little inclination to understand the centrality
of violence in the political field, Chad seems to be a playground
and an object of speculation for armed gangs that offer themselves
to the highest bidder. This is to forget that so-called 'warlords' are
professionals of politics in Weber's sense:[1] moving in a non-pacified
professional market, they do not reject the use of force. Chadians
call these political entrepreneurs who have decided on a career in
arms 'politico-military'.[2] Politico-military leaders adapt to the rules
of the country's political game as much as they help to produce these
same rules. In this sense, Chad is in the grip not of chaos but of a
political field that has never excluded war. In order to understand
this political field, we need to look at the intertwined local, regional
and postcolonial roots of the revolts and conflicts that broke out
after independence. I will show how peasants and nomads who were
engaged in the first revolts became professionalised men in arms,
and how rebellions fuelled by the financial and material support of
regional allies recurred. I will stress the role played not only by the
regional powers but also by the United States and France. Chad has
not experienced any anticolonial war of the kind that afflicted its
neighbour, Cameroon.[3] But France has led counter-insurrectional
campaigns in Chad and has carried out dirty wars there.

From peasant revolts to the war of 'tendencies' (1960–78)

How the national army became a regional faction

The first Chadian army inherited the troops created by the colonisers.
It was mainly formed of veterans from the French army and young

men trained in the Ecole des enfants de troupe in Brazzaville. In 1960, the army comprised just one company of 200 men, who acquired their military experience on campaigns in Indochina, Madagascar, Algeria and Cameroon.[4] The vast majority of career soldiers, and of veterans from the French army, came from the south of the country. There were many sons and nephews of veterans among the first soldiers of independent Chad. This transmission was linked to a very particular element: their wages, although modest in comparison with what their French brothers in arms could earn, represented a significant sum in Chad.

Upon independence, the veteran from the French army was a successful figure in the south of the country. The military profession then became an attractive one for young men. Ganda, the former career soldier who was with me in the taxi stopped by the *bogobogos* in Ngueli,[5] told me of the time he signed up for the Chadian army. While living in Fort-Archambault (Sarh), he took the exam that would enable him to join the military: 'I was seventeen, but I pretended I was eighteen. There were a lot of openings. My uncle on my father's side used to be in the French army. I saw his uniform, and he earned a regular pension. This was what really got me interested.'[6]

The Sara dominated the Chadian army (and the civil service) until 1979. The Hadjarai of the centre of the country, who also served in the colonial troops, form another important group. In the BET regions, there were unsuccessful attempts at mobilisation, and recruits often deserted as soon as their training was over.[7] Most of the officers came from the south. The lack of education of the 'northerners' is only part of the reason why the 'southerners' grabbed the commanding positions: the Tombalbaye regime was characterised by a strong 'political tribalism', i.e. the political use of ethnicity by a particular group in its struggle with other groups.[8]

The regime was also marked by its repressive authoritarian character. In January 1962, all political parties apart from the PPT were banned. The first repressive operation undertaken by the Chadian army was the bloody crushing of the 16 September 1963 demonstration. On that day, in Fort-Lamy, the opposition leaders were arrested and there were some thirty deaths.[9] The commander of the Chadian army at the time was a Frenchman,

Colonel Leverest. The gendarmerie of Fort-Lamy was led by another Frenchman, Adjutant-Chef Gelino: the day after the repression of the 16 September demonstration, he 'hunted opponents down with unequalled energy and with such method and success that the hierarchy marked him out for distinction'.[10]

In addition to the military interventions of the former colonial power (to which we shall be returning shortly), the French played a key role in the training of the first army of independent Chad. Officers were sent to train in France and the influence of the French was considerable:

> the ideal profile of the Chadian military institution was the Général Leclerc School in Brazzaville and then the different military schools in France ... All the soldiers and officers had been cast in the same mould and were familiar with just one tradition, the same for most of the former French colonies, i.e. Saint-Maixent, Saumur, Fontainebleau, Melun, Montpellier, Saint-Cyr-Coëtquidan, Fréjus, and Antsirabe.[11]

Not until 1969 did Chad create its own officers' school. The French also played a key part in intelligence. In the retinue of Tombalbaye, there were elements of French military security. The Frenchman Camille Gourvennec led the intelligence office known as the Bureau de Coordination et de Synthèse du Renseignement (BCSR, or Bureau for the Coordination and Synthesis of Intelligence). Known for his brutal practices, he was appreciated by Paris.[12] As the historian Jean-Pierre Bat explains, Gourvennec set up an intelligence network; this network was structured by officers from the French army, placed at the disposal of the Chadian government, and sent to each prefecture to provide intelligence for the struggle against the Front de Libération Nationale du Tchad (National Liberation Front of Chad), known as Frolinat. In 1968, Gourvennec retired from the French army and took up a contract in Chad. He became the confidential adviser of Tombalbaye, at the crossroads of the interests of Chad and France. His services were suspected of being involved in the assassination of Outel Bono, one of the leaders of the Chadian opposition, on the streets of Paris in 1973.[13]

The Chadian army recruited, organised and armed in 1965 and 1966, when there was an increase in the number of peasant revolts. The Compagnies Tchadiennes de Sécurité (CTS or Chadian Security Companies – the name recalls the French Compagnies Républicaines de Sécurité or CRS, a branch of the police force responsible for civil order, especially in demonstrations) constituted a well-equipped praetorian guard. In 1972, the different components of the army were reorganised and placed under a single command. They assumed the name Forces Armées Tchadiennes (FAT or Chadian Armed Forces).[14] The national gendarmerie created in 1961 initially recruited from the Sara, as did other corps in the coercive forces. The army, the gendarmerie and the Garde Territoriale – later known as the Garde Nationale et Nomade du Tchad – contained 3,500, 2,000 and 4,000 men respectively. In 1979, the army reached a complement of 11,000 men.[15] In tandem with this, the figures in the budget for defence and French military aid expanded considerably. Budgetary expenditure for military and security purposes rose from 18 per cent of total state expenditure in 1968 and 1969 to over 40 per cent between 1973 and 1977.[16] The Chadian state was becoming militarised.

Tombalbaye was overthrown by the army on 13 April 1975, with the support of France. General Félix Malloum, at the head of the Conseil Supérieur Militaire (CSM or Supreme Military Council), assumed power. The seven years following the fall of Tombalbaye were a period of great instability. The CSM, which hesitated between a political settlement of the crisis and the pursuit of repressive measures, finally accepted negotiations in the face of the rebel advance. These negotiations led, on 17 September 1977, to the Khartoum agreement, which gave birth to the Fundamental Charter of August 1978 that organised a sharing of power between Félix Malloum, President of the Republic, and Hissène Habré, the Prime Minister. However, this cohabitation was not a success: dissensions between Malloum and Habré, aggravated by the contradictions and vagueness of the Fundamental Charter, quickly came to light. When civil war broke out in 1979, the regular forces that had developed and professionalised in the 1960s and 1970s became a mere regional faction, on the same level as the different groups composing the Frolinat.

The mobilisation of Muslim peasants and cadres

In the first years of independence, rebellions were organised in the centre, the east and then the north of the country. The Frolinat and its various factions have already been studied in great detail by Robert Buijtenhuijs. Without going into all the complexities of this history, I will analyse how the experience of the Frolinat reinvented armed violence as a practical occupation.

It was in the mid-1960s that a new type of man in arms emerged: the *suwaar* (in Chadian Arabic) or revolutionary, the Frolinat rebel. The peasants of the centre of the country rose up against the civil servants from the south who had adopted the violent methods of the colonial administrators who had preceded them. The fiscal burden grew heavier and the launch of the national lending scheme in April 1964 was met with outright hostility in the countryside. In October 1965, peasants in the Mangalmé region[17] rebelled against the tax collectors who were taking advantage of the levying of taxes to rob them. The repression imposed by the Chadian army created several hundred victims. Other peasant rebellions broke out in the centre and east of the country. These were led by peasants who had no experience of combat: 'those rebel gangs rarely [leave] their original region and, as they do not have any modern weapons at their disposal, they [avoid] as often as possible any contact with the Chadian army'.[18] The demands of the insurgents were restricted to the local level.

It was in the context of these peasant *jacqueries* that members of the Muslim elite organised. On 22 June 1966, Ibrahim Abatcha created the Frolinat in Nyala, a town in the south of Darfur. The Frolinat was in fact a fusion of two organisations: the Union Nationale Tchadienne (UNT) of Ibrahim Abatcha and the Front de Libération du Tchad (FLT) of Ahmed Hassan Moussa. This movement, which recruited almost exclusively among Muslims, tried to federate the local insurrections. While the Muslim elites reacted to their exclusion from positions of power and accumulation, we need to avoid any utilitarian reading of the emergence of the Frolinat, which was also the product of the humiliation experienced by those elites in a country marked by the domination of the south. The Frolinat adopted a revolutionary anti-imperialist programme with a strongly religious subtext.

In 1968, the rebellion, initially based in the centre and east of the country, spread to the desert region of BET. The inhabitants of the far north of Chad were also subjected to the coercive and humiliating policies of the new administration. This led to the creation of the 'second army', distinct from and independent of the 'first army' created in the centre-east (i.e. in the prefectures of Guéra, Batha, Salamat, Chari-Baguirmi and Wadai) following the peasant *jacqueries*. The army of the north was commanded by Goukouni Oueddeï, son of the *derdé* Kihidémi, the traditional chief of the Toubou,[19] who had been forced into exile in Libya. In the first years of the rebellion, equipment was extremely basic, as the documentaries by Raymond Depardon[20] and the photographs of Marie-Laure de Decker[21] show. The brutal repression led by Chadian and French soldiers, far from crushing the rebellion, roused a considerable mobilisation, and a growing number of young men joined the resistance.

The Frolinat was riven by significant dissensions in 1968 when its founder died. The new general secretary, Abba Siddick, was far from able to gain unanimous support. Mohamed al-Baghalani, who had been the Frolinat second in command, rejected the authority of Abatcha's replacement. In 1970, he was expelled from the Frolinat and created his own faction, 'the Volcano Army' or 'Frolinat Volcan', which shortly afterwards became the Conseil Démocratique Révolutionnaire (CDR or Revolutionary Democratic Council). Internal rivalries and conflicts aggravated the division in the Frolinat between the members from the centre-east and those from the north: in spite of political alliances, the first and second army were never integrated in the field. Abba Siddick's attempt to 'mix up' the combatants in 1971 immediately met with resistance from the Toubou. Goukouni, joined by Hissène Habré, a Goran Anakazza, broke away from Abba Siddick, and in 1972 the two men created the Conseil de Commandement des Forces Armées du Nord (CCFAN or the Council of Command of the Armed Forces of the North). But their relations were somewhat rocky. A conflict broke out between the two leaders in 1976, when Habré found himself in a minority within the CCFAN; he created his own faction, the Forces Armées du Nord (FAN or Armed Forces of the North). At the same time, Abba Siddick's authority over the first army was undermined: far from their exiled leader, the military commanders and the combatants from the centre and the east formed de facto an autonomous faction. At the beginning of 1978, a third front was opened in the west of the country, near Lake Chad, with the 'third army', also known as Forces Armées Occidentales (FAO or Western Armed Forces).[22] The FAO, with support from Nigeria, recruited mainly from Kanem and the prefecture of Lake Chad, but it was not recognised by the other elements in the rebellion. The Frolinat was then divided into factions known as 'tendencies'.

The French, who considered the border territory with Libya and Sudan as a strategic military position, intervened directly in the conflict. They actively supported President Tombalbaye, committing themselves to the struggle against the Frolinat. The French army intervened in 1968, and Tombalbaye invoked the 1960 defence agreement and the 1964 technical military assistance agreement. The French army's intervention went almost unnoticed in the French media,[23] even though troops were directly involved in the fighting. Between April 1969 and August 1971, France launched Operation Limousin, followed by Operation Bison between 1971 and 1972. Interviewed by a journalist several decades later, Goukouni testified to the 'huge' human and material damage caused by French soldiers.

Villages and palm groves were destroyed and burnt down across the BET regions. At that time, the legionnaires were fighting alongside the Chadian forces. We didn't know who was doing what. We attributed the responsibility for all this damage to the French forces, as they were the ones directing the operations.[24]

The numerous French military councillors continued to supervise and sometimes command the Chadians after the official end of the operations.

The military mission was reinforced by a 'Mission de Réforme Administrative' (MRA or 'Mission of Administrative Reform') in the BET. This mission was meant to be a technical assistance force comprising some sixty civilian administrators. It involved, however, mainly soldiers, embedded in prefectures, sub-prefectures and certain cantons. The MRA, supposedly bringing help to civilians, in fact re-established the local administration, including the traditional chiefdoms, created militias at village level (over a hundred at the end of 1971) and provided them with weapons.[25] This intervention weakened the Frolinat factions considerably, without eliminating them entirely. While France was heavily involved in Chad, the war featured in the French (and international) media only on 21 April 1974, with the capture by Habré and Goukouni of two French people, Françoise Claustre and Marc Combe, and a German, Dr Staewen. The archaeologist Françoise Claustre was kept hostage by the rebels for twenty-seven months in the desert massif of Tibesti.

In 1973, Libya, which backed the rebels, occupied the Aouzou Strip in the far north of Chad. From 1977 onwards, it provided huge amounts of aid to the rebels. Colonel Gaddafi, who had exploited the divisions in the movement by supporting the different factions successively or simultaneously, now turned to the Toubou. These obtained most of the weapons and munitions, depriving the first army in the centre-east of equipment. As for Sudan, it provided 'discreet but effective' support[26] to Habré. After expelling the Chadian combatants from Darfur in 1971, the pro-American regime of Gaafar Mohamed al-Nimeiry changed its mind and from 1975 supported the Chadian rebels, especially the nationalist Habré, in a context of worsening relations between Sudan and Libya. In 1978, internationalisation took on a new, broader role: after the seizure, in February, of Faya-Largeau by the rebels of Goukouni Oueddeï supported by Libya, the French sent military forces to prop up the Chadian army. Operation Tacaud, whose aim was to restore the control of Libya's border regions, continued until May 1980. At the same time, Libya supported the latest of the rebel factions to arrive on the scene: the FAO.

The increase in human and material resources at the end of the 1970s marked a break in the history of the Frolinat, fostering as it did a form of professionalisation among the rebels. These rebels were no longer peasants and herders who were short of everything (clothes and shoes but also weapons and munitions):[27] now they could live off rebellion. This process of professionalisation in many ways resembles the same process as it affected, nearly ten years later, the Afghan mujahidin as they confronted the pro-Soviet regime in Kabul.[28] The growth of American aid to Afghanistan in the mid-1980s entailed a modernisation of rebel equipment and the increasing independence of the guerrillas from the civilian population; the combatants, better armed and sometimes able to draw on their military training, gradually became more distinct from the civilians. In Chad, as in Afghanistan, the rebels who had to face ever more powerful and organised armies learned how to handle the weapons provided by their sources of external support.

In 1978, the rebels managed to capture, in three weeks, the garrisons of Faya-Largeau and Fada, thus controlling the BET regions. As Acheikh Ibn Oumar, one of the protagonists in this episode in Chadian history, explains 'the failure of the Chadian armed movement on the political and organisational level [was] directly caused by its successes on the military level'.[29] The victories did indeed lead to new divisions: the movement was not prepared to manage a 'liberated zone', and recruitment gained a new impetus as Libyan equipment came in. The enthusiasm aroused by the victories and the availability of weapons encouraged people to join one of the Frolinat tendencies. Local chiefs joined in the recruiting drive so as to gain authority, and the groups they mobilised were relatively independent of each other. The political leadership was no longer able to control the extension and dispersal of the movement.

However, while the factions recruited massively, few women were enrolled as combatants. There were some exceptions: Hadjé Halimé, a former PPT-RDA activist, joined the Forces Armées Populaires (Popular Armed Forces or FAP) in 1978. She fought as a combatant and was considered the 'mother of the revolution'. Another exception was Halimé Kana Moussa, who joined the FAN in 1978 and was known as 'madame bazooka'. But while few women took up arms, they supported the combatants and encouraged them to join the rebellion.[30]

The mass enrolments of the late 1970s were also partly the result of the destruction of traditional economic structures: as the country became bogged down in war, the men in the eastern regions were forced to choose between exile to Sudan and the rebellion.

Rebellion became an ordinary mode of subsistence: 'day-to-day survival and defending themselves against the neighbouring rebels were the sole preoccupations of the *suwaar* in the east of Chad in 1978 and the following years'.[31] The rebels imposed exorbitant taxes on civilians and practised a summary form of justice. In one of history's ironies, they reproduced the methods of their enemies, such as '*arbatachar*', a torture consisting of binding together the victim's arms and legs behind his or her back. While such practices as forced hospitality and extortion were commonplace from the outbreak of the rebellion onwards, they became widespread at the end of the 1970s when the civilian population shrank due to deaths and migrations to neighbouring countries. As the war continued, the boundary between political violence and criminal violence blurred. At the end of the 1970s, the Frolinat was, in the severe words of Buijtenhuijs, 'a disorganised set of groups of *guerrilleros*, without any "civilian" supporters'.[32] When attempts to unify the movement in 1978 failed, factional fighting broke out, especially between the Gorans and the Arabs in July and August of that year. Inter-factional struggles led to more deaths than the struggle between rebels and government forces. Thus, civilians started to ask themselves the following question, as did the young 'Pale Face' in the novel by Baba Moustapha who saw the combatants fighting at N'Djamena in 1979: 'But what combatants? Combatants fighting for whom?'[33] If, in their discussions of this episode in Chad's history, historians and political scientists have insisted on the fragmentation of rebel movements and the proliferation of weapons, the 1960s and 1970s were also a time of major changes in the composition of the rebellions, and the behaviour and daily practices of the combatants. The processes at work over these two decades, the factionalisation of rebellion and the professionalisation of the combatants, would leave their mark on Chad right up until the present.

The generations of the Frolinat

The singular experience of the Frolinat shaped a whole generation. As Karl Mannheim explains,[34] it is not the class of age that creates a generation, but the shared experience of those who have taken part in the same history. A generation is formed in a particular historical process, but assumes concrete form through contacts, discussions, handshakes and shared meals. Lived experience and its re-appropriations form a way of being in the world and a social *imaginaire*. The reference points of a particular generation are not stable: they are eroded by time, reformulated as new events occur, and reinterpreted by each person in accordance with his or her social and political trajectory. However, they still comprise a common repertoire for those who have experienced the event together.

From this perspective, the Frolinat was not simply a politico-military movement, but also an event that marked a break in the history of the right bank of the River Chari, destabilising hierarchies, forming new authorities and reinventing the rules of politics and war. The generation formed by and within this event was not monolithic, however. There was a gap between the political leaders and the rank-and-file combatants.

Who were the first rebel leaders? They included militants who had fled to Sudan, Chadian students abroad (many of them in France and Egypt), and the group of the seven 'Koreans' (seven men who had undertaken politico-military training in North Korea in 1965). Every group had its own particular experience. The students in France engaged in dialogue and worked with militants of the Fédération des Etudiants d'Afrique Noire en France (FEANF or Federation of Students from Black Africa in France), the Algerian National Liberation Front, or the Polisario Front of Western Sahara. Their eyes were turned to the socialist revolutions and anti-imperialist struggles then taking place. 'We were influenced by Indochina and Vietnam. We wanted a revolution in the meaning of the word thirty years ago,'[35] Ibni Oumar Mahamat Saleh told me. Although there were no combatants from the south, a few militants from that region involved in the anti-imperialist struggle (Gali Ngothé Gatta, Manassé Guéalbaye, Nadji Bassiguet and several others) joined the movement. They were, as one of them told me, 'to some extent the product of May 1968 in France'.[36]

In addition to their socialist-inclined, anti-imperialist socialisation, the first political cadres of the Frolinat had some other features in common. First and foremost, they were young: apart from former Sudanese militants of Chadian origin who supported the movement, the Frolinat cadres were barely thirty years old at the time the organisation was created.[37] They then formed an Arabic-speaking Muslim elite (apart from a few southern militants) that broke away from its elders. The young cadres of the Frolinat had not been involved in the political parties that existed before, or at the time of, independence.

The history of this generation, which was shaped by politics and war while still young, was, however, extremely fraught. Certain conflicts, such as those that set Habré against Goukouni, to mention just the best-known case, would never be resolved. The Frolinat rapidly split up into different tendencies and politico-military entrepreneurs ended up fighting for their own fiefdoms more often than they defended the revolution. However, their paths crossed when they formed ad hoc alliances and during peace talks with the government. In spite of the conflicts that divided them, the former members of the Frolinat tendencies form a generation because they were socialised together into political life, armed struggle and anti-imperialist ideologies, and because they turned against their elders together. Those who created the history of the Frolinat were at odds with each other more than they were mutually supportive, but the bonds they established led to a group in which everyone knew the others.

The survival of the Frolinat and its 'spirit' was the subject of a series of lectures organised in N'Djamena by the Al Mouna cultural centre in 1999. One thing that emerged from the debates was the way in which the political generation shaped by the Frolinat was perceived as such by southerners, who felt that the Frolinat was not part of their history.[38] Intellectuals who did not play an active part in this history attributed to this 'generation of immovable dinosaurs of the political scene'[39] the perpetuation of armed struggle: for them, the supporters of the regime and the revolutionaries were as bad as each other. Finally, we should note that the cadres of the Frolinat tendencies are also viewed as a 'generation' by the 'children of the Frolinat' and the 'children of the enemies of the Frolinat', who are currently trying to gain the upper hand over their elders in politico-military movements, legal parties and civil society associations.[40]

The experience of the Frolinat did not form just the political cadres of the country, however. The Frolinat leaders, who were 'African intellectuals and petits bourgeois',[41] did not wage the same war as those combatants who fought in the bush. The 'intellectuals' held meetings and endeavoured to politicise the population. Combatants sang political songs: 'Socialist Chad of tomorrow! Our young socialist state that will see the light of day at the end of the rifle. The peasant will close his door, once and for all, on the imperialist struggles and the anti-popular regimes ...'[42] There was still, however, a significant gap between the cadres and the troops. The encounter between the 'intellectual Frolinat' and the 'real Frolinat'[43] was far from easy, as the Frolinat needed to federate the insurrections that were being carried out without any overall organisation.

The war years affected all the populations in the combat zones in the centre, east and north of the country. 'Who has not been a rebel in Chad?' wondered a friend whose father and uncles had joined the Frolinat.[44] Factional conflicts often set brothers, cousins and friends against each other: buffeted and mauled by events, they ended up in enemy camps. Some fought in different tendencies. Prisoners were often forced to continue their fighting in the other camp, and to turn their weapons against their former companions.

The struggles of the Frolinat constituted spaces of regional and national integration. The combatants were socialised into the state by fighting against Tombalbaye, then Malloum. The men – more rarely the women – emerged from the bush to discover the towns and cities in their regions, and the capital city. They learned the common languages of their country. Yaya is a Goran from the north of Kanem who joined the FAP of Goukouni at the beginning of 1979. He did not choose the FAP rather than the other tendencies: he was enlisted by rebels who were active in the zone where his village was situated. His experience in rebellion and then in the regular forces – after he joined the army in the mid-1980s – was a testing time for him, but also an opportunity to discover the country and its languages. 'I am more open-minded than my brothers who stayed in the bush,' he explains. 'Before, I was a raw fellow, without any army experience. Now I can speak Arabic. And I understand a bit of French.'[45]

Former members of the various Frolinat tendencies have not just survived the same wars; they have also grown old together. This is the case of those who were incorporated into the regular army after 1982. They also belong to the generation that vanquished the Libyans in 1987, a national event in which many soldiers from the south also took part. The identity of former combatants is built on the shared experience of war and violence. Of course, they may nurse (as many civilians do) deep-rooted prejudices against Chadians from other regions or ethnic groups, but they do not express any resentment against ex-combatants from other tendencies. As the years go by and they are made part of the regular army, any animosity between combatants from different tendencies evaporates. Struggles between different factions are now just a distant memory.

The shared experience of ex-combatants from the factions of the 1970s becomes clear from my discussions with the 'old hands' of the associations of demobilised soldiers in N'Djamena. I had long discussions on this subject with Abdoulaye Chedi,[46] who joined the FAP at a young age and stayed loyal to Goukouni until 1990 (he lived in exile until Idriss Déby's seizure of power). One day in September 2005, in an outlying part of N'Djamena far from the hubbub of the city centre, he told me his story and the story of his generation:

> People ended up in different tendencies. After that, everyone ended up in the army. And when you're a soldier, you don't belong to one tendency or another. You're a soldier, that's all! ... We realised that they'd made us fight so they could win power ... Today, we've realised that, and we won't fight any more. People killed us, we killed them. But at the end of the day, we're on more familiar terms with each other than those who are in civilian life.

When I underlined the way in which ex-combatants never described themselves as heroes, he replied:

> Heroism? No way! Who did you fight in order to be a hero? You can't be a hero if you fight your brother ... Of course, we chat about things! We say, on such and such a day, you were there in such and such a battle. You burnt this vehicle in this

place. It was that person who saved me. But we're not all that interested. Before then, we weren't enemies. A soldier who's fought isn't going to have another soldier as his enemy.

Since the Frolinat years, the armed groups have split away from the rest of the civilian population. The reputation of men in arms further declined with the proliferation of rebellions and the increasing number of lucrative peace agreements, but the history of Frolinat tendencies and the formation of a generation of combatants have left an enduring mark on the country's political and social history.

Soldiers and combatants: blurred boundaries (1979–90)

Civil war and the assignation of ethnic identities (1979–82)

The civil war (1979–82) constitutes the crucial moment when the boundaries between soldiers and combatants were blurred. The Chadian armed forces (FAT) – that is, the regular army – became de facto one armed group among others. To begin with, all the movements that had emerged from the Frolinat joined in an alliance against the national army. But in June 1979 the factions split up: the CDR of Acyl Ahmat joined with Colonel Kamougué, while the factions of Goukouni Oueddeï and Hissène Habré fought against the FAO of Moussa Medela, even though these too had emerged from the Frolinat. Thus, the country was divided. Colonel Kamougué fell back on Moundou with what was left of the FAT and the gendarmerie, and organised the resistance. He became the self-proclaimed president of the Permanent Committee, a veritable parallel administration that exercised power in the south. The Colonel was accused of large-scale embezzlement and his authority was contested and combated: there were clashes between his supporters and his opponents, all of whom came from the south. As for the north, this was controlled by different factions of the Frolinat who fought among themselves mercilessly. Conferences aimed at reconciliation met in Kano and then in Lagos[47] in Nigeria and attempted to impose on the different politico-military tendencies ceasefires that were never respected.

General Malloum went into exile in Nigeria and, after the Lagos accord of August 1979, the Gouvernement d'Union Nationale de Transition (GUNT or Transitional Government of National Unity) was formed, with Lol Mahamat Choua at the helm (from April to September 1979), followed by Goukouni Oueddeï. The authority of the GUNT, however, was immediately demolished by faction leaders. In March 1980, fighting resumed in the capital, this time between Habré and Goukouni, the latter being given lukewarm support by Acyl and Kamougué. Goukouni was also supported by Libya, whose troops got as far as N'Djamena; Habré retreated to the Sudanese border. But the GUNT, weak and divided, could not resist the withdrawal of the Libyan troops in October 1981. Habré launched a new and, this time, decisive attack on the capital: on 7 June 1982, his troops made their triumphal entry into N'Djamena. Habré, defending an anti-Libyan policy, was surreptitiously aided by France and the United States: the Cold War was the prism through which African politics was read by the West at that time. The forces of the Organisation of African Unity stationed in Chad after the departure of the Libyans were ordered to observe a strict neutrality. The FAN then assumed control of the country. Hissène Habré was the first African rebel leader to take power by force of arms outside the context of struggles for national liberation.

Up until now, I have been examining the collective trajectories of two groups of men in arms: on the one hand, career soldiers who were the heirs of veterans from the French army, and, on the other, the Frolinat rebels who became professionalised as the war dragged on. The former mainly came from the south, and the latter from the east, the centre and the north. But just as the distinction between soldiers and combatants was losing its clarity, the identities 'southerner' and 'northerner', 'Christian' and 'Muslim' became sharper. The polarisation of identities was initially a matter for town dwellers and 'intellectuals' (i.e. those who could read and write French).[48] During the civil war, people were increasingly forced to choose their ethnic and religious identities. In February, the southerners were victims of a pogrom. For the first time, the capital was divided between northern- and southern-controlled districts; those originally from the south headed back to their homelands in their tens of thousands. The war now spread to the whole of the country.

The civil war radically reshaped the composition of the armed groups and the political geography of the country and the capital. The pejorative and insulting terms '*kirdi*' (non-Muslim or pagan) and '*doum*' (Muslim), used to designate the Other, started to spread. However, the conflict cannot be reduced to a break along religious lines; that would be an over-simplistic interpretation. Religious and ethnic divisions and splits between herders and farmers, or between sedentary and nomadic peoples, cannot be mapped onto one another. In the south-east of the country, there was a significant Muslim minority (the descendants of populations forcibly converted by Rabah) – one that was thus both 'southern' and 'Muslim'. In the Guéra region, in the middle of the country, the population was composed of a Muslim majority and a Christian minority, while everyone worshipped the *margay* (mountain divinities).[49] But if the identities 'southerner', 'northerner', 'Christian' and 'Muslim' do not help us to explain the behaviour of groups and individuals, the civil war made one's identity an important matter. What we see is less a mechanical, ancestral attachment to an immutable identity than a dramatically modern process in which identities were reinvented and became more fixed. Identities are defined and crystallised in specific circumstances; they are more often a product than a cause of war.

Rebellions and repressions (1982–90)

The trajectories of men in arms during the presidency of Habré need to be understood within the context of a violent and authoritarian mode of government. In 1984, a single party was created: the Union Nationale pour l'Indépendence et la Révolution (UNIR or National Union for Independence and Revolution). Satellite organisations were set up in tandem (for women, young people and traders) and contributed to the control of the population. Habré undertook to reconstruct the state and the administration. The repression was appalling: the Direction de la Documentation et de la Sécurité (DDS or Documentation and Security Directorate), created in 1983, was controlled by the President. It locked down the territory with its armed wing, the Brigade Spéciale d'Intervention Rapide, and, on a mere say-so, arrested anyone rightly or wrongly suspected of belonging to the opposition. The presidential security force, both the President's praetorian guard and an elite corps of the army, was another pillar of the regime.

Prisons, especially the notorious 'swimming pool' of N'Djamena,[50] had a terrifying reputation: few prisoners came out alive. Women activists were also imprisoned,[51] and some women who were not activists themselves were imprisoned because of their husbands' political activities.[52] According to the Commission of Inquiry into Habré's crimes, the regime was responsible for the deaths of nearly 40,000 Chadians.[53]

Despite the systematic use of violence, Habré continued to enjoy the active support of the French and Americans, who had no hesitation in offering massive assistance. Habré was the centrepiece of the Reagan administration's covert effort to undermine Gaddafi. He was able to count on solid US support throughout his rule: he received large provisions of military aid, training and intelligence, as well as support for the DDS.[54] The US also conscripted a small army of anti-Gaddafi Libyan fighters – interestingly, their leader, General Khalifa Haftar, reappeared on the Libyan political scene during the uprising against Gaddafi.

How did Habré restructure the Chadian armed forces? In December 1984, he created the Forces Armées Nationales Tchadiennes (FANT or Chadian National Armed Forces), uniting former FAN members and previous enemies who had agreed to defect to the regime. The ex-rebels of the FAN now comprised the bulk of the troops. The gendarmerie, which was reminiscent of the resistance of the southerners during the civil war, became the military police. The war continued on all fronts. In 1982, the ex-FAT members who had not gone over to Habré organised self-defence movements in the south, which gradually transformed themselves into rebellions. The 'codos' (an abbreviation for commandos) were divided into various groups: the 'green', 'red', 'hope', 'coconut tree' and 'log-tan'[55] codos. They were supported by the rebels from the north and Libya – proof, if any were still needed, of the ineptness of reading Chadian conflicts in terms of a north–south opposition. The repression of the codo movements was bloody: in 1984, government troops massacred civilians in the Moyen-Chari and the two Logones. These events, known as Black September, left an enduring imprint on people's memories.

In the first half of the 1980s, the entire south was plunged into warfare. Entire villages fled into the bush. Young men and boys were quickly trained to use weapons, while the women and girls took care of the combatants and took over delicate operations such as intelligence.[56] The training of militiamen was conducted by former soldiers. People lived in the bush and launched ambushes against the soldiers patrolling the zone. It was a war of movement. The political economy of the rebellion was decentralised, and rivalries between chiefs from different regions were intense. Colonel Kotiga Guerina's attempts at unification were undermined by the fact that Habré held out his hand to his enemies, many of whom gradually went over to his side. Little by little, the codos were integrated or reintegrated into the regular forces, and the movement died out in 1986.

While the codos were organising in the south, the war continued between the new government forces and the former Frolinat tendencies that had refused to join Habré. In June 1983, the Toubou brought together by Goukouni Oueddeï and the Arabs led by Acheikh Ibn Oumar and Rakhis Mannany, supported by the Libyans, launched offensives aimed at recapturing the north and east of the country. A month later, the Libyans engaged in a massive, overt operation that deployed considerable forces. In reaction, France launched Operation Manta (August 1983–November 1984). This operation, ordered by France's Socialist President François Mitterrand (elected in 1981), was at the time the most important French use of force overseas since the end of the war in Algeria. In 1986 came Operation Epervier (Sparrowhawk),[57] a deterrent campaign conducted mainly from the air. These interventions marked the defeat within the French Socialist Party of those who wished to break with the policy of President Valéry Giscard d'Estaing, according to which France was 'Africa's gendarme'. The supporters of intervention referred at the time to the danger represented by Libyan expansionism. French intellectuals who claimed to be on the left (Bernard Kouchner,

André Glucksmann) lined up behind Mitterrand's interventionist policy,[58] provoking the ire of their former fellow traveller from May 1968, Guy Hocquenghem.[59] Thus, the foreign policy of the French left-wing government was hardly any different from that of the right. The strategy of containment applied to Libya, and the desire to maintain a French presence on the continent, soon led to the brutality of Habré's policies being forgotten. And although the French strive to keep Chad within their exclusive sphere of influence, Habré was also actively supported by the United States.

In 1987, the Chadian army defeated the Libyan army and liberated the Aouzou Strip, on the northern border of Chad. Although the support of the French and the Americans was a factor in the outcome of the battle, the victory of the Chadian soldiers mounted on their pickup trucks was a moment of national pride. The ex-GUNT tendencies split during the 1980s: factional logics undermined the armed opposition. After the defeat of the Libyans, Acheikh Ibn Oumar moved to the government side, while Rakhis Mannany and his troops remained in their bases in Darfur and in the south of Libya. Under Habré, the Arabs were viewed as close to the Libyan enemy; many of them fled from the repression and settled in neighbouring Darfur (especially between 1982 and 1984).

Past splits continued to fuel violence, but there were also new divisions with equally terrible consequences in human terms. In 1984, Idriss Miskine, a Hadjarai and a former companion in arms of Habré who had become Foreign Minister, was assassinated. Habré had considered him to be a dangerous figure: Miskine was in a position to overshadow Habré, and he also enjoyed support from sources in France. The Hadjarai, who were one of the main components of Habré's FAN at the time of his victory over Goukouni, rose up in revolt. In 1986, a small group of cadres from Guéra, together with allies from other regions in the country, created the Mouvement pour le Salut National du Tchad (MOSANAT or Movement for the National Salvation of Chad).[60] The insurrection was led by another Hadjarai, Maldome Bada Abbas. Maldome went underground in May 1987. The repression of the Hadjarai movement was harsh and Hadjarai men of an age to fight joined the rebellion in great numbers in order to escape it.

It was then the Zaghawa (or Beri)[61] who fomented a coup d'état. The Zaghawa, who with the Hadjarai formed one of the pillars of the regime, rebelled. The Action du premier avril (Action of 1 April) was launched by Idriss Déby (who was at that time councillor to the President and a former Commander in Chief of the FANT), Ibrahim Mahamat Itno (the Interior Minister) and Hassan Djamous, who had previously led the recapture of the BET against the Libyans. Only Idriss Déby managed to reach Sudan. The abortive coup d'état sparked a new wave of arrests. Under Habré, responsibility was collective: whole families were decimated.[62] The rebellion recruited from the Zaghawa of Chad who wanted to avenge their dead and save their own lives, as well as from the Sudanese Zaghawa of Darfur who supported their cause and/or expected to be rewarded. The Hadjarai of the MOSANAT and the Zaghawa of the Action du premier avril rebel group ended up in Darfur with other dissidents: the supporters of Rakhis Mannany (mainly Arabs) who had refused to change sides and a small group of southerners led by Djibrine Dassert and Nadjita Beassoumal – the latter called their armed group the Forces Armées Tchadiennes–Mouvement Révolutionnaire du Peuple (FAT–MRP), taking over the name 'FAT' that had been borne by the regular army before the civil war. In March 1990 in Bamina, a locality in Darfur, the insurgents formed an alliance called the Mouvement Patriotique du Salut or Patriotic Salvation Movement, known by its French acronym MPS. The army, poorly paid, put up little resistance to the MPS combatants, who were supported by three countries: primarily France but also Sudan and Libya – even though the interests of these countries diverged.

The spread of armed groups (1990–2009)

The 'authoritarian restoration'[63] under Idriss Déby

After a period of hesitation, the French did in fact give their support to Idriss Déby: Paul Fontbonne, a colonel of the Direction Générale de la Sécurité Extérieure (DGSE or General Directorate for External Security, the French intelligence service), accompanied Déby from the *maquis* of Darfur to N'Djamena. Fontbonne would play a key political role as presidential adviser until 1994. On the evening of

1 December 1990, as the MPS troops were making a triumphal entry into N'Djamena, the capital was cordoned off by the French army. Habré had already fled to Cameroon. One politico-military entrepreneur had driven away another, yet again with the support of France.

The new occupant of the presidential palace declared, in his 'message to the nation' on 4 December 1990: 'I bring you neither gold nor money, but freedom.' This speech, although it was given by an officer who had never held any civilian responsibility, initially roused everyone's hopes. Adapting to the new demands of financial backers and responding to the expectations of the Chadians, Idriss Déby embarked on a process of reform. The organisations set up by Habré were dissolved and the prison doors were opened. Following the practices in force on the international scene, a commission of inquiry into the crimes of Hissène Habré was set up. But its recommendations were soon ignored.[64] The DDS became the Centre de Recherche et de Coordination des Renseignements (CRCR or Centre for Research and Coordination of Intelligence), then the Agence Nationale de Sécurité (ANS or National Security Agency). The ANS employed a great number of former agents from Habré's political police force.

With the adoption of a multiparty system in October 1991, opposition parties were established. Trade unions and new human rights associations were tolerated. The press, followed by independent radio stations, developed in spite of pressures and threats. Like many other countries in French-speaking Africa, in 1993 Chad organised a Conférence Nationale Souveraine (CNS or Sovereign National Conference).[65] The decisions of the CNS that aimed to limit the President's power were emptied of their substance. In March 1996, a referendum approved the new constitution. The same year, in July, Idriss Déby was elected President. Chadians were still living in a tense atmosphere. While Déby's mode of government was less brutal than Habré's, arbitrary arrests and assassinations – which could not be blamed on any particular person for lack of evidence – continued to occur.

It was in this context of authoritarian restoration that armed groups became more numerous. Ever since 1990, in fact, new groups had come into existence while the old ones fragmented.[66] No region of the country was spared. I will not inflict upon the reader an exhaustive list of the dozens of armed groups that came into being after 1990. The first significant rebellion, which brought together former supporters of Habré, broke out shortly after the MPS victory. The Mouvement pour la Démocratie et le Développement (MDD or Movement for Democracy and Development) of Goukouni Guet and Moussa Medela was based in the west, around Lake Chad. After the MDD military defeat, its cadres were extradited from Nigeria to Chad, where they were assassinated (1991–92).[67] It was then the turn of the centre, with the Front d'Action pour l'Instauration de la Démocratie au Tchad (FAIDT or Action Front for Establishing Democracy in Chad; 1991); then of the east, with the Comité National de Redressement (CNR or National Recovery Committee; 1992–93) under Abbas Koty, and the Front National du Tchad (FNT or National Front of Chad) of Dr Al-Harris Bachar (1991–1992–1994).[68] In 1996, a dissident faction of the FNT created the Front National du Tchad Rénové (FNTR or Renovated National Front of Chad). In 1994, Mahamat Garfa defected and attempted to federate the movements in the east in the Alliance Nationale pour la Résistance (ANR or National Alliance for Resistance; 1994–1998–2003).[69] There was also unrest in the south, with the Comité de Sursaut National pour la Paix et la Démocratie (CSNPD or National Revival Committee for Peace and Democracy; 1992–94) of Moïse Ketté and the Forces Armées pour la République Fédérale (FARF or Armed Forces for the Federal Republic; 1994–98) of Laokein Bardé Frisson. Finally, the war affected the Tibesti area with the rebellion launched by Youssouf Togoïmi: the Mouvement pour la Démocratie et la Justice au Tchad (MDJT or Movement for Democracy and Justice in Chad; 1998–2002).

After only a few years of peace, armed movements in eastern Chad re-emerged between 2005 and 2009. The escalation of the politico-military crisis initially sprang from within. In 2003, Idriss Déby decided to amend the provisions of the 1996 constitution that allowed only two consecutive terms of five years for the head of state. While the measure was unpopular both in the political class and within his own ethnic group, Idriss Déby, who had promised not to seek a third term, still undertook a hasty constitutional revision. Voters largely boycotted the constitutional referendum in June 2005[70] and the presidential elections in May 2006, which, however, allowed Déby to stay in power. The President's political base narrowed considerably. Social discontent was even more acute as the population expected to reap the benefits of the oil that had begun to be extracted in 2003.

However, the reconstruction of a rebel coalition was also linked to the regional context. Chad and Sudan would wage war by proxy, with each country supporting the rebels in its neighbouring country. The Sudanese President Omar al-Bashir accused Déby of supporting Darfur rebel groups such as the Justice and Equality Movement (JEM). The JEM, whose leaders are ethnic Zaghawa, formed rear bases inside Chadian territory. In retaliation, Sudan backed Chadian rebel groups, which also formed rear bases in Sudan's western region. The Chadian rebel coalitions that succeeded one another varied in type. Some factions were led by Idriss Déby's former allies, others by various politico-military figures who were at loose. They brought together combatants from ethnic groups with differing political histories.[71] The rebels launched two attacks on the capital in April 2006 and February 2008, but Idriss Déby won in military terms thanks to the superior weaponry of government forces and because of rebel divisions.

We should also note the decisive support of the former colonial power. The military cooperation agreement that had linked the two countries since 1976 was interpreted very broadly. In February 2008, the battle seemed lost for a few hours. However, Déby stayed in his palace and refused to be evacuated. France protected the airport in the capital during the rebel attack and also played a facilitating role in the supply of ammunition from Libya. In addition, French military officers helped plan the counter-offensive.[72] French interference raised very little debate in France at the time. As Roland Marchal explains: 'The French state is not as transparent as the US Administration: there is no counter power, the Parliament and the Senate hardly play their role and the political opposition has little taste to argue about foreign policy, not to mention African policy.'[73]

Other key international players were the European Union (EU) and the United Nations (UN). In September 2007, the UN Security Council endorsed the French proposal to deploy a joint EU and UN force in eastern Chad and the north-eastern CAR. The EUFOR Chad/ CAR mission was actually deployed in March 2008. The neutrality of the force was questionable given the pre-eminence of French troops in its ranks. As Bruno Charbonneau argues, 'the French colonial tradition of military intervention is not necessarily incompatible with a multilateral approach'.[74] However, EUFOR's impact has not been solely negative: European forces secured their zones of operation, thereby facilitating the work of humanitarians. And, to Idriss Déby's chagrin, the European mission was more impartial than many observers and diplomats had expected: Déby accused EUFOR of not defending Chad against rebels. A year after its deployment, EUFOR was replaced with a UN mission called MINURCAT. In January 2010, Chad demanded that the blue helmets leave at the end of their mandate in March 2010. By the end of May, all peacekeepers had already departed. Both operations were deprived of political mandate and were wasted opportunities to implement a political process to settle the conflict. Déby had remained in a position to refuse any 'inclusive dialogue' that would have involved not only the rebel coalitions but also the civilian opposition and civil society organisations.

Chadian rebels suffered a last military defeat in May 2009. They were then definitively undermined by the rapprochement between Chad and Sudan; the two countries signed an agreement in January 2010 that terminated the proxy war. They agreed to a joint border patrol force to replace MINURCAT. Four of the main Chadian rebel leaders then left their Sudanese refuge under pressure from their protectors and the combatants gradually returned to Chad.[75] The emergency measures taken in the aftermath of the attack of February 2008 were lifted. The 'democratic dictator' had successfully regained power.[76]

A few years later, in 2015, suicide bombers struck N'Djamena. The attacks were attributed to Boko Haram, as Chad was playing a leading role in the regional war against the group. The Chadian parliament adopted a stringent law on the suppression of acts of terrorism and ten suspected members of Boko Haram were executed following a swift process that did not respect international human rights standards. In Chad, as in many countries in Africa and beyond, the measures adopted as a response to the terror attacks paved the way for additional human rights violations.

Political entrepreneurs and professionals of war

The structural weakness of the civilian opposition

Armed rebels are not the only opponents: a civilian opposition has developed since 1991. But what do political parties look like in a country that has never experienced a free and fair transfer of power through elections? As long as armed rebellions were central in the political field, civilian leaders and non-violent political campaigning were relegated to a secondary role. The relationships between civilian and politico-military opponents were uneasy. Opponents who chose not to take up arms (or to relinquish them) needed to keep their distance from the rebels. Being too close to rebel leaders would have reduced their credibility – and would have been a risk for their own safety. However, they felt that rebels were the only political actors likely to trigger change. Rebels, for their part, were eager to attract political leaders and 'civil society' activists within their ranks: for example, Djibrine Assali, a trade union leader, was welcomed by the rebel coalition when he fled Chad in 2009.

The defeat of the rebellion in 2009 does not imply that the civilian opposition has acquired a central role. Political parties are numerous and weak. They have to face the powerful clientelist machine of the ruling party. Only the presidential MPS is able to conduct electoral campaigns in all regions of the country. Moreover, the boundary between the majority and the opposition is blurred. Opponents regularly defect to the ruling party, while fake opposition parties are manufactured to create the perception of political competition.[77] The problem does not lie in the political opponents' alleged lack of commitment: the very functioning of the political field prevents the formation of powerful coalitions that would be able to defy the ruling party.

What are the effects of elections in such a context? They are unlikely to bring any significant change. However, international actors have put their efforts and resources into organising elections in Chad. In 2007, the EU encouraged and facilitated an agreement that brought together government officials, the ruling party and the civilian opposition – five years earlier the opposition had called for a boycott of all electoral consultations in response to Déby's decision to amend the constitution. By signing the 13 August 2007 agreement, the main opposition parties agreed to participate in the electoral process. A few months later, in February 2008, as the rebel coalition launched an unsuccessful attack on the capital, the leader of the coalition of opposition parties, Ibni Oumar Mahamat Saleh (known as Ibni), was arrested by governmental forces. He is still considered 'disappeared'. The assassination of this respected political leader has dramatically changed the political life of the country.[78]

However, after a short period of unease, negotiations resumed and the EU pushed for the implementation of the agreement. As a result, presidential and legislative elections were organised in 2011. The MPS won an absolute majority at the parliamentary election. A few months later, major opposition figures boycotted the presidential election. It came as no surprise that President Idriss Déby was re-elected. In 2012, local elections were held. The opposition was able to take several neighbourhoods (*arrondissements*) of N'Djamena as well as two major cities in the south, Moundou and Bébédjia. The devil, however, is in the detail. While some opposition parties were able to win elections in specific areas of the capital city and in the south, they did not have the same room for manoeuvre in the north and the east, regions that are considered strategic by N'Djamena. For example, in the Dar Tama department, the only candidates in the legislative elections belonged to the ruling party. Why bother falsifying the elections when it is easier to co-opt opponents and to prevent the emergence of a strong civilian opposition?

The 2007 agreement's aim was also to promote an appropriate environment for participatory politics and credible elections. The de-politicisation and de-militarisation of the public administration were among its most ambitious provisions. However, these have never been implemented. Interestingly, the EU, as well as political parties, focused on the elections and have not pushed for the implementation of these provisions. In Chad, as elsewhere, it is easier to organise elections than to restructure the state administration and to alter the mode of government. Previous elections have not modified the rules of the militarised political field.

Political entrepreneurs' repertoires of legitimacy

Outside observers often interpret the recurrence of rebellion as the result of a lack of virtue on the part of a politico-military personnel prepared to make any compromise in order to win power. However, rebellions cannot be explained by any predisposition to violence on the part of protagonists, or by a dubious morality. It is less the opportunism of individuals and their personal relationships to violence that are at stake, and more the formation of the political field in Chad. Politico-military entrepreneurs sought to take control of the state by following in the footsteps of their predecessors, on a path that leads from the *maquis* to the presidential palace.

The recent rebellions, which were confined to their rear bases in Darfur between attacks, had no political plans for establishing hegemony over populations. Their ambition was to take power or, alternatively, to raise the price of their loyalty in the political market. The rebellions that were organised in the south in the early 1990s from the embers of the codos did, however, formulate a plan for the state. With the slogan 'federation or death' adopted by the movement of Moïse Ketté Nodji in 1992, the urgent need to protect one's own people gave way to a federalist cause. For the rebels and their supporters, federation was meant to open the door to greater autonomy in the south. The discourse of the southern rebels, more sophisticated than that of the other rebel groups, was also more worrying: the federal solution they advocated presupposed the division of the country along ethnic divides. The tracts produced by the rebels and the writings of intellectuals close to these groups – primarily those of Roné Beyem[79] – reflect their distrust of 'northerners'.

As political entrepreneurs, the rebel leaders draw as much from local repertoires of legitimacy as from the kind of language and ideologies that are in vogue on the international stage. The Chadian rebellions of 1990 and 2000 displayed, more or less clumsily, their commitment to 'democracy', or, less often, 'development'. In the game of acronyms, we often find the letter 'D': the Mouvement pour la Démocratie et le Développement (MDD), the Comité de Sursaut National pour la Paix et la Démocratie (CSNPD), the Front d'Action pour l'Instauration de la Démocratie au Tchad (FAIDT), the Mouvement pour la Démocratie et la Justice au Tchad (MDJT), the Union des Forces pour la Démocratie et le Développement (UFDD), the Union des Forces pour le Changement et la Démocratie (UFCD), and so on.[80] Chadian political actors finessed their images. In the April 2006 and February 2008 attacks, combatants were instructed not to attack civilians or those providing humanitarian aid in the cities through which they passed, while spokesmen sent out more and more reassuring messages to France and to other international participants. For example, in February 2008, they declared that they were not opposed to the deployment of EUFOR.

Faced with the rebels, Déby too showed an ability to seize the opportunities of the moment. He found in the post-11 September 2001 context and in the stigmatisation of the Sudanese regime of Omar al-Bashir inspiration for his speeches on 'mercenaries in the pay of Sudan' – for, since 1993, Sudan had been on the American list of state sponsors of 'terrorism'. After the April 2006 attack, Idriss Déby stated that 'the real reason for the attack on Chad is the desire to extend Arab influence south of the Sahara, on the part of the fanatical, fundamentalist regime of Khartoum'.[81] A few years later, Sudan was yet again an ally of Chad. The regional context then provided another enemy and another justification: the jihadist sect Boko Haram in Nigeria. While the violence committed by the armed group is a tragic reality, Déby also knows how to use it to escape international pressure.

The local root causes of rebellions

The armed struggles led by political entrepreneurs develop from local conflicts. The practices of power with which Chadians must live on a daily basis fuel contestations: the way in which those close to power have a quasi-monopoly on state resources, as well as the violence committed by soldiers and the impunity they enjoy. Issues such as cattle rustling and inter-communal violence, which seem at first sight to be far removed from politics in N'Djamena, are of considerable importance. The injustice, violence and humiliation suffered by civilians provide fertile ground for wars. Taking up arms after a violent repression directed against your family, your village or your community means that you are both defending yourself and participating in a political struggle.

In the 1990s, Wadai suffered a cycle of violence that, although having a local origin, quickly took on a national dimension. In August 1993, a cattle-rustling operation dating back to the early 1990s triggered a feud between Zaghawa and Wadaians. The Zaghawa, who wanted to avenge their dead, attacked the village of Gniguilim. The shootings left thirty dead and over a hundred injured:[82] most of the victims were Wadaian. The assailants were never arrested. Demonstrations in support of the victims organised by Wadaians in Abéché[83] and then in N'Djamena were violently repressed. After a few months of calm, Wadaian former rebels from the FNT stationed in Abéché rose up.[84] Their mutiny was severely repressed: there were a thousand victims among the rebels and the civilians who were accused of supporting them.[85] One part of the FNT eventually joined the government; another created the movement called the FNTR. The violence of the years 1993–94 is not enough to explain the Wadaian armed uprisings, but it was one of the root causes. As Johanne Favre notes, 'though the unrest began in the village, it became a national problem'.[86]

In the Dar Tama, too, local conflicts had a highly political dimension.[87] The arrival in the area of herders driven south by drought and the destruction of their pastures led to tensions. Some of these herders were protected by local authorities, and conflict with farmers could reach no negotiated settlement. Tama resentment increased further with the intensification of cattle rustling, which they attributed to the Zaghawa – whose territory is located north of Dar Tama. This rustling was not perceived as a mere criminal activity, but as a manifestation of the daily brutality of the state. The Zaghawa, who since 1990 had benefited from the protection of local authorities, no longer compensated the owners of the stolen animals as they had done before. Although the Zaghawa do not automatically enjoy impunity, they are considered 'untouchables' ('*intouchables*'). One sign of their dominance is the fact that the *diya*, the amount that must be paid by the community of the perpetrator to the community of the victim in cases of murder, is not the same for a Tama as for a Zaghawa.[88] The 'Tama are dropping like flies', I was told by one former commander from a gendarmerie in Guéréda, the main city in Dar Tama.[89] This violence has exacerbated the poverty of the Tama and has encouraged young people to take up arms. All ex-combatants I interviewed in Guéréda had been victims of theft and violence.[90] Many of them said that they had engaged in rebellion to avenge murdered members of their families.[91] Whole groups of siblings were mobilised by the rebellion. Girls and women took up arms too. Women were the first victims of violence and impunity, and those who joined the rebellion fled the Dar Tama because they had been raped or because they feared that they would be raped. According to Human Rights Watch, the 3rd Brigade of the Front Uni du Changement (FUC or United Front for Change) was entirely female, comprising fifty-two women and girls. There is little information available on how they were treated in the rebellion.[92] Minors were also recruited: sadly, this was a common phenomenon in both the rebel forces and the regular forces.[93] After the failure of the FUC raid on N'Djamena in April 2006 and the signing of a peace agreement at the end of the year, between 4,000 and 6,000 combatants returned to Chad.[94] The former rebels, who feared further violence against civilians, formed militias in Dar Tama. They attacked thieves and those who had the misfortune to be considered as such. The militias also attacked civilians and Sudanese refugees suspected of belonging to 'untouchable' ethnic groups – and the latter retaliated, with weapons. The violence of the militias was then considered by the Tama as legitimate revenge against their oppressors.

The south of the country was not immune to local conflicts. As in other areas of contact between farmers and herders, the increased migration to the south and the militarisation of local government aggravated conflicts between communities that nevertheless had a long history of cooperation. These conflicts regularly set farmers against herders, but also, in cities, those who called themselves 'natives' against those considered to be 'northerners'. While people living in the north do not benefit from any special treatment (the south, conversely, is more developed economically than the north), those who live in the south view the 'northerners' as privileged. Under such conditions, local disputes quickly gain momentum. They are likely to fuel desires for revenge that can take a military form.

Revenge, which is linked to the political context, is also a powerful motive for mobilisation. In a country where peace agreements rarely end wars, and where (war) criminals are never tried (with the notable exception of Habré), old divisions reappear and become militarised. Revenge is a legacy for the children of the victims of violence, a theme that has been brought to the screen by Mahamat Saleh Haroun.[95] We can measure the importance of this phenomenon when we hear young Chadians who have lost loved ones saying, 'Now, we do human rights stuff, but only until we have our own front.'[96]

A last pattern of Chadian rebellions needs to be examined. In a context of routinised violence, the bush is also a viable option for those who seek to access the state and its resources. Writing about rebellions in the north-east of the CAR, Louisa Lombard explains that people 'lament the absence of a state capable of building roads, operating schools and clinics, and employing people. At the same time, their only way of getting "the state" to pay attention to them is by threatening rebellion and armed disorder.'[97] This description reflects a common feature of the politics of Chad. Both political entrepreneurs and rank-and-file combatants may resort to armed violence, or to the staging of armed violence, to claim their 'rights'. The second part of the book aims to explore how such an economy of war and peace-making has developed.

PART II
FROM ONE WAR TO
THE NEXT: REBELLION,
REINTEGRATION, DEFECTION

. . . .

When I asked a demobilised soldier who had served as both a rebel and a member of the army what happened to the young men who had been demobilised like him, he answered: 'Half are in the garrisons, half are in the rebellions, half are road bandits.'[1] This spontaneous response suggests that experience in soldiering is usefully recycled as work in the army, the rebellion or road banditry. The interviewee did not discount combining one activity with another. Because of this fluidity between the statuses of combatant, soldier and road bandit, people use the vocabulary of disguise and cross-dressing to talk about men in arms. Regular soldiers are said to 'dress up as' or to 'transform into' road bandits. Civilians who are enrolled in the army are said to 'dress up as enlisted men' for payday – they live as farmers, herders, merchants or taxi men and go to the garrison only when they expect to be paid. Moreover, the verb 'to go out' has become synonymous with 'to take up arms'. 'Going out' refers to leaving the town, the village or the *ferig* (a nomadic herders' camp) and entering the bush for a few months or a few years. In a country where combatants often take up arms more than once, 'going out' alludes to the possibility of 'coming back' to the government fold and to the regular army. The terms 'to dress up' and 'to go out' denote the porous borders between the status of rebels and soldiers, soldiers and road bandits, civilians and men in arms.

How do men in arms circulate between different factions? From the army to a rebel group, and back to the army? Combatants' tumultuous trajectories, which are puzzling to observers with a Western perspective on conflicts, are often associated with disorder and chaos. Yet in a factional system, warfare is not unregulated. In Chapter 3, I analyse the logics of armed factionalism and the fluid loyalties of both rebel leaders and their followers. I will show how rebel leaders were integrated into regional and global patronage networks, while their followers had to deal with multiple social identities and complex political loyalties. In Chapter 4, I focus on the dozens of peace agreements that have been signed since the 1980s. I show how these peace agreements, which have been reduced to political bargaining among prominent actors, benefited some and excluded others. Political entrepreneurs traded their political loyalty for lucrative positions. Intermediate elites negotiated to make a good deal, while rank-and-file combatants did not have much to negotiate. Combatants dreamed of upward social mobility, but they seldom experienced it with weapons in hand.

CHAPTER 3

. . . .

Fluid loyalties

War was waged in Chad – indeed, it was waged rather often – but war was not waged in just random ways. The tactics, tricks and moves were integral parts of a fluid political field that developed at the end of the 1960s. Rebel factions were forever forming alliances, splitting, negotiating and renegotiating coalition agreements. How should we understand the unstable loyalties of the belligerents? The political field was unstable, but it was far from being chaotic. Apart from the violence and the apparent disorder, certain rules characteristic of the politico-military field were imposed upon the actors. This chapter studies the itineraries of politico-military personnel and highlights their spatial, political and social mobility to suggest ways of interpreting them. After a first part on the rules of the political game and the ways of waging, and understanding, war, the chapter focuses on the use of arms as a practical occupation from the point of view of both rebel leaders and their followers. We shall see that rebel leaders were politico-military entrepreneurs who sought to appropriate resources on the regional and global scene, and we shall go on to analyse, on the basis of the case of combatants on the Chad–Darfur border, the way in which combatants' loyalties were manufactured.

Armed factionalism

The term 'faction', which comes from political anthropology, refers to groups or quasi-groups that are politically oriented and weakly institutionalised, and whose members are recruited by a leader.[1] Factions may have an ethnic, territorial or clientelist basis – and these modes of relation are combined and mutually reinforce one another. Ethnicity and kinship, often mistakenly considered as stable identities, are themselves subject to a process of political mobilisation. They are neither primordial nor apolitical, as the previous chapter has shown.

Unlike the concept of the 'warlord', which emphasises the authority of leaders,[2] the concept of factionalism allows us to place rebellions in their social context and to highlight the logic of division at work. Applied for the first time to the situation in Chad by René Lemarchand, the concept of factionalism refers to the process whereby rebellions fragment in ways that go beyond ethno-regional polarisation. Lemarchand used the concept to make sense of the rivalries and confrontations breaking out within the Frolinat at the end of the 1970s.[3] Sam Nolutshungu, who studied conflicts in Chad in the 1970s and 1980s, then pointed out that armed factionalism is a self-perpetuating political system that resembles 'a balance of power system in an "anarchic" world'.[4] He stressed five key features of Chadian factional politics. First, no player, internal or external, is ultimately unacceptable as a coalition partner (non-exclusion). Second, no coalition is permanent; each can be undone by the defection of any coalition member, or destabilised by the addition of new allies or resources (open coalition). Third, the bargaining power in alliance formation depends crucially on each leader's command of combatants and external supplies of arms (the primacy of force). Fourth, the 'fair' distribution of military positions and weapons is crucial to the cohesion of a governing coalition (armed pluralism). Fifth, every winning coalition is multi-ethnic in composition and must be seen to be non-sectarian (diversity).

This analysis of the rules of the political game needs, however, to be complemented by an analysis of the relations between the different levels of the rebel hierarchy. Nolutshungu notes in passing that the foot soldiers do not always follow their leaders,[5] but his analysis largely ignores intermediate commanders and combatants. The history of armed movements, however, cannot be reduced to the interplay of alliances and negotiations conducted by those in charge of these movements. Dissent and support are frequent at every hierarchical level of the rebellion, and the political decisions taken by the leaders do not fully reflect the complexity of their troops' allegiances. Indeed, the fragmentation of rebellions has become so significant that the politico-military leaders themselves are unable to draw up a list of groups demanding their participation in the country's insurrectional activities. Groups form and reform, and may change name several times over. Conversely, when the acronym associated with the name of a particular politico-military personality lasts for several decades, this apparent permanence is deceptive. Certain political entrepreneurs continue the combat on the internet when their troops have abandoned them to join a less virtual form of struggle. In the final analysis, the way in which acronyms are used tells us little about the reality of rebellions.

Studies of the role of 'big men' have provided a fresh perspective on the instability of African rebel movements. The big man, a rather loose label, highlights a position within social relations. A big man is a man (in patriarchal societies, whether in Africa or elsewhere, big men are always men, not women) who is able to create his faction by using social relations and by transforming them into strategic power and control.[6] In Chad, rebel leaders and mid-level commanders use patronage networks to build up groups of fighters. Interpersonal relations and informal networks are key in politics. Anybody who wishes to have a career in politics, with or without arms, at the head of a rebellion or of a political party also needs to be at the head of a huge clientele, to have friends in the political class and access to resources. As we shall see in the next section, being part of global networks and being able to tap into resources from outside the country are also necessary conditions for being a major player on the insurrectional scene.

Tripoli, Khartoum, Paris: rebel leaders as global entrepreneurs

As one politico-military cadre, exiled to Canada, writes: 'Opposition is like the beyond. Everyone can find his way there.'[7] However, not everybody can play a major role. How does one become a rebel leader in Chad? How does one create a politico-military movement able to have an impact on the country's history? While politico-military leaders often follow trajectories that involve frequent changes of camp, they are far from being erratic. By choosing three contrasting biographies, I attempt to grasp the logics that govern defections, alliances and switches in alliance. The careers of Acheikh Ibn Oumar, Mahamat Nour and Djibrine Dassert show different ways of conquering (or trying to conquer) the politico-military milieu. They show that, if the roads to Tripoli, Khartoum and Paris constitute almost obligatory stages on the way, these are particularly risky strategies; and the precarious profession of being a rebel leader requires an intense capacity for adaptation and an aptitude for managing rebellious teams. This analysis of their trajectories does not aim to create the illusion of a logic that applies to each of their routes,[8] but rather to bring out the constraints weighing on the leaders and the strategies they implement to move within an unstable political system.

Acheikh Ibn Oumar: the long journey of a Frolinat leader

Acheikh Ibn Oumar is one of the politico-military leaders to have been a witness and an actor in all the conflicts in Chad. His itinerary has passed through N'Djamena, Tripoli, Khartoum and Paris. An alternating pattern of defections from and rapprochement with the powers that be, characteristic of Acheikh's career, is the rule rather than the exception.

Acheikh's political history began in Paris, in the Latin Quarter, with the left-wing, anti-imperialist atmosphere that marked the French capital in the early 1970s. The young Arab, Awlad Rashid from Batha (a region in central Chad), had come to continue his studies in France. In 1975, together with other students including Ibni Oumar Mahamat Saleh, Nadji Bassiguet and Mahamat Ali Younouss, he took part in setting up an underground group whose mission was to transform the Frolinat into a revolutionary movement. Acheikh joined the armed struggle in the field in 1977, at which point he discovered the discrepancy between the theoretical analyses made by the student movement on the socio-economic mechanisms of the revolution on the one hand, and the actual motivations and experiences of the combatants on the other.

In 1978, when the Frolinat was already split into several factions, Acheikh decided to support Goukouni Oueddeï. He joined the CDR, a tendency within the Frolinat that recruited from among Arab circles and that was the heir of a faction created by Mohamed al-Baghalani. After the death of its founder in 1977, the CDR was directed by another Arab leader, Ahmat Acyl. Although, according to Buijtenhuijs, the CDR was the most 'ethnic' faction in the Chadian rebellion,[9] it was not homogeneous, and it also recruited from among the non-Arab groups in the centre. The CDR also allied with other groups, including southern groups. At the beginning of 1979, the CDR, then led by Ahmat Acyl, concluded an alliance with the southerners of the Chadian armed forces: this accord set a precedent and Acheikh Ibn Oumar would relaunch this alliance in 1982. Between 1981 and 1982, under the GUNT (Government of National Unity) led by Goukouni, Acheikh Ibn Oumar occupied the post of Minister of Education. Acheikh took over the CDR in 1982 when the movement's founder, Ahmat Acyl, was cut down by the propeller of a helicopter. Acheikh presented himself as Acyl's heir. Gaddafi remained the movement's main supporter. While Acheikh was accused of adopting a more conciliatory position towards Libya than Acyl, he was still less pro-Libyan than the rebel leader Rakhis Mannany.[10] The trajectory of Acheikh and his movement passed via Libya but also Darfur, where in the 1980s the first rear-guard base of the CDR was set up. This was in fact a refugee camp, Amjikoti, which provided shelter for Chadian Arabs who were the victims of the repression organised against them by the Habré regime.[11] After a joint attack of Chadian forces supported by France, the combatants of the CDR made for the interior of Darfur.

Relations between Acheikh, Goukouni and their Libyan godfather were stormy. In 1984, Acheikh was removed from his post in the GUNT and put under house arrest in Tripoli. The conflict intensified between Goukouni and Acheikh, who for a while had been considered by Gaddafi as a possible replacement for Goukouni as leader of the rebellion: their troops clashed, and Acheikh was arrested and detained until November 1985.[12] After the defeat of Libya by troops under Habré, Acheikh broke off with Gaddafi. In November 1988, he signed an agreement with the government and became Minister of Foreign Affairs, a post he would keep until Habré's fall. Some CDR combatants, loyal to Rakhis Mannany, refused to support the government and joined the rebels who took part in the action of 1 April led by Idriss Déby.

Under Déby, Acheikh was offered several prestigious posts. He became a special adviser to the President (1990–91), then Chad's Ambassador to the United States and the High Representative to the United Nations (1992–93). However, he broke with Déby and went into exile in France. To explain his defection, he stated that he felt threatened: rumours were circulating in N'Djamena about his supposed links with armed opposition leaders.[13] In May 1995, he announced on Radio France Internationale that he had re-joined the politico-military. In Cotonou and then in Paris he met Mahamat Garfa from the ANR and Brahim Mallah from the MDD. They were joined by Hissène Koty and Bichara Idriss Haggar, from the CNR, Adoum Yacoub Kougou, and Dr Al-Harris Bachar, Ousmane Gam and Adoun Moussa Seïf.[14] Acheikh's politico-military endeavours at this time were modest, and the fallout from his activism in exile was quite insignificant. The CDR and the dormant politico-military groups were not to be buried so quickly, however. In March 2006, while he was merely a politico-military leader without troops and a member of a coalition of cyber-rebels, the Union des Forces du Changement (UFC or Union of Forces for Change), Acheikh Ibn Oumar told me: 'Even in the movements that no longer exist, we are still there and can stage a comeback at any time.'[15] And he was indeed back on the politico-military scene a few months later. The man who returned to Khartoum in July 2006 found his former comrades in arms and his political adversaries in the 'liberated zones' of the Chadian rebellion (in Darfur!). They included other Arab rebel leaders who had also passed via the CDR, such as Hassan Al Djinedi.

Acheikh's return to business was possible only once Sudan approved it. Acheikh could take advantage of Sudanese support from summer 2006 onwards, on condition that he agreed to form an alliance with Mahamat Nouri, a former follower of Habré whom he had fought for a long time. Acheikh agreed to collaborate with his former enemy: the CDR that he led joined the new coalition. However, the UFDD, the product of an ad hoc alliance, could not hold out for long against internal dissent. A faction composed mainly of Arabs, the UFDD-Fondamentale (UFDD-F or the Fundamental UFDD), left the coalition in May 2007. The UFDD-F brought together the CDR of Acheikh and a wing of the FUC led by Abdel Wahid Aboud Mackaye. The misadventures of the rebellious intellectual continued as Aboud Mackaye rose to power in the ranks of the UFDD-F. Acheikh was finally expelled from the movement in February 2008,[16] at the time of the raid on N'Djamena – in which the UFDD-F took part. Acheikh went back to his French exile. In January 2009, as a new rebel coalition was being formed, Albadour Acyl Ahmad Aghbach became the official General Secretary of the CDR within which Acheikh had, in his own words, 'become just another militant'.[17] Five months later, as the new rebel coalition that had been given the name Union des Forces de la Résistance (UFR or Union of Forces of Resistance) launched an attack on the east of Chad (which was rapidly halted by government forces), Acheikh was once more centre stage in the media when he accepted the post of representative of the rebellion in Europe. With the defeat of the rebellion in 2009, Acheikh was relegated to his status as a member of the opposition and an intellectual in exile. His excursions in support of the rebellion did not stop him being invited as an expert to seminars and conferences on Chad and the countries of the Sahel-Saharan strip. He is regularly asked to give his opinion on current affairs in the French media.

Acheikh's career is of interest in several respects. It mainly illustrates the longevity of certain politicians who had been trained at the time of the first mobilisations for the Frolinat. Acheikh passed through every post: leader of a politico-military movement, minister, ambassador, exiled opposition figure. His trajectory also shows the absolutely crucial role played by regional sources of support: Libya and Sudan. It was not his popularity in Chad that governed the different stages of his politico-military career, but rather the benevolence of his sponsors. These influenced the loyalties of politico-military leaders: in 2006, Acheikh did not forge an alliance with Mahamat Nour with a light heart. While the support of neighbouring countries played a key role on the insurrectional scene, regional godfathers also encountered a great deal of resistance. And thus, in spite of – or because of – the money and effort invested in the reunification of Chadian armed groups, the Sudanese were unable to unite them behind the leaders they had chosen. The Sudanese could impose a leader, and could force the various pretenders to the presidency to join up provisionally, but they were in no position to dictate the policies of their Chadian allies.

Another lesson can be learned from these trajectories: ethnic origin does count, but alliances between armed groups do not simply follow ethnic or clan logics. Although the Arabs comprise one of the demographically most significant groups in Chad, they have never been all that important on the Chadian political scene. They have never been united. For one thing, the ethnic groups are not culturally homogeneous. The Arabs of the Salamat, who before the civil war stayed in the Tombalbaye camp, and the Arabs of the central region, including Acheikh, do not share the same history as the Arabs from the east, who, like Hassaballah Soubiane (a former member of the MPS who was Chad's Ambassador to Washington before joining the rebellion in 2003),[18] have relatives on the other side of the border. As for the Arabs of Chari-Baguirmi, they are more in evidence in the civilian political class than in rebel circles. Apart from the case of the Arabs, we need to note that no Chadian ethnic group has been united in the political arena. The most violent and longest-lasting conflict in Chad in the 1970s and 1980s was the one between Habré and Goukouni, even though both of them originally came from the far north of Chad. More recently, in 2005, the presidential clan split: relatives of Déby took up arms against him. Finally, ad hoc alliances may unite armed groups even when they have different historical and social trajectories behind them. What better example could there be than the alliance forged during the civil war against Acyl Ahmat and the southerner Kamougué and then renewed by Acheikh when he took over the CDR?

One final point needs to be made: the man who embodies the CDR made a brief reappearance on the insurrectional scene at a time when his groups seemed to be a thing of the past. After his split with Déby, Acheikh, who no longer had any combatants to count on, took part in several little politico-military enterprises. There was nothing very out of the ordinary about this: isolated leaders and cyber-rebels are legion in African and Western towns. The proliferation of press communiqués and conferences that are meant to spread the message of the opposition in exile may seem to the uninformed observer so many useless gestures, but they do make it possible to maintain a presence on the insurrectional scene. The exiled opposition member continues to have people talking about him, while the real leaders of movements – those who are in contact with commanders in the field – can boast of their collaboration with cadres from other regions and ethnic groups and foreground their movement's multi-ethnic character. A politico-military leader without any troops in the field cannot, however, be more than a fellow traveller of rebellions, and cannot claim to play a decisive political role, whatever his past in these circles may have been. With regard to Acheikh, a politico-military figure twenty years his junior told me this: 'He does have a whole load of qualifications. But it's the armed men who go around with the man who count, not qualifications.'[19] This is a lesson that Mahamat Nour has taken to heart.

Mahamat Nour: the east face of the rebels' rise

Mahamat Nour Abdelkarim also led a rebellion and then a ministry. However, his trajectory represents a different route taken by the rebel hierarchy as he rose up the social ladder. While Acheikh Ibn Oumar was an intellectual who took over a rebellion, Nour, who belonged to the new generation of politico-military entrepreneurs, climbed the east face of the politico-military milieu, on the Chad–Darfur border.[20] Mahamat Nour belongs to the small group of Chadian politico-military figures who hit the headlines not only in Chad, but across the world. The man who was at the head of the FUC when the movement launched an unsuccessful attack on N'Djamena on 13 April 2006 already had a long politico-military career behind him. Born in the Dar Tama, and nicknamed 'Abtantama' ('The Stammerer') due to a speech defect, he spent a good part of his younger years in the home of one of his relatives, Mahamat Garfa, who was at that time one of the most significant Tama personalities.

Nour's politico-military career began in 1989, when he took up arms and joined the Patriotic Salvation Movement, the rebel coalition led by Idriss Déby. Nour was barely twenty at the time. After the MPS victory in 1990, he became sub-prefect in Biltine, near his home region. But when his uncle Garfa founded the ANR in 1994, he followed him and resumed the armed struggle. Garfa went into exile in Benin in 1998, while Mahamat Nour remained with the combatants in Darfur. Nour, who had good relations with the Sudanese authorities, lived with his troops between Darfur and Khartoum. In 1998, he was recruited by the Sudanese intelligence services and operated in the oil-producing regions of the Western Upper Nile. After 2003, when the repression of the Darfur movements was organised, he pursued his career as an auxiliary in the Sudanese armed forces in Darfur. Under the authority of an officer of the Sudanese services, he gave a helping hand to the pro-government militias known as the Janjaweed. The Tama whom he recruited attacked the rebel positions of the Sudan Liberation Army (SLA) and villages in the west of Darfur. His troops, like many pro-government militias, were integrated into the Popular Defence Forces (PDF). He rose to the rank of general coordinator of the PDF of West Darfur.

During this time, Mahamat Garfa, from his exile in Benin, did not have the means to implement his political ambitions. Isolated from his combatants, he signed a peace accord with Idriss Déby in 2003. However, he had to face the rivalry of his own cousin, Mahamat Abbo Sileck, who had taken refuge a long time before in the Paris region. Hardly had he arrived in Khartoum than the latter found himself in the jails of the Sudanese services, leaving the field open for Nour. Mahamat Abbo Sileck was freed nine months later. Although he was accused in politico-military circles of having orchestrated the arrest of his troublesome relative,[21] Nour became the leader of the movement, which he renamed the Rassemblement pour la Démocratie et les Libertés (RDL or Rally for Democracy and Freedom – RDL) in 2005. The worsening relations between Déby and Al-Bashir were a real stroke of luck for the Chadian rebels. The Sudanese supplied Mahamat Nour with the military equipment and necessary resources to maintain his troops. In December 2005, the RDL became the spearhead of the rebel coalition of the FUC. The FUC recruited on a large scale in the Dar Tama and other regions in the east of Chad as well as in Darfur, where many Tama live. The coalition was forced back on 13 April 2006 when the rebels reached the outskirts of N'Djamena. Rumour has it that the combatants attacked the Palais du 15 Janvier, the seat of the parliament in the north-east district of the capital, thinking mistakenly that it was the presidential palace.

The failure of the April 2006 attack marked a turning point in Nour's trajectory. He lost the confidence of the other politico-military leaders: in July, the Concorde Nationale Tchadienne (Chadian National Concord or CNT) of Al-Djineidi broke away from the FUC, followed in September by the group under Adouma Hassaballah. Nour was soon no longer the protégé of the Sudanese, whose support shifted to Mahamat Nouri. Although their names differed by only a single letter, the two rivals belonged to different worlds: Nouri was a Goran, a former collaborator of Habré and senior to Nour. The ambitious young Nour was forced to face facts: the road to the presidency of Chad was now strewn with obstacles and he was obliged to make a strategic withdrawal. He negotiated and signed an agreement with Idriss Déby at the end of 2006 with Libya as a mediating presence. In March 2007, Déby made him Defence Minister.

A rapprochement is not the same thing as a reconciliation, especially in Chad, where peace negotiations boil down to mere horse-trading between leaders. The ex-rebels, fearful of renewed violence against the Tama civilians, organised militias in the Dar Tama. Nour's relations with the regime deteriorated in the rainy season (summer in Europe) of 2007, when former members of the FUC refused to allow their militia to be dismantled so that they could be (re)incorporated into the regular army. In autumn 2007, government troops entered Guéréda and some militia managed to flee to nearby Darfur. Former FUC military commanders were arrested. Mahamat Nour was sacked in December, while his entourage claimed that he had been the victim of a poisoning – and, in a sign of the climate of mistrust, Nour stayed in a luxury hotel in N'Djamena before taking refuge in the Libyan Embassy. He returned to Khartoum at the end of 2009, hoping to find the support he had once enjoyed, but after a few days he was expelled. His reintegration into politico-military circles was now compromised, and he took refuge in the Gulf States, where he became a trader. In February 2014, he decided to change camp and go over to Idriss Déby. He returned to Chad.

What stands out from this itinerary that followed the roads and trails of Chad as well as of Darfur? It was the backing of a foreign supporter that made Nour's meteoric rise possible: he was in a position to threaten the Chadian regime at the age of thirty-five, when he had been more or less unknown just six months previously. Sudan recently played for Mahamat Nour the role that Libya had played for Acheikh Ibn Oumar in the 1980s. The regional political context – the expansionist ambitions of Gaddafi in one case, Al-Bashir's desire to overturn Déby in the other[22] – were real windfalls for their politico-military endeavours. Like Acheikh, Nour had passed through Darfur. Nour's collaboration with his sponsor, however, went beyond a mere coincidence of interests: Nour, as a member of the Janjaweed militias, played an active part in the repression that was inflicted on Darfur, with unprecedented violence, from 2003 onwards. This was a Sudanese affair, but Nour and his men found, in the Darfur war, an opportunity to take revenge for the exaction committed by the Chadian Zaghawa who acted with complete impunity in the Dar Tama. It mattered little that the Zaghawa of Darfur and their allies were not involved. However terrible, the result was clear: Nour had managed to make himself indispensable in the eyes of the Sudanese when the latter were seeking to destabilise Idriss Déby.

Nour's trajectory also shows that the main rivals of the politico-military figures came from their own ethnic group and sometimes from their own family. Nour took up the torch from his uncle, while his own cousin was in no position to cause any harm thanks to his imprisonment in Khartoum. For Acheikh, Nour and the rest, the members of their ethnic group or clan and their closest relatives were indispensable. However, they knew that they could also trigger their destruction. In this sense, family members represent a real dilemma: the politico-military figure who relies on them can encounter nasty surprises, while anyone who fails to seek their support is isolated and weakened. So loyalties need to be understood in a context in which the optimum solution does not exist: there are only compromises.

Djibrine Dassert: the routing of an isolated leader

While Acheikh and Nour got people talking, others, such as Djibrine Dassert, one of the last rebels from the south, did not hit the headlines. However, the *sortie* or 'going out' led by Colonel Dassert, a member of the Boua (an ethnic group from the Moyen-Chari region), was sensational. On the night of 13–14 November 2005, Dassert and his men, apparently recruited from near Sarh, Kouno and Bosso,[23] stormed the Garde Nationale et Nomade du Tchad (GNNT or the National and Nomadic Guard of Chad), a stone's throw away from the presidential palace. They wanted to collect weapons and stage a coup d'état. But they were betrayed: the weapons were no longer there and the attempt to topple Déby failed. The rebels left the city and seized the reserve of weapons and munitions in the officers' school in Koundoul, to the south of N'Djamena, before heading to the bush. The next day, the capital was a little more restless than usual: military pickup trucks were heading south and east. Rumours were circulating and the author of the attempted coup the night before was soon identified. In the southern districts of N'Djamena, there were fears of repression, but people could not help thinking that the presence of combatants from the south among the rebels might constitute an advantage when it came to defending the interests of the region if the government was toppled or if there were negotiations with the government.[24]

The adventure of this military officer from the Moyen-Chari region, accompanied by commanders and combatants from the centre of the country, soon petered out, however, in the sparsely inhabited zones between the centre and the south of Chad. A few months after his coup attempt, Dassert was barely spoken of any more. In March 2006, he published a manifesto that was soon forgotten. The Chadian press occasionally reminded readers of his existence, and international observers believed that they had sighted him in the north of the CAR.[25] In 2006, there was some talk of a possible alliance with the rebels in the east, but this came to nothing. Dassert and his troops had no resources. Sudan had a very limited interest in this group, which in turn mistrusted anything coming from the east. The Mouvement pour la Paix, la Reconstruction et le Développement (MPRD or Movement for Peace, Reconstruction and Progress), which was not able to launch attacks, transformed itself into a dormant network. The government did not even bother to engage in negotiations but simply ordered the arrest of soldiers suspected of complicity with the rebels.[26] In 2010, Dassert was arrested in the bush by the army. He had no more combatants to count on. He spent one year in jail and died in April 2012, a few months after being freed.

Djibrine Dassert was no newcomer on the politico-military scene. This officer, trained in the 1960s in the Ecole des enfants de troupe in Brazzaville, was a career soldier.[27] He had his first experience of rebellion with the codo movements of the 1980s. When Déby formed the MPS, Dassert was, with Nadjita Beassoumal, the man in charge of the FAT–MRP, a group that brought together the combatants from the south. At the Congress of Bamina, Dassert was appointed Commissioner for Arms, a position with which, as the leader of a small faction, he had to be satisfied.[28] After the MPS victory, Dassert became Defence Minister, but he did not stay long in this post. Since he had not been given the responsibilities and the influence that he thought he could justly lay claim to, and disappointed by the politics conducted by the MPS, he slammed the door of the party behind him in 1992. His defection also seems to have been based on a contentious sharing out of the government's resources. So he declared with his fellow traveller and friend Ousmane Gam, who had also resigned from the MPS: 'We do not wish to be accountable for the dictatorship in the eyes of history.'[29] The man who took up arms in 2005 had thus been retired from political life for over ten years. He had not been able to provide himself with a social base.

What does the history of this abortive politico-military enterprise teach us? Rebellions have little chance of making any impact on the politico-military scene if they cannot draw on any external support. The absence (or weakness) of external support is a recurrent problem for the politico-military movements of the south of the country. Admittedly, in 1979, the so-called codo movements could count on the support of Libya, thanks to an alliance with the CDR.

But the southern rebellions that sprang back to life in the 1990s and 2000s could not draw on any significant financial or material resources; they were unable to establish, in the CAR, rear bases and training camps that were as efficient as those the rebels in the north and east set up in Libya and Sudan. This brings us to the heart of the debate affecting the opposition in the south. About ten years ago, a former fellow traveller of Moïse Ketté, who had been contacted by candidates for the armed struggle, told me that he shared their ideas but did not want to commit himself to a new war without resources. 'I'm fed up of hanging around under the trees,'[30] he said. Creating a rebellion without external backing implies that you can live off the population and expose it to repression: the question is not just strategic, but ethical too.

Managing the possibilities in an uncertain environment

What can we learn from the trajectories of these three politico-military entrepreneurs? It is immediately apparent that we are dealing with professionals of politics, even if they entered politics in different ways. Acheikh joined the Frolinat when he was a student; the young Nour took up arms when he followed his uncle Garfa to Darfur. As for the career soldier Dassert, he went underground for the first time when the army disintegrated following the unleashing of the civil war. Politicised or mobilised by circumstances, they became professionals of politics in its armed variety.

One element shared by all these trajectories is spatial, political and social mobility. The rebel leaders travelled between N'Djamena, Tripoli and Khartoum, with time spent in Paris. All three of them alternated between periods in government and time spent in rebellion. Unstable alliances need to be understood as the product of the way in which possibilities are managed by actors who interact in a difficult and ever-changing milieu. Those involved adapt, sometimes from day to day, to a set of constraints and resources that incite them to break and then renew their alliances on a regular basis. Alliances are the result of a weighing-up of sometimes contradictory demands. They need to reckon with social obligations and material imperatives.

The resources that are indispensable to the maintenance of an armed movement are those of extraversion.[31] Chadian armed groups are not in a position to draw on natural resources in order to finance their activities. The combatants can temporarily go back to being peasants or herders, but growing crops and herding have never been enough to arm a rebellion. Resources mainly come from external support. And this is significant: Libya invested massively in Chadian rebellions after the 1970s even if its role has been less important since the end of the 1980s. Sudan, a player since the beginning of the Frolinat, recently became a key actor when it armed and supported Chadian politico-military figures. Access to resources influences the trajectories of rebel leaders and the future of armed movements. Likewise, support from France and other Western states has played a key role in the financing of the regular army.

The process of political mobilisation is never separate from the question of material resources: the maintenance of a social base is another crucial rule of the politico-military profession. In the tropics, as elsewhere, you will not succeed in politics if you pay no heed to the survival, and indeed the well-being, of your supporters. Rebel leaders and the combatants who follow them have relations of asymmetric mutual dependence. It is indeed possible to see the rise of rebel leaders as the result of their ability to attract foreign capital and to forge alliances with movements that have wind in their sails. There is indeed, to use the words of another such cadre, a 'permanent hiring fair for rebellion'[32] at which recruits and support can be bought. An armed movement that has suffered heavily from defections can soon reconstitute itself if it can draw on powerful supporters.

We should note at this point that politico-military leaders do not negotiate directly with combatants from their base: these are organised by commanders who are big men and who play the role of intermediaries in the rebellions. One politico-military leader described recruitment in his group in these terms:

> The com' zones [commanders of zones] negotiate with the cadres and the cadres negotiate among themselves. Sometimes we are contacted. People can contact us saying: 'I've got fifteen or twenty men. If we join you, what have you got to offer?'[33]

The supply of work (the number of potential recruits) can be higher than the demand (the number of combatants that a rebellion can recruit). Recruitment depends on the number of candidates who wish to join the rebellion but also, and above all, on the group's ability to maintain them and arm them. There is also a large discrepancy between the popular support a movement may (or may not) enjoy and the probability that it will manage to be a successful presence on the insurrectional scene. The number of men mobilised depends only marginally on the movement's popularity. Access to resources can never be counted on and a movement can pass quickly from being an important, high-profile organisation to a straitened group when resources are scarce. In other words, movements can go through 'opportunistic' and 'activist' phases according to the distinction proposed by Jeremy Weinstein.[34] They change profile with the circumstances.

Last but not least, we should note that none of the three politico-military leaders whose trajectories have been set out here has actually taken power. None was supported by France; none benefited from the advice and backing of anyone like the French intelligence services officer Paul Fontbonne. Their rebellions roused a few ripples in N'Djamena, but they ended in military defeat or rapprochement with the government. The support of a regional godfather makes a great number of things possible, but it does not ensure victory. Until now, all regime change has been approved by Paris. So it comes as no surprise that both politico-military leaders and the leaders of the civilian opposition invest time and energy in their French networks.

Kin-based social networks and political loyalties

Political loyalties, however, are not only a question of resources. They are also linked to identities and to social networks that pre-exist the war. In this respect, the question of loyalty cannot be separated from the question of scale. As we have seen in the previous section, ethnic solidarity is never automatic and alliances among rebel groups do not follow ethnic lines: at the macro level, ethnicity cannot explain the logic of alliances. However, at the micro level, kin-based social networks are crucial to understanding combatants' loyalties. The most common reply to the question 'How did you take up arms?' is 'I followed my uncle' or 'I left with my brother, my cousin …' A combatant will not, after all, place his or her life in the hands of a stranger, but will trust a person who belongs to his or her circle of acquaintances, and often to his or her wider family circle. In this section, I try to understand combatants' loyalties by investigating the role of identities and social networks in political relations, without seeing ethnicity and kinship as the sole explanations for particular loyalties.

Between 2003 and 2009, the loyalties of the combatants were of great complexity. As we saw in the previous chapter, a regional system of conflicts[35] developed with the support of Chad for the JEM armed movement and the support of Sudan for the Chadian rebels.[36] At the time, many Chadian and Darfuri combatants had family and ethnic connections with rebels and/or soldiers who were not only on the other side of the border but also in the enemy camp in the conflict between the two countries. On the Sudanese side of the border, Chadian rebels could be found who had kinship links with Janjaweed militias, with whom they had forged alliances. On the Chadian side, there were JEM combatants in officers' posts in the Chadian army. They changed uniform depending on the person they were talking to. But this imbroglio does not mean that the entrepreneurs of war form alliances with anyone and everyone. The allegiances and function of men in arms are many and varied, but not just a matter of calculation: they are linked to political alliances and ethnic, clan[37] and kinship identities. Combatants will identify, at different times in their social navigation, with their state of origin, their region, their clan or a network of ex-comrades in arms. They redefine and renegotiate their social and political identities on a day-to-day basis, while politico-military entrepreneurs attempt to play on these identities in order to raise troops.

Our analysis of identities in wartime will be pursued here in relation to Zaghawa men in arms. Their trajectories, which should not be seen as representative of the wider set of trajectories of Chadian combatants, show, more modestly, the complexity of commitments undertaken by individuals who are caught up in complex skeins of political and kinship alliances. Who should you support when your family is split between different camps – that of President Déby, that of the Chadian rebels led by his cousin[38] Timan Erdimi, and that of the Darfur rebels who sealed an alliance with N'Djamena? One answer was given to me on a Sunday in May 2008, when the JEM withdrew from a raid launched on Omdurman, a city opposite the capital Khartoum, on the Nile. That day, I was with Mahamat, a Zaghawa of about thirty years old. He had spent his time between France and Chad before joining the Chadian rebellion in Sudan. The JEM attack was suicidal, but its political impact obviously delighted Mahamat and his friends. The man who was introduced to me as a member of Timan Erdimi's Rassemblement des Forces du Changement (RFC or Rally of Forces for Change) took two cards out of his wallet and told me:

> I am a Chadian military officer, but I am also with JEM. And, as you know, I support RFC.

He showed me his identity card as an officer in the Chadian army, placing it on the table next to his JEM card, and explained:

> On JEM's side, there are my maternal uncles, on Déby's side as well as on RFC's side, there are my paternal uncles. If any of them call me, I can't refuse.[39]

Mahamat's relatives were indeed close to the leader of the JEM rebellion. Khalil Ibrahim visited them on a regular basis, in their village near the Sudanese border. As a Darfuri rebel, Khalil Ibrahim was also a militiaman in the service of Idriss Déby. Mahamat, who was in the RFC – the Chadian rebel movement composed of Zaghawa – did not approve of his uncle's position; however, he did support the cause of the Zaghawa in Darfur. Thus Mahamat was connected to armed groups whose political aims were not just different but also opposed. This complex situation had an advantage: it meant that he was in the victor's camp, whoever won.[40] Family and ethnic ties are crucial for an understanding of the shifting loyalties of the combatants and soldiers in the rebellions. Loyalties are all the more unstable and complex as individuals may be linked to groups that the historical moment has set against one another. These relationships do not entirely explain the political decisions that are made – Mahamat's brothers with the 'same mother, same father' did not follow him when he went over to the RFC. However, they do mean that we can make sense of situations that initially seem unlikely.

Mahamat was very preoccupied by visits to those wounded in combat who had been repatriated to hospitals in the Paris region. Some of his cousins had been wounded while fighting on the government side, others while they were defending the rebellion. This radical split within the family is not exceptional in Chad and it is good manners, especially for those abroad, not to do your political dirty washing in front of the rest of the family. Mahamat told me:

> We don't mix family and politics. I have cousins on the government side. When we meet, we don't talk politics. But afterwards, they talk on their side, and I do the same on mine. There's even a guy from the rebellion who told a relative to go and give a million [CFA francs, i.e. 1,500 euros] to his wife so she could get treatment. The relative is on Déby's side, but he still went. It's his cousin and Déby can't do anything about it [i.e. can't stop him helping his cousin even though the latter has joined the rebellion].

Mahamat's story shows that identities alone do not determine loyalties. But, conversely, combatants do not forge alliances with just anyone. Individual choices are not completely open: while kinship links do not dictate political loyalties, they circumscribe possible alliances. It is all a matter of negotiations and improvisations in an unstable environment. Identities are constantly being redefined. While Mahamat could not completely cobble together a southern identity (nobody would have believed in it), he did belong simultaneously to several worlds with which he could identify in turn: Chad, the transnational ethnic group of the Zaghawa, and his father's or his mother's clan.

However, it is not simply a matter of identity: one also needs to deal with the 'little problems'. Thus, Mahamat explained:

There are relatives of Timan [Erdimi] who are with Déby and want to hang Timan out to dry. And there are relatives of Déby who are with Timan and who want to hang Déby out to dry, too. A guy says that someone's been to look for his wife and he goes off and joins the rebellion. You see, with us, little problems turn into big problems. Big problems turn into little problems.

The 'little problems' that turn into 'big problems' are not, however, all about women. There are plenty of personal reasons for taking up arms, even if people rarely boast about the fact: there may be an account to settle, an instance of corruption that turns out badly, a trial you are going to lose. These commonplace stories assume a particular dimension in a country such as Chad where violence has become routine and where arms have almost become just one means among others for settling a dispute.

Loyalties are not purely instrumental. Personal and family strategies are not the products of cold calculations; they are not founded on certainties and they do not always succeed. The combatants find their way and determine their political affiliations by means of the resources available and the constraints imposed by the group to which they belong, but also by means of social representations that are always ambiguous. Loyalties are the products of unstable social and political identities as well as of individual arrangements in a constantly changing environment. The rules of war are not completely different from those of times of peace. Quite the opposite: they are continuous with ordinary social life. Going to war is never a landslide that wipes out all trace of social routines. And, as the next chapter will show, the return to peace (or, in the case of Chad, to the ordinary life of the inter-war periods) does not follow a straight and direct path.

CHAPTER 4

· ·

Benefiting from war:
the unequal share of
war dividends

Watching, with former rebels exiled in France, videos of the peace negotiations held in Libya in 2007 between the Chadian government and the main rebel factions helped me to grasp the extent and effects of post-war clientelism. After a few comments on the acts of war carried out by each side, one of the ex-rebels endeavoured to retrace the career of each of the cadres of the rebellion (all male) as they appeared on screen: apart from a few leaders who had remained in exile, they had all been co-opted into the military or the civilian administration. The posts handed out to politico-military cadres demonstrated the relative importance given to the different factions and their social basis. The ex-rebels and civilians who watched the videos on that day were neither astonished nor angry about these rapid promotions: it was all part of the ordinary life of politics.[1] Alex de Waal's analysis of the 'political marketplace' makes sense of such an anecdote. De Waal defines the political marketplace as 'a contemporary system of governance in which politics is conducted as the exchange of political services or loyalty for payment or license'.[2] The political marketplace has emerged as an alternative form of governance in the Horn of Africa, even though patterns of monetised politics can be found elsewhere in the world. This political system resembles an 'auction of loyalties'[3] in which political entrepreneurs seek to obtain the best price for their loyalty to the central power. Peace negotiations are thus a market on which loyalty can be bought and sold.

Negotiating to better continue the war

The rents of war

In Chadian wars, the price of loyalty depended on the evaluations of force and resources that the rebels thought they could lay claim to as they negotiated their rapprochement with the government. War could also provide a veritable rent for notables and traders who benefited from its dividends while keeping a sensible distance from the fighting. War maintained pressure on the regime and enabled the notables in the regions in conflict to gain influence on the national marketplace: they became strategically significant actors. The peace negotiations themselves became businesses. A former commander from the CSNPD of Moïse Ketté explained:

> There are people who remain in the city but say they have connections with people in the rebellion. They say they have influence, and the authorities place means at their disposal to negotiate and they sell off jobs in the administration.[4]

Not only mediators but rebels as well could live off the suitcases stuffed with banknotes that were meant to support the arguments of the emissaries of the regime. While we should not go as far as to reduce the pursuit of war to economic preoccupations, we should acknowledge that peace and reconciliation were not in everyone's best interests.

There was, on the rebel side as well as on the government side, a kind of stock exchange on which weapons and networks of combatants could be negotiated over and bought. So there was a constant ebb and flow between government and rebel forces. The economy that had grown up around the war had encouraged the development of 'rent-seeking rebellions', 'namely the mutiny of army commanders or local political leaders with armed constituents, seeking a larger share of the resources dispensed by government'.[5] Between 2005 and 2009, men in arms circulated from west to east and then from east to west. 'Sorties' or occasions of 'going out' could be extremely brief and rapprochements relatively insignificant. For example, one officer from a family that had influence among the Bideyats, Idriss Abderamane Dicko, joined the rebels for a few months between March and July 2006. On his return to N'Djamena, with just eight companions, he told the press that he had realised that Sudan was seeking to destabilise his country. However, his rapprochement had more than a little to do with strong pressure from his relatives.

The rebels who joined the government forces negotiated the price for their materials (especially weapons) to be bought back. These rapprochements also gave rise to ceremonies at which the ex-rebels used what was clearly the same kind of language: they had decided to become law-abiding citizens again when they realised they had been duped. Conversely, when a small group of army recruits defected, the rebels sometimes bought up their vehicles and their weapons – thanks to Sudanese funds that were also boosted by oil revenues. 'If we don't do the same as the other side are doing, the vehicles and weapons will only go in one direction,' a politico-military cadre told me.[6] Money played a central role in the war: one consequence was the lucrative traffic that sprang up around the rebel rear bases. Between 2005 and 2009, on the Chad–Darfur border, weapons circulated between all the armed forces, whether these were Chadian or Sudanese, governmental or rebel.[7] While the Sudanese armed the Chadian rebels, weapons from Chadian government stocks ended up in the hands of rebels in Darfur.

As already noticed, Chadian conflicts also involved actors outside the sub-region. Chad received substantial military assistance from France and the US. Moreover, arms bought with oil revenues were a major boost to Chad's military strength (see Chapter 5). In May 2009, the army equipped with newly purchased planes and helicopters defeated the rebels, who were still using 4 × 4 vehicles with machine guns mounted on the back (Sudan supplied the rebel groups with small arms and multiple rocket launchers).

Bargaining and partial peace accords

The escalation of a conflict even after the signing of an accord is not a problem specific to Chad. The list of counterproductive accords in Africa (and beyond) is unfortunately a long one. In Chad, the pursuit of war after a peace agreement, however, was not just the sign of a one-off failure on the part of those involved in trying to resolve the conflict. Accords signed by politico-military entrepreneurs who handed over their weapons only temporarily were the rule rather than the exception.

Chadian wars did not exclude dialogue. They resembled wars between friends and brothers in arms: networks of acquaintance facilitated dialogue but did not prevent conflict. Indeed, observers were struck by the powerful bonds that united the leaders of rival factions: 'They fall into each other's arms, they exchange family news, they fraternise outside the official sessions, while hurling insults at each other when they are "on stage".'[8] This was still true during the last politico-military crisis; when they met up to negotiate, 'Chadian rebels and soldiers fell into one another's arms, remembered old battles, mutual acquaintances ...'[9]

In Chad, as in many other countries,[10] accords were reduced to being mere bargaining between government forces and rebels – who were sometimes old comrades in arms or former allies, as in the case of Idriss Déby and the main protagonists of the events of 2006 and 2008, Mahamat Nour, Mahamat Nouri and Timan Erdimi. Apart from questions about the security of the signatories, the most important debates were concerned with political appointments and lucrative positions in the army and the civil service that would be offered to the cadres. The number of combatants recognised by the government was also a matter for negotiation, with politico-military leaders having an interest in swelling their troops when they staged a rapprochement with the government. Accords made provision for the reintegration of combatants in the regular forces but they did not envisage any measures for the regions from which the combatants originally came.

While it would not be sensible to expect a peace accord to deal with all the root causes of a conflict, we nonetheless have to admit that the accords signed in Chad were still far from achieving this aim. How did peace negotiations become mere stages and strategic moments in what seemed to be endless wars?

The first difficulty is this: peace negotiations brought together several armed factions that did not succeed in forming lasting alliances. In 1977, the first inter-Chadian negotiations began in Sudan; they led to the Khartoum accords. These accords did not make it possible to put an end to the conflict, and several rounds of peace talks continued without reaching a conclusion. During the civil war, all the belligerents – whether or not they were representative or powerful in the field – were invited to negotiate. The division between rebel groups has remained an obstacle to the resolution of the conflicts. Furthermore, when a movement sealed an alliance, one faction often defected to continue the armed struggle. In Chad – as in Darfur, with the partial signing of the Abuja accord in May 2006[11] – the fragmentation of armed groups and their inability to form a coherent bloc in negotiations undermined every effort to build a lasting peace.

The practice of partial agreements and separate rapprochements started after Habré's rise to power. He soon came to understand the benefits he could derive from an ever increasing number of negotiations and accords. After the failure of the reconciliation conference in Brazzaville in October 1984 that brought together the government and the GUNT factions, Habré opted for what Buijtenhuijs picturesquely calls the 'technique of whittling away'.[12] Negotiations with the codos in the south were held in no particular order, and some fifteen or so separate accords were signed between the end of 1985 and the beginning of 1986 – the different movements were in any case divided, despite Colonel Kotiga's attempts to place them under his own command.

After 1990, Idriss Déby also negotiated separately with the rebel factions as soon as this became possible. One exception needs to be noted: the conference in Franceville, Gabon, in 1996, which brought together the head of state, the MPS, fourteen Chadian armed movements and a few representatives of political parties and civil society. President Omar Bongo of Gabon and President Ange-Félix Patassé of the CAR, the main mediators, were unable to reach any significant result. The armed opposition immediately raised the stakes by demanding Déby's resignation, while the government was not prepared to make more than minor concessions. Apart from the MPS and allied parties, only two of the fourteen politico-military movements present signed the final declaration: one of the MDD factions led by Moussa Medela and a small group led by Béchir Bisco.[13]

The partial accords were also linked to the inability of armed protagonists to forge lasting coalitions as well as to the techniques employed by the regime, which were aimed at deepening the rivalries between the rebel leaders and the armed factions. Déby turned out to be a cunning strategist when it came to fomenting dissidence. At the peace negotiations table, every move was permitted: using family and clan connections, corrupting the rebel cadres, setting traps with the complicity of allied countries, and spreading rumours on negotiations being held with the leaders of factions who might be getting ready to desert.[14] Habré and Déby had long since realised that, as the political scientist Stathis Kalyvas explains, defection – especially ethnic defection – depends more on demand than on supply.[15] In other words, individuals and factions that break away from the rebellion to join the government side rarely do so spontaneously: the incitement usually comes from outside.

The accords were already extremely limited; furthermore, they were not even respected. It is not enough for an accord to be signed: the signatories need to believe in it as well. Idriss Déby has a bad track record when it comes to respecting accords. Certain signatories were assassinated: the ex-leader of the CNR, Abbas Koty, was killed in October 1993 at his home in N'Djamena, a few months after his return from exile and the signing of an accord negotiated with the guarantee of Sudan and Libya. The reconciliation accord signed in 1992 with the FNT of Dr Al-Harris Bachar was broken in 1994, shortly after the massacre of Gniguilim,[16] when violent conflicts broke out in Abéché. The head of the movement had apparently waited eight months in N'Djamena, at the hotel Le Chari, before being made to sign the accord.[17] Another event also left its mark on people's memories, this time in the south. In October 1997, government forces attacked FARF combatants confined to Moundou after the signing of an agreement; the confrontations caused heavy losses among the rebels but also among civilians.[18] This accord immediately caused problems: Laokein Bardé demanded that federalism be made part of the constitution, something that was difficult to do in the framework of a peace accord.[19] N'Djamena was not prepared to make more than minimal concessions. Apart from the ill will of the FARF and the government, deplorable working conditions hampered the work of the committee set up to monitor the accord. It is symptomatic of the lack of interest shown in this committee that its chair, Colonel Daoud Soumaïn, was sent to a new post in Bangui a few months after the accord was signed. The combatants went back underground. They set up deadly ambushes, and the army inflicted bloody repressions: the prospect of oil being drilled in the south did not encourage the regime to hold back. In May 1998, the FARF signed a new accord, but Bardé, who refused to support the regime, disappeared in the bush, most likely assassinated.

In such a context, it is hardly surprising if penitent rebels join the government side rather than creating an opposition party. All peace accords have authorised rebel movements to transform themselves into political parties, but no party has actually emerged from a rebellion. Only two attempts have been made: the first by Abbas Koty, who created a party a short while before he was assassinated, and the second by Moïse Ketté from the CSNPD, who, in 1994, founded a party that immediately forged an alliance with the MPS. The rebels were political entrepreneurs who did not believe in civilian struggle – or had abandoned any belief in it. As a former cadre from the federalist groups of the 1990s told me: 'After the rapprochement, I did not want to set up a party. I'm from the military; I went back to barracks. And to set up a party, you need to have a solid financial basis. If not you'll just be a complete laughing stock.'[20] When politico-military figures came in out of the cold, the rules of the political game had not changed. It was not in their interests to set up a political party in a saturated political field.

The practice of making separate accords with the civilian opposition and the military opposition put the government in a strong position. Apart from the Franceville conference, negotiations did not involve either the political parties or the organisations of civil society. The politico-military groups that came to the negotiating table were in any case in no position to demand anything other than compensation. Generally, negotiations began when the politico-military leaders had been weakened by the loss of their external support. This was true of Mahamat Nour, who signed an accord after losing the – invaluable – support of Khartoum in 2006. The rebel leaders before him had negotiated in similar conditions: Dr Al-Harris Bachar (1992), the federalist leaders Moïse Ketté (1994) and Laokein Bardé (1997 and 1998), as well as Adoum Togoï (2003), who had inherited the leadership of the MDJT after the death of its founder, Youssouf Togoïmi, in 2002. Whether or not this was part of their plans, the rebels who went over to the government did not have the means to bring about any significant change in the way it operated.

The failure of the Sirte accord of October 2007 shows, yet again, the emptiness of accords signed by divided rebel coalitions and participants who do not actually believe in them. The negotiations that led to the accord were held away from the civilian opposition and civil society organisations, even though these were militating in favour of an 'inclusive dialogue'. These negotiations involved the four main rebel factions from the eastern front, who were at the time led by Timan Erdimi, Mahamat Nouri, Aboud Mackaye and Hassan Saleh Al-Gaddam, better known as Al Djineidi. One month after signing, three of the four rebel factions took up arms again. In February 2008, the signatories launched a lightning attack on the capital. The only signatory to the accord who actually joined the government side was Al Djineidi. However, the rapprochement of this politico-military entrepreneur and some 1,600 combatants from his faction did little for the cause of peace in Chad.

In the first place, over half the rebels from the CNT, a movement composed mainly of Arabs, stayed on the side of the rebellion. The commanders who had remained underground, such as Captain Ismaïl Moussa, attempted to reconstitute the CNT. The Sudanese gave them to understand that, in order to benefit from their support, they would need to forge an alliance with another Arab politico-military entrepreneur: Ahmat Hassaballah Soubiane. The former members of Al Djineidi's movement resignedly joined the Front du Salut pour la République (FSR or Front for the Salvation of the Republic). Captain Ismaïl became the second in command of the movement. One year later, when Soubiane refused to join the UFR (the new rebel coalition led by Timan Erdimi), Captain Ismaïl broke with Soubiane and went over to the coalition side.[21] Far from abandoning their weapons, Al Djineidi's combatants stayed underground with the FSR and/or the UFR after their former leader had entered the government. In the second place, in one of history's sad ironies, Al Djineidi, who was suspected of being responsible for the death and displacement of many civilians,[22] was appointed Secretary of State for National Defence in charge of ex-combatants and war victims. In May 2009, he was named General Chief of Staff of the Army, and was thus organising the war against his own former allies. Buying the loyalty of a rebel leader poses two main problems: on the one hand, it is inadequate if the intermediary commanders and combatants do not also stick to the peace accords, and, on the other, it rewards the entrepreneurs of violence.

Finally, the regionalisation of the market for political loyalties made peace negotiations even more complex. Between 2003 and 2009, Sudan and Chad bore their respective share of responsibility for the failure of the negotiations and the lack of respect for the accords signed in each other's neighbouring country. Khartoum complicated the Chadian political process by offering the rebel leaders more interesting opportunities than peace. Why go to the negotiating table when there was still some hope of winning the war with the help of Sudan? While supporting the Chadian rebels, Sudan raised the price of their loyalty. Although the situations in Chad and Sudan were not symmetrical, Chad also had a high potential for damaging its neighbour in the east. Chad remained the official mediator and then co-mediator (with the African Union) in the Darfur conflict right up until the beginning of 2006, in spite of the support of Idriss Déby's followers in the Darfur rebellions. Last but not least, the fact that the rebellion ended in 2009 does not contradict this analysis of the peace negotiations as a means to better continue the war. The war did not end with peace agreements between the government and the rebels but when the rebel coalition was defeated and when Chad and Sudan agreed to stop their proxy war.

State repression and post-war clientelism: the case of the Dar Tama

'They split the leaders'

The succession of accords since 1990 has produced a swollen class of senior officers, ministers and special advisers to the President. As Dobian Assingar, a defender of human rights who was one of the main mediators in the accords between the government and the FARF, put it: 'There is a huge number of accords in this country. In order to respect all of them, we would need 2,000 ministers and 10,000 delegates.'[23] Depending on their position in the rebellion, their social base and their political influence, former rebels were appointed to key posts in the army and the government, but also in the local state administration. They became regional governors, prefects or sub-prefects. However, co-opting them like this is often a short-lived affair. Swift but ephemeral promotions play a part in controlling those who have switched support to the government: they know that their social rise is due only to the goodwill of the prince, who can withdraw his favours just as easily as he granted them.

The description of these mechanisms might suggest that the state apparatus is simply being manipulated in a process that occurs far from the people. However, co-optation is not just a matter for the elites. Those who gain positions of power and accumulation have the social obligation to redistribute the accumulated resources. Thus the beneficiaries are not just the co-opted but also large swathes of the social body. One former politico-military cadre awaiting a position in the civil service explained the situation to me in these terms: 'You don't know how long you're going to remain in a position, so you gobble up what you can. If not, after a year or two, you walk – and you end up like some bloody idiot.'[24] And the 'idiot' in question will be criticised by his base for not having taken advantage of the position he obtained when the time was ripe! The 'administrative belly' – which, in the spoken French of Chad, symbolises the way in which local state officials get rich – presupposes a certain economic trickery that goes beyond the legal economy. Remunerations in the local state administrations are not high, but these posts can still turn out to be lucrative as they can give you access to the illegal as well as the legal economy.

As Béatrice Hibou emphasises: 'These networks of clientelism and patronage are also mechanisms that legitimise political life because they help to establish norms for the recruitment and mobility of elites.'[25] In Chad, the clientelist distribution of positions of power and accumulation belongs to the routine framework of politics. The appointment of rebel leaders and commanders to government posts, in the civilian administration and the army, is not in itself considered a problem. Admittedly, there are many debates and confrontations between the various registers of legitimation: clientelism is criticised by those whose academic capital is higher than their social capital or their capital as warriors. All the same, this mode of government belongs to the ordinary workings of the political field. The clientelist manufacture of allegiances after the signature of a peace accord is part of the legitimatisation of the accord.

In the previous chapter, I traced the trajectory of the former FUC leader. Mahamat Nour is, however, not the only one to have been co-opted after the signing of the peace accord in December 2006. The political cadres of his movement were also co-opted after they had shifted their support to the government. Two of them were appointed to positions as state secretaries,[26] while the military commanders were given new ranks in the army. Not all the ex-rebels were treated in the same way, however. Some were given important positions, while others were marginalised after the signing of the accord. In the Dar Tama, as in other regions of Chad, the distribution of posts, sinecures and cushy jobs is not used as a reward for faithful allies alone: it also fuels the division of families and clans whose members have played a part in armed groups. The inhabitants of the Dar Tama, both civilians and ex-rebels, interpreted the unequal sharing out of posts and the promotion of defectors as a policy aimed at stirring discord among former armed opponents. 'Once the rapprochement with the government had been made, they split the leaders,' a former FUC member told me.[27]

The frequent re-allocation of posts is another instrument for controlling loyalties and dissuading people who might be tempted to rebel. Former cadres of the Tama rebellion appointed to key posts in the administration and the army were swiftly sacked. The only FUC cadre who made a career in politics was the former spokesman of the rebellion. Raoul Laona Gong obtained the rank of general despite having no military training or any experience of combat. He enjoyed the privileges associated with his rank: an expensive car, a driver and a bodyguard. He was a member of several governments. He was also appointed as adviser to the Chadian High Court in 2009. The former spokesman, who had joined the ruling party, owed his career to the fact that he had split with old members of the FUC. He came from another region in the country and had no bond of kinship with the leaders of the former rebellion.

The lower ranks in the rebellion, on the other hand, did not rise in society. After the end of hostilities, most of them went back to agricultural labour. A few lucky ones were recruited by non-governmental organisations (NGOs) or by the UN peacekeeping mission in subaltern posts (as guards, for example), and less frequently in qualified posts: one ex-rebel, for instance, worked as an instructor for an NGO in charge of reintegrating children who had been associated with armed groups. Back in civilian life, ex-combatants make no bones about their time spent in armed struggle. In any case, their rebel pasts are known to everyone – to the inhabitants as well as the authorities. However, the return to civilian life has been more difficult for women who took part in the rebellion. In Tama patriarchal society, they are not in a position to claim their 'rights'. Moreover, as I already emphasised in the introduction to this book, the assassination in 2010 of the woman who had obtained the status of a 'commander' encouraged other former female members of the rebellion to keep a low profile.

The prefects' and sultans' war

Post-war clientelism also modified the power relations in the Dar Tama. After the signing of the peace accord of 2006, a former FUC member was appointed prefect of Assongha (an administrative department close to the Dar Tama, on the border with Darfur), and then made governor of the Wadi Fira region (the Dar Tama is one of the three departments in the Wadi Fira). However, he was stripped of his functions a few months later for 'bad behaviour'.[28] As for the prefecture of the Dar Tama, it was given to a former rebel: Abdel-Kerim Mahamat Toraye. The appointment of a former military commander to the post of prefect was probably one of the clauses not made public in the peace accord. Toraye was chosen from among the commandants of the FUC; he was one of the few commandants who had taken their baccalaureate and was considered to be one of the best qualified.

However, the prefecture did not remain in the hands of the Tama ex-rebel for long. In autumn 2007, while the former members of the FUC refused to dismantle their militias, government troops entered Guéréda. Confrontations broke out. Former FUC military commanders, including the prefect, were arrested. They were sent to Koro Toro, a prison located in the desert region of the Borku that is viewed by the prison service as a top security jail and by members of the opposition as a penal colony.[29] The prefect was replaced by one of the sub-prefects of the Dar Tama, a relative of the mayor of Guéréda. The mayor himself had not been elected but appointed (in Chad, mayors were appointed until the first communal elections in 2013, although elections were not organised in Guéréda).[30] The new local authorities were viewed as acting on behalf of the government. One inhabitant of Guéréda, for example, told me that the local government officials 'talk about the MPS to intimidate people, they use the name of the President [i.e. the President of the Republic] indiscriminately'.[31]

The sultanate is also at the heart of local politics. As the politico-military crisis was escalating, Sultan Haroun Mahamat Abdoulaye (known as Sultan Haroun), regularly denounced the violence in the Dar Tama. This traditional leader, who succeeded his father in 1997, studied in France before becoming a senior civil servant in Chad. He held a political post (he was Minister for Commerce and Industry under Habré in 1986–87) and worked for the United Nations Development Programme (UNDP) and the World Bank. Sultan Haroun was viewed as a troublemaker as he was a French speaker and in contact with defenders of human rights and with international journalists. He was arrested for the first time in November 2007 on the pretext of his supposed connection to the rebellion – he is a close relative of the rebel leader Mahamat Nour. He was then stripped of his functions by the Minister of the Interior and Public Security. Yaya Garfa, brother of the former rebel leader Mahamat Garfa, was made sultan. The appointment of Yaya Garfa was a piece of state interference that undermined the principle whereby the election of the sultan was a matter concerning the Tama. Here, the state relied on pre-existing rivalries within the clan (for several years, Haroun had been involved in a conflict with the two brothers Mahamat and Yaya Garfa) to impose a trusted servant of its own.

Sultan Haroun was freed in May 2008, but he was kept under house arrest in N'Djamena without any charges being laid against him. In July 2009, the High Court annulled the decree of the Interior Ministry stripping the Sultan of his functions and ruled that the government should pay him damages of 20 million CFA francs (about 30,500 euros). The decision of the High Court was never applied. Indeed, it was overruled by a decree signed by the President, again relieving Sultan Haroun of his functions. A few days after the court's ruling, the Sultan was again arrested, and his brother, who had hitherto been Deputy Secretary General to the government, was removed from office (he had allegedly been outspokenly critical, during a council of ministers, of the treatment meted out to Haroun). The Sultan was then detained for several months by the Chadian Special Branch. Upon his release, he remained in N'Djamena, as a visit to the Dar Tama would risk aggravating a delicate situation. The Tama interpreted the fact that Sultan Haroun had been deposed and arrested twice as a form of reprisal against his family and, more broadly, as a policy aimed at discouraging any stirrings of revolt.

This mode of government is particularly effective in that the affairs of the elites concern the population as a whole. The Sultan's 'family' includes a great number of individuals – let alone the countless number of people I have met who claim some link of kinship with Sultan Haroun. The networks created by kinship links are especially dense, and the co-opting of elites has an impact on the weave of personal, family, clan and ethnic relations. Furthermore, the Sultan is an authority both traditional and administrative, who is called upon to settle problems involving the daily lives of residents: Tama, but also members of other ethnic groups who live in the Dar Tama. Despite the support on which the fallen Sultan could count, the inhabitants of the Dar Tama had to come to terms with the new leader of their traditional authorities. It was out of the question to boycott the new Sultan. Social obligations were strong, and residents could not avoid the Sultan if, for example, they were party to a conflict that needed to be resolved by the traditional authorities.

Of course, clientelism in the management of local authorities is not specific to Chad. It is a common phenomenon in African countries at peace[32] and elsewhere in the world, even if not always to the same extent. However, it is a phenomenon that has a specific meaning and specific effects in a context of inter-war, when those who hold positions of power are linked to the trajectory of the victors of the most recent war. In the Dar Tama, people interpreted the undermining of routinised norms in connection with the co-opting of people into the local state and the traditional chiefdom as a policy aimed at dividing and silencing those in rebel circles and rewarding the trusted servants of power. The end of the shootings and the apparent 'normalisation' of the situation concealed the retaking of control over the Dar Tama.

Difficult returns from the front line

Rebelling against one's former leader

After the failure of the attack on N'Djamena in February 2008, and even more so since the rapprochement between Chad and Sudan, the rebels, weakened and divided, were not in a position to negotiate their shift of support to the Chadian government, which refused to initiate new peace talks on the pretext that the accord signed at Sirte in October 2007 was still valid. It therefore negotiated separately with the factions that were abandoning the armed struggle. Those who went over to the government side after 2008 did not receive the rewards that had accompanied the signature of peace accords since 1990.

Let us analyse the case of the Mouvement National (MN or National Movement), a rebel movement that comprised about 1,800 combatants.[33] In 2009, the leader of the MN, Ahmat Hassaballah Soubiane, split from the rebel coalition and negotiated with the government. Soubiane was appointed special adviser to the President, a position without any real influence. He kept a low profile and avoided being seen with his former brothers in arms.[34] Soubiane was said to have received a lot of money, which he did not share. This kind of rumour is the norm rather than the exception. Combatants accused him of 'eating' alone the fruits of the armed struggle: they expected more than the 400,000 CFA francs (about US$820) they received from the government as a discharge payment.[35] They also expected their integration into the army. They waited for months in the Moussoro military camp where they had been confined – in vain. They lost patience. A section of them crossed the Sudanese border again to join another rebel faction: they were back on the politico-military job market. The others left the camp, went to the capital city or their home regions, and resumed civilian life.

Former MN combatants gathered within the 'great strategic commission of the national movement', a movement that claimed to have some 350 members. The dozens of former combatants of the 'commission' whom I interviewed in N'Djamena told me about the idleness they faced in the camp at Moussoro and the way their hopes had been dashed. After tumultuous trajectories (most of them had moved from one faction to another during several years spent underground), they had expected to be (re)integrated into the army, like their predecessors. Once they had returned to civilian life, they claimed their 'rights': (re)integration and a specific rank, as well as a car for those who had been in positions of 'responsibility'. The insistence on 'rights' or 'entitlements' (or 'hagg' in Chadian Arabic) shows how commonplace it was to take up arms when renegotiating one's social status. In their view, the man responsible for their disappointments was not the President or the government, but their old leader. After fighting Idriss Déby, they proclaimed loud and clear their support for the President and their grudge against Soubiane. This was a strategic move: to negotiate anything in a post-war situation, it is better to side with the regime and show as many signs of loyalty as you can.

This 'commission' composed of disgruntled ex-combatants (all male) was led by a woman. Halime had already had a long career as a politician. This divorced woman with a single child, who was the head of her household, had used rebellion, a tactic of the male repertoire, in her social navigation. When I met her in May 2010, less than a year after she had left the rebel coalition, she proudly showed me her brand-new car with air conditioning, a 'gift from the President'. Filled with gratitude, she had affixed an Idriss Déby bumper sticker to the car. In addition to the car, Halime had received cash as a reward for joining the government fold. She was, however, far from rich. She lived in a modest house with her mother, her daughter, one of her sisters, and several of her relatives' children. There was no tap water. She had no generator even though she lived in a neighbourhood of N'Djamena that seldom had access to electricity. Her story is representative of the use of rebellion as a means to claim one's 'rights': that is, what she thought she was entitled to. Before opting for the rebellion, she was a local party official of the ruling party, which she had joined at the beginning of the 1990s. As she explained to me: 'I have worked for years, darling, but never received my due [*droit*].'[36] She talked about her decision to join the rebellion as a legitimate and ordinary means to let MPS officials know that she was upset and disappointed by the meagre benefits of her activism. She had spent only a year in rebellion, between 2008 and 2009. During that year, Halime had stayed in Khartoum: she belonged to the political leadership and did not go to the combatants' camps. After her return to the government fold, she claimed that Soubiane had deceived the combatants and herself. Most importantly, she hoped that her new anti-Soubiane and pro-Déby stance might help improve her personal situation. Despite the multiple signs of loyalty she had given to the government, Halime was not reappointed as an official of the ruling party. Halime's trajectory shows that war was a means of contestation that was sometimes used by politicians who pursued a career in the civilian opposition or the ruling party. The recourse to violence – or to the threat of violence – was commonplace; combatants and rebel leaders spoke openly about both the cause they defended and the benefits they expected from war. War had become a means of claiming one's entitlements. However, this tactical repertoire should not be reduced to a mere means of achieving personal ends. Rebellions and threats of rebellion remained a form of political protest.

Back from the bush: expectations and intimidations

Not all rapprochements with the government are equal. It could be difficult for combatants from Chad's eastern front to return, but it was even more difficult for rebels from the south, the poor relations of the Chadian insurrectional scene. At the turn of 2009–10, two politico-military movements abandoned the armed struggle: the Front Démocratique Populaire (FDP or Popular Democratic Front) and Telssi Résistance Nationale (Telssi National Resistance – *telssi* means 'we have returned' in Sara). The FDP, set up in 1997 by Dr Mammouth Nahor N'gawara, kidnapped some French people in the south of the country. While the hostages survived, the government repression was extremely violent and there were many civilian deaths. Once the insurrection had been crushed, Nahor took refuge in the CAR and then in France, where he took part in the various coalitions that brought together the exiled politico-military figures. As for Telssi, this was a movement launched in 2004 by Colonel Michel Mbaïlemal, who at that time already had a long experience of rebellion and rapprochement behind him. This former codo took up arms again in the 1990s with the CSNPD and the FARF, before being arrested in 1999 as he was preparing the ground for a new insurrection. Mbaïlemal's movement operated on the border between Chad and the CAR. The contingents of this rebellion without vehicles hardly even fought: they often lived as civilians in the villages. Their deeds of arms extended to a few ambushes. Nahor came back to Chad in December 2009, and Mbaïlemal agreed to give up armed struggle a few months later. They formed an alliance so that they could together negotiate the terms of their rapprochement with the government.

I visited Nahor in April 2010 in N'Djamena, after seeing him regularly in Paris. He lived in a modest house without electricity with members of his family and eight of his supporters.[37] These men were military and political cadres aged between about twenty and fifty. They were not all 'combatants' – some of them had been refugees in West Africa, far from any underground activities. Former soldiers are called by their rank (the rank they had in the army before they deserted or the rank they would like to have when they go over to the government): thus, there was a lieutenant, a sub-lieutenant and a general. Nahor, who had come home after twelve years in exile, received visitors. Once a doctor, he was now a politico-military cadre, but he was still asked to treat the sick. However, many of his former acquaintances, he told me, were still wary and were waiting until he had been reintegrated before they would make contact with him again.

The negotiations were, in Nahor's terms, 'a veritable obstacle course'.[38] Michel Mbaïlemal, the movement's vice-president, was being urged to move away from Nahor, his president. Mbaïlemal, who refused to break his alliance with Nahor, saw the conditions in which the Telssi delegation was lodging deteriorating: the cadres of the movement were staying in one of the capital's finest hotels, but they quickly had to pack their bags and move to a less comfortable one. Those who had recently re-joined the government side then had to wait. Months went by without their 'case' making any progress. Nahor was subjected to several attempts at intimidation. It was as if the government were telling them that they were in no position to demand anything. The two leaders negotiated to have nearly a thousand combatants officially recognised. The number of rebels is always the product of a discussion between the government and the former rebels – the latter have every interest in swelling their ranks at the time of demobilisation. After months in the bush, half of them went back to the Moussoro camp that was already taking in the remnants of other rebel factions. They received a bonus of 300,000 CFA francs (about 457 euros) – a little less than the amount Soubiane's combatants were offered, even though they were confined to the same camp. The (re)integration they were expecting would not happen; reintegration was no longer the order of the day. They were asked to leave the camp and go back to civilian life.

On the other hand, after a period of waiting, the former rebel leaders obtained significant positions through negotiation. Mbaïlemal was appointed prefect in the south of the country, before being sent to a job in the east, then in the north. Nahor was finally authorised to resume his job as a doctor at the hospital in January 2011, over a year after his return from exile. In December, he was appointed Minister for Health – which shows, yet again, that time spent in politico-military opposition does not stop one being co-opted at the highest level. A year later, after a ministerial reshuffle, he lost his post and went back to being a doctor. The last rebel from the south, Babba Laddé, who was leading Chad's Front Populaire pour le Redressement (Popular Front for Recovery or FPR), was arrested in northern CAR in December 2014.

As I moved from the best air-conditioned restaurants in the capital to modest houses, I gained a sense of the ex-rebels' divergent social trajectories and realised that the phrase 'to live by the gun' might be misleading. It homogenises divergent situations and careers. While a section of the male population was able to make a living in war and through war, only a few of those who engaged in armed violence actually benefited from it.

PART III
GOVERNING WITH ARMS:
THE 'UNNUMBERED DECREE'

....

One day in December 2004 I was in Moundou talking with former soldiers about illegal roadblocks (known as 'anarchic barriers'), where men in uniform hold travellers to ransom. One of them, a demobilised soldier and now a policeman, exclaimed: 'But who is going to condemn them? They are decreed without a number. You can shout that it's bad, but in the shadows, it's all right.' The decree that authorised the racket is 'without a number', or unnumbered, insofar as it cannot be found in the state bureaucracy's registers. Its effects are nonetheless palpable. Despite 'shouted' protests, the racketeering practised by my interlocutors is commonplace and institutionalised. Nearly a year later, I spoke with residents in Mongo, a small town in the Guéra region, about the racket operated by elements of Chad's National and Nomadic Guard. Resignedly, one of them told me: 'A decree or a spoken word, it makes no difference; these guys are in power, they do what they want.' These feelings about the 'spoken word' that has the force of a decree not only express the lassitude of civilians confronted with the practices of unscrupulous armed men, but also indicate that state power is practised as much by those unwritten rules that can be grasped by the metaphor of the 'unnumbered decree' as by laws and official decrees. In this metaphor, the 'decree' indicates state power, while the absence of a number reflects that such practices are illegal and unofficial.

The military's illegal and violent practices are often seen as the result of the weakness of the state. According to this view, the state has failed to control the men in arms (or in uniform) on its territory. The realities are more complex. An incomplete control over personnel, flexible chains of command, an absence of *esprit de corps* and of discipline are not necessarily weaknesses. Unnumbered decrees are also a fully fledged mode of government. This mode of government, erratic at first sight, obeys rules that are known to all and has some advantages.

There is obviously no *deus ex machina* that could implement such a mode of government. Unnumbered decrees cannot be reduced to a deliberate strategy formulated by an individual or group of individuals. The state's practices are neither unambiguous nor coherent; they are the product of many decisions, sometimes contradictory, taken by various actors at different levels. However, the intentions of the known and unknown architects of this mode of government count less than their effects. Governing with arms and unnumbered decrees constitutes a cheap but nonetheless efficient mode of government. Only a non-normative analysis of concrete forms of the exercise of power and of violence will help us understand how it actually works. How are men in arms governed? Who are those men in arms who work for the state without being officially integrated into its apparatus? What is their place and their role in the governing of society and the control of populations? What are the effects of the impunity granted to powerful men within the military and beyond? In the following chapters, I suggest a response to these questions by focusing on the army and then on these men in arms who live in the margins of the state.

CHAPTER 5

. . . .

A 'militianised' army

For some years, the Chadian army has been considered one of the best in the Sahel. In 2013, the military played a decisive role during the French-led action in Mali. In early 2016, Chadians comprised the first contingent of MINUSMA, the UN Multidimensional Mission in Mali, with more than 1,200 soldiers.[1] The same army participated in military operations against Boko Haram[2] as part of the Multinational Joint Task Force (MNJTF),[3] which it provided with one-third of its troops (about 3,000 out of 8,700 soldiers, police and civilians). The Chadian army is praised for its effectiveness and 'robustness', to borrow a term used by the Foreign Affairs Committee of the French National Assembly.[4] The way in which the supposed qualities of this army are described reactivate the old cliché of the Chadian desert warrior who has been a source of fascination for the French military since the colonial period. Behind this picture, however, there lie less glorious realities. Chadian forces also enjoy a reputation in Chad – and Central Africa – for their brutality and human rights violations. In April 2014, Chadian forces had to withdraw from the UN Multidimensional Integrated Stabilisation Mission in the CAR (MINUSCA) because of accusations that they had killed thirty unarmed civilians. Moreover, Chad has a long history of interference in the CAR and there were reports of financial and military support being given to the Séléka rebels. In Mali, allegations of rape and sexual violence have been levelled against Chadian soldiers.[5] This chapter places these recent events within the history of the army under Idriss Déby.

From the perspective of the social sciences, the following analysis aims to grasp the operation and routine practices of the regular forces by moving beyond the limits of two dominant frameworks: the influence of culture, and the resilience of warrior values. First, the apparent disarray of the regular forces is too often considered a cultural trait of Sahelian and Saharan societies. And second, the rebel past of the soldiers is too often used as a replacement for any real explanation of their practices once they have been integrated into the regular forces. But, here again, there is nothing inevitable about this process. The practices of veterans cannot be reduced to the mere transposition of a warrior habitus, nor to a refusal to demobilise wartime values and attitudes. I show in this chapter that the army has been shaped by war, but also by a form of militianisation in the form of unnumbered decrees. To understand the Chadian army, we must look at how it is governed and not see cultural elements where what really is at stake is politics. While the army has been partly transformed by oil money and by the opportunities associated with the Western counter-terrorism operations in the Sahel–Saharan zone, it is still affected by the politicisation of ethnicity, a militianisation process, and impunity.

An army shaped by and for wars

Uncontrolled numbers of troops

Since the collapse of the Chadian armed forces in 1979, the regular army has been a space of coexistence for men (and a minority of women) from different generations and different backgrounds. Professional soldiers coexist with former rebels. Under Habré, the army has given pride of place to the former combatants of the FAN. Ex-rebels reinstated in the army were given the interim rank of 'assimilated officers' or 'assimilated non-commissioned officer' or NCOs ('officiers assimilés' and 'sous-officiers assimilés' in the jargon of the Chadian army). Under Déby, in 2005 they represented a significant part of the troops: 31 per cent of officers and 21 per cent of NCOs were 'assimilated'.[6] The pyramid of ranks was almost completely turned upside down: there were almost the same number of officers and NCOs as enlisted men. The granting of the rank of NCO and officer status to combatants stopped in 2008, however, when it was no longer necessary to buy the rebels' loyalty.

It is difficult to know the actual size of the regular forces. The numbers have fluctuated as men have deserted or re-joined, or have been recruited locally by commanders. In 1991, the number of soldiers counted was 47,000.[7] The numbers of the former army had been augmented by the 'liberators' of the MPS and those who had managed to enlist during the confusion entailed by the change in regime. During the 1990s, the size of the army was halved thanks to the implementation of a programme of disarmament, demobilisation and reintegration (DDR), to which I shall return later in this chapter. However, numbers continued to fluctuate. In 2005, an audit report drawn up by a team of French and Chadian soldiers indicated that the figures given by officials in the central administration of the army were between 24,500 and 27,500 men. The army was now composed of the following: 12,500 men in the land army; 350 in the air force; 6,000 in the National Gendarmerie; and just over 7,000 in the Republican Guard. However, the size of the army changed rapidly from 2005 onwards, due to the worsening political and military crisis. In 2008, the Defence Minister, Wadal Abdelkader Kamougué, proposed a wide possible range of figures: he said that there were between 50,000 and 80,000 soldiers.[8] In 2011, a census was organised: the army was then composed of 18,000 soldiers, with a total of 36,575 individuals if the gendarmerie and the GNNT were also included.[9] A few years later, in 2014, a report by the French National Assembly suggested that the ANT (Armée Nationale Tchadienne, Chad's actual military force) and the presidential guard both had about 14,000 soldiers.[10] In comparison, if one takes into account the soldiers of the ANT and the presidential guard, the numbers in the Chadian armed forces are about twice as many as those of the armed forces of neighbouring Niger – even though Niger has a somewhat larger population than Chad.

Until recently, the Chadian army employed minors. The presence of these minors was related to the leeway left to certain military leaders who could recruit their own elements, including minors. Others were recruited from camps for refugees and internally displaced persons from the east of the country.[11] This issue was particularly sensitive. In 2006, while minors were being deployed in the field during clashes with the rebels, Chadian and international journalists were urged not to talk about it. A former correspondent for Radio France Internationale (RFI) in Chad reports that Chadian authorities had warned her that she would be expelled if she spoke out – the Frenchwoman was eventually expelled from the country two years later after covering the attack of February 2008. The Chadian journalist Evariste Ngaralbaye, from the newspaper *Notre Temps*, was imprisoned for denouncing the massive presence of minors in the ranks of the army. He was released following the mobilisation of professional organisations and associations for the protection of human rights.[12] In 2011, the government renewed its commitment to halting the recruitment of minors into the regular forces by signing an agreement with the UN. Members of the government had then recognised the presence of minors in the regular forces while stating that their recruitment was the result of individual initiatives taken by local commanders. In 2015, the UN considered that the Chadian government had fully implemented the action plan to end the recruitment and use of children.

A two-class army

What is called the Chadian army is in fact two armies: the ANT and the presidential guard. The latter was renamed the General Directorate of Security Services for National Institutions (DGSSIE) in 2005. In ten years, its numbers have almost doubled, since there are now at least as many troops in the DGSSIE as in the ANT. The DGSSIE receives disproportionate funding in comparison with the rest of the army. It is much better equipped and its troops are better trained. Members of the DGSSIE are also much better paid than those of the ANT.[13] The DGSSIE depends on the presidency and is not under the command of the army's General Chief of Staff. The elements of the DGSSIE are recruited from the Zaghawa and to a lesser extent from the Gorans and Arabs.[14] General Mahamat Idriss Déby Itno, the son of the head of state, is in charge of the DGSSIE. He was appointed to this position in April 2014, by presidential decree. In 2013, aged twenty-nine, he was appointed second-in-command of the Chadian armed forces intervening in Mali (*Fatim*).[15] Most of the Chadian armed forces in Mali came from the DGSSIE. As for the ANT, it is the ordinary military force; it recruits among all ethnic groups but it is also controlled by Idriss Déby's close relatives. The GNNT,[16] whose official mission is homeland security,[17] has long been used as an auxiliary army force, with some 4,000 troops.

The politicisation of ethnicity and the gap between the treatment of the presidential guard and that reserved for other bodies of the armed forces have sparked discontent since the earliest days of Idriss Déby's regime. In the early 1990s, a group of forty-three soldiers, all from the south, drafted a memorandum on the problems of the army: they protested against the fact that professional soldiers did not benefit from the same promotions as those awarded to ex-combatants who had returned to the army.[18] They were arrested and released following the mobilisation of political parties and civil society organisations.[19] Several articles were later published pseudonymously in the press by professional soldiers who denounced the disorganisation of the army; they claimed that it had become a 'monster', a 'hideous creature' in the eyes of 'brave warriors'.[20] However, it is in the freedom of private conversations that the denunciation of the moral decay of the army finds its most virulent expression. Soldiers challenge not only the differences in pay and status, but also what they see as a perversion of military 'values': professionalism, discipline and respect for hierarchy. They denounce and reject the model of an army of combatants.

Politicisation of ethnicity

The politicisation of ethnicity has characterised all the regimes that have succeeded one another since independence. At the Gardolé Congress in July 1991, the former allies from the MPS were marginalised, while the Zaghawa (representing approximately 1.5 per cent of the population of Chad)[21] took control of positions of power and accumulation. We should immediately note, however, that there are two limits to the politicisation of ethnicity. First, while the private press in Chad tends to present the Zaghawa as a group occupying all positions and enjoying all privileges, not all the Zaghawa have benefited from this path to power. Solidarity within the group is not automatic. The Zaghawa include three main subgroups that are themselves divided: the Kobé, living mainly in Chad; the Wogi, who have settled in Darfur; and the Bideyat, who inhabit the Saharan areas of Chad.[22] The political and personal conflicts between them are intense. Out in the bush, the Chadian and Sudanese Kobé, who massively mobilised in support of the MPS, criticised Idriss Déby for favouring the members of his subgroup, the Bideyat, and of his clan, the Bilia. Conflicts within the Zaghawa took military form on two occasions: in 1992, with the creation of a political and military movement comprised basically of Kobé; and more recently in 2005, when the Bideyat and the relatives of Déby went out into the bush to fight from there. Second, the politicisation of ethnicity is associated with the appointment of individuals from all ethnic groups and all regions of the country. In the Chadian political system, alliances are always open. Thus, contrary to what is often argued, the 'southerners' are not excluded from the exercise of power; or, more exactly, they are no more excluded than other non-Zaghawa groups in Chad. Under Habré, as under Déby, the Prime Minister, who admittedly does not have a great deal of power, has almost always been from the south, which is a way of respecting a principle that Chadians call geopolitical (or regional) equilibrium. Since 1990, there have been only two exceptions.[23] Similarly, individuals from all regions of the country have been able to make a career in the regular forces and reach positions of power and accumulation. Nevertheless, the fact remains: while the politicisation of ethnicity does not rule out the establishment of alliances with other groups, many Zaghawa and members of the President's family clan have remained in key positions.

The politicisation of ethnicity has an impact on the organisation of the army and the daily practices of the military. The geographer Johanne Favre notes that there is a high level of segregation in the Koulbous military camp on the Sudanese border. She describes life in the camp, as observed in March 2004, after the departure of the residents of Koulbous village, who fled the Sudanese bombing:

> The dwellings of the Chadian soldiers and their families were removed from the border and rebuilt to the rear of the camp. It would be more accurate to speak of the 'camps', as the Koulbous camp was very obviously partitioned: there were, on the one side, the Zaghawa 'leaders', the non-French-speaking 'colonels', and on the other side the junior officers, NCOs and

other soldiers from the ranks of the 'southerners'. According to the latter, the relationship between the two groups was strained. They remained in separate parts of the military camp. The Zaghawa banned the wives of their subordinates from accessing the only water point in the camp; they had to go to the well of a *wadi* [river] further off. To reach the market, they were also forbidden to cross the territory reserved for the leaders.[24]

The politicisation of the police and other bodies of law enforcement is not a taboo subject. It has been vehemently denounced by opposition MPs. In 2005, they challenged the Minister of Public Safety and Immigration during oral questions to the government in the National Assembly. For example, MP Adoum Mahamat Konto protested:

> Since the numbers of the National Police have been swelled by thousands of fighters from the same region and the same clan, the majority of them illiterate, this organ of security has started murdering the population. An inadmissible line is crossed by the behaviour of some of these 'policemen' who are outlaws and who enjoy total impunity.[25]

Ex-combatants and civilians are indeed incorporated by decree, under a policy of unnumbered decree: men affiliated to the inner circle of power by their ethnic origin benefit more than their fair share from opportunities for integration and promotion in the army or the police. Many Zaghawa have benefited, from the early 1990s onwards, from fast promotions that cannot be explained by either their skills or their seniority. Some were able, within just a few years, to reach a higher rank than that of their instructors from other ethnic groups.[26] High school pupils and students aged twenty or so, without military training or combat experience, were appointed colonels, something of which they did not fail to inform their classmates and teachers.[27] Young men who enjoy meteoric promotions in the military without having spent time in the bush often adopt, through a chameleon effect, the haughty attitude of their elders.

If integration in the army or the police is a means of providing an income for people close to state power, it can also be used to transform violent behaviours into acts of war. For example, a commander in a gendarmerie brigade in Guéréda was forced to recruit a former combatant from the MPS who was related to one of his men. The commander, who did not wish to recruit the man, had to yield to the pressure of his subordinates. The new recruit, who was, in the commander's words, a 'Zaghawa with a murky past', then climbed up the hierarchy much faster than the commander did.[28] Actual hierarchies do not represent official positions and ranks: the man who has the power to get his friends and relatives recruited is not always the official leader.

The three dimensions of militianisation

In examining the regular forces, we must free ourselves from the idea that their mode of operation is radically different in principle from that of the irregular forces. Furthermore, contrary to conventional wisdom, the practices of the regular forces are not necessarily less brutal than those of the irregular forces. In the case of Chad, the armed forces themselves have been militianised. The army has an administrative and bureaucratic appearance inspired by the former colonial power, but the way in which it actually works is quite different. I propose to understand the militianisation of the Chadian army as a combination of three processes: factionalisation, outsourcing and informalisation. By *factionalisation* I mean the process of fragmentation of the regular forces into different factions. Chadian regular forces were reconstructed through a process of fragmentation: the army is divided into several groups based on kinship or patronage. This kind of faction within the army – like those of the rebellion – are dynamic configurations renegotiated according to the political context of the moment. I then use the term *outsourcing* for the use, by the state, of armed groups formed outside the regular forces, whether they be self-defence militias or armed groups from neighbouring Sudan. In both Chad and Sudan, the outsourcing of regular forces is a terribly lethal form of 'counter-insurgency on the cheap'.[29] I finally distinguish these two processes from the *informalisation* of the armed forces: that is, the mechanisms, neither unilinear nor irreversible, for getting past rules and official institutions. The three processes are part of the mode of government and rely on unnumbered decrees. The following sections are based on fieldwork conducted before the 2011 census and reform. However, as we will see in the last part of this chapter, past and recent reform programmes have had limited impact on the armed forces.

Factionalisation: the power of the commanders

In the years 2005–09, life in the rebel forces and government forces respectively was often less different than we imagine. During periods of fighting, rebels and soldiers lived – or died – in similar conditions. Between two offensives, the idleness of the soldiers' lives was the counterpart to the boredom of the rebels as they waited in their rear bases for the end of the rainy season so that they could (re)open fire. Some interviewees told me that there was little difference between their lives in the regular and irregular armies. One of them, a demobilised soldier of just thirty or so, who was about to be recruited into the GNNT in December 2005, expressed this very clearly: '[The army and the rebellion] are the same. You're with your brothers in both cases.'[30]

The social networks that existed prior to the war were the backbone of the rebel forces – and, to some extent, of the regular forces. The role of commanders in the army was close to that of local commanders in the rebel movements. They recruited and managed troops and were de facto heads of what could be called regular factions: 'Military discipline often comes down to obedience to a specific leader, often a parent.'[31] All factions were not equal. Some soldiers, who enjoyed a popularity and an authority superior to that of the others, could mobilise large numbers of troops. They could also generate a significant wave of defection if they join a rebel group. When an officer such as General Séby Aguid joined the rebellion in February 2006, this was a major blow to the regime because of the networks he was able to mobilise.[32] The officers with broad social bases were the keystones of the army.

In a factionalised army not governed by bureaucratic rules, the chain of command changes depending on the political circumstances and loyalties of the moment. To take a recent example, Chad was not able to provide a chart of registered battalion commanders, even though this was necessary if the country was to benefit from an assistance programme from the US government.[33] The hierarchy has not disappeared, but there is considerable vagueness about the missions and responsibilities of the officers. Those who make the decisions are not always those who, according to official texts, should be making them. Recruitment, placement and career advancement obey a logic of patronage. The high number of senior officers demonstrates the need to constantly thank the faithful and the new recruits. Professional soldiers are often relegated to technical jobs.

The regime uses the forces available more than it seeks to control them. In this sense, it leaves things alone when it would be too expensive to intervene, and it intervenes directly or indirectly when the preservation of the balance of forces is at stake. If it is difficult to obtain accurate information on the composition of the army when clashes took place, one can argue that the troops mobilised were not always the same: the army's profile was adapted, on a case-by-case basis, to the profile of its enemies. When the rebels attacked in April 2006, only soldiers loyal to the regime (or rather, in a context marked by uncertainty, those who were rightly or wrongly considered reliable) were required to fight. The others were not called upon.[34] However, the army was reinforced by police contingents led by the director general of this institution, a police officer close to Idriss Déby.[35] Government forces also drew on the support of Zaghawa civilians who mobilised against the threat posed to them by a rebellion led by a Tama: the Zaghawa feared that the rebel leader, who had worked with the Sudanese and had participated in bloody repressions against the people of Darfur, particularly the Zaghawa, might seize the presidential palace.[36] In February 2008, during the second rebel attack on N'Djamena, it was already not quite the same army that was engaged in the fighting. This time, there were Zaghawa on the rebel side. Contrary to the calculations made by the insurgents, who were relying on huge support for the rebellion from the

Zaghawa,[37] only a minority of them defected. The clashes led to many deaths among the Zaghawa.

War techniques were themselves marked more by mobility than by discipline. The Chadian army has been known for its technique of *rezzou* (plural of *razzia*, the word for 'raid'), whereby pickup columns launch rapid attacks. This technique of lightning offensives allowed the Chadians to beat the Libyan tanks in 1987 in the desert of Ennedi. Against all the odds, small groups of pickups that each carried a dozen fighters equipped with small arms and rocket launchers managed to take the garrison of Fada, which had been occupied by the Libyans: 'an ancestral survival tactic designed to save encampments from looting was transformed into an offensive strategy'.[38] During the last period of the war, government and rebel columns came together and clashed, and fighters fired in a piecemeal way – it seems that they also often missed their targets.[39] War techniques, however, have modernised and use new equipment. Columns of the army are now equipped with heavy tanks and multiple rocket launchers and can draw on air support. These techniques all come at a high human cost.

Outsourcing: supplemental militias

Factionalisation was closely related to the outsourcing of the army: that is, the use of supplemental militias and mercenaries. Between 2005 and 2009, when the crises in Chad and Darfur were intertwined, Chadian regular forces were supported by the JEM of Darfur. N'Djamena provided the JEM with a rear base in eastern Chad and enabled the movement to recruit in the Sudanese refugee camps set up in Chad. The JEM rebels were not, however, mere puppets of N'Djamena. Nor were they mere mercenaries: their claims concerned Sudanese politics and their involvement in Chad was only a means to achieve their ends. Conversely, Idriss Déby's support for the JEM did not mean that N'Djamena wished to interfere even more in Sudanese affairs: their alliance was strategic. In April 2006, this Darfuri armed movement supported the Chadian army during the FUC attack. In February 2008, some of the JEM men took the road to N'Djamena. But by the time they had arrived in the capital, the coalition rebels had already been defeated. In early 2009, some of the JEM troops based near the border with Darfur participated in the defensive line formed by the Chadian army and its elite corps. The Darfuri groups were known in eastern Chad as the 'Toro Boro', a term imported from Darfur that referred to Osama bin Laden's resistance in the Afghan mountains – although there was no link between these groups and the transnational network of al-Qaeda.

As well as the use of rebel groups from a neighbouring country as supplementary forces, we must take into account the formation of local armed groups even when they are not systematically co-opted or used by the regime. In the Dar Sila region, to the south-east of Abéché, self-defence groups were set up because of the polarisation of local conflicts and the proliferation of Janjaweed attacks (often coordinated with those launched by Chadian rebels).[40] These militias formed by the Dadjo (and other such groups, including the Masalit and Sinyar) were comprised mainly of peasants.[41] They were based on a local organisation called the *warnang*, which in each village mobilised young men for different types of work, particularly farm work. These *warnang*, whose mission was to defend the village in wartime, had been militarised since 2006. In late 2006, they asked the government to provide them with weapons, but the government refused, less out of a concern to limit communal conflicts than for fear that this strategy might be turned against N'Djamena. At this time, the Dadjo were not considered reliable allies. Moreover, the regime did not want to take the risk of arousing a wave of defection among the Arabs with whom it still maintained good relations, despite the presence of Arab groups in the rebellion. The militiamen also turned to the Darfuri armed groups. The JEM and SLA provided them with training but not with weapons. The Sudanese rebels had no interest in arming groups that did not intend to fight in Darfur.[42] Dadjo militias had already been violently destroyed by the Janjaweed and Chadian rebels of the CNT in March 2007. After their defeat and the murderous destruction of the villages of Tiero and Marena, some militiamen gave up their weapons, while others were integrated into the regular army.

Informalisation: the profits drawn from sinecures and disguises

The army was not simply a factionalised force that used militias to quell rebellions at home and to make war abroad; it was also an informalised institution that generated cushy jobs and offered sinecures – that is, the granting of positions that provide a salary with no work being done in exchange – at all levels of the social and political hierarchy. The rules in force in the army were far removed from those contained in official documents or in written manuals for military schools. Soldiers were supposed to wear red berets, gendarmes blue berets, customs officers and policemen black berets (albeit with different badges), members of the National and Nomadic Guards beige berets, and officials of the Forestry Commission green berets. However, a large amount of confusion reigned in the world of these men with their mismatched uniforms. The boundaries between different bodies of law enforcement were blurred: individuals could pass with great ease from one body to another. 'Today, you have a weapon, you're a soldier, a customs officer, a policeman, an official of the Forestry Commission. All at the same time! In the bush, they do what they want,' an old man told me in Abéché.[43] The changing of berets was, then, a metaphor more than a practice: it was not the uniform that made the soldier, but his weapon and his social position that enabled him to pull rank over civilians.

Chadians and seasoned visitors could recognise powerful soldiers from the others, regardless of their attire. In 2005, the minibus in which I was travelling was stopped at Koumra, a small town between Moundou and Sarh in southern Chad. It was a period in which weapons searches were frequent. A first group of soldiers, who were quickly identified by travellers as people from the region, stood some way off from the operation. The searches were carried out by a weak-looking man in plain clothes, surrounded by a second group of men in uniform. He grabbed my French passport, held it upside down and proudly announced: 'Ah! I see that you're American!' The man in plain clothes, identified by my travelling companions as part of the ANS, impelled by a keen interest in my first aid kit, began to carry out a zealous search of my bag in the hope that I would offer him money to shorten the procedure – which I did not do. He was the one really in charge here, at the entrance to Koumra. The soldiers from the region just stood by and watched. This search of the minibus, a commonplace operation, revealed the hierarchies at work in the regular forces: the plain-clothes man directing the operation did not bother to present himself as an agent of the ANS or of any of the other coercive forces; he did not state his position, but nobody doubted that he was the leader.

The armed forces played a central role in economic and social life. The circles surrounding those in power could do good business while ordinary Chadians derived a small amount of revenue from the situation. Logistical problems were less related to lack of resources or incompetence than to practices of corruption and embezzlement that redirected available resources to other purposes. Informalisation was a mode of human resources management: the vagueness of troop numbers allowed the distribution of rewards and a series of more or less profitable activities. The use of sinecures was common. Those who were well placed in the social hierarchy could recruit their relatives or people who had done them favours. They were able to demand a fee for admission to the profession, which often corresponded to two or three months' pay. In a country where much of the money circulated as cash, local commanders picked up the wages of fictional soldiers and deceased soldiers whose names had not been removed from the troop lists. Furthermore, they got part of the general food bonus (known as the PGA or '*prime générale d'alimentation*') that was meant to feed the troops. This phenomenon was not unique to the armed forces but also applied to the whole of the civil service: some officials contributed part of their salaries to their superiors so that the latter would allow them to undertake their other occupations. There were therefore several rationales for recruitment: to thank an individual, to comply with social obligations (helping one's relatives, for example), or to levy a tax on the pay or salary of the new recruit.

Corruption and income from fictitious jobs were widespread phenomena. An officer who worked in the supply corps of the army told me the following:

When I was in the supply corps, I went to the north, to Tibesti, to pay people. But we don't know who we're paying! We sit at the table and people come. We don't know the numbers involved, we don't know who's a soldier. We pay the soldiers, but also their wives, their children, their cousins. We pay everyone. In the end, we're told: 'Leave the money for here. No need to go to the other barracks.'[44]

This phenomenon, however, did not concern the BET alone, but all the regions in the country. In early 2004, after the 'mysterious disappearance'[45] of money for the payment of wages for December 2003, a census of the armed forces was undertaken. It showed the extent of fraud involving the troops. The number of registered soldiers was much lower than the number of people paid. In Military Region no. 1, which included the garrisons of Tanoua and Bardaï, fewer than 1,300 soldiers were registered while more than 3,000 had been paid. In Sarh Military Region, 2,000 soldiers were registered, but the actual number was only 700. Depending on the military region, between a third and a half of the soldiers habitually paid actually turned up on the census day. This census and the timid measures that followed it failed to rationalise numbers or to clean up army finances. From 2005, when defections grew and the rebels became more organised, the army recruited and the old methods of management (or non-management) reappeared. In contrast, the census aroused much discontent. Because of the income made possible by the vagueness of numbers, efforts to control it could be dangerous for the regime. The Zaghawa rebels who attempted to overthrow Déby in May 2004 were motivated by various considerations. While Déby's policies were then being heavily criticised (in particular his policy in Darfur), the census, which deprived some senior officers of part of their income, played some part in the wave of desertions that then swept the army and the presidential guard.

The irregularly paid soldiers were idle when they were not engaged in combat. Except for the elite corps, the soldiers did not train and were not quartered. In N'Djamena, idle soldiers were part of the scenery: you saw them at roundabouts, sitting under trees or in bars, in sandals and turbans, on bikes and motorbikes and in cars. Soldiers and officials without jobs and without offices were said to sleep 'under the *nimiers*': they killed time under these trees while waiting to be paid. The portraits that Chadian journalists sketched of these idle soldiers were often even more harsh than mine.

In 2004, I talked to a *bogobogo* who was reminiscing about his daily life as a soldier. Until recently, he had been a regular at the Camp des Martyrs, a barracks that was then located in the centre of N'Djamena. I asked him:

What were you doing at the camp?

It's like at school: you go there to see if there's anything happening.

Is it tiring?

It's tiring. Staying like that doing nothing is always tiring.

One day, this soldier decided to leave the regular forces. He 'didn't say goodbye': rather, he simply stopped going to the barracks. He kept his outfit to work in the mobile brigade of the customs office, where one of his relatives worked. He became a 'volunteer officer' for the customs office – in other words a *bogobogo*.[46]

The idleness of soldiers fostered absenteeism and the hierarchy was not interested in the work carried out by new recruits. Many soldiers and officers therefore never joined their duty stations. For example, in 2005, 15 per cent of cadres of the General Staff of the Land Army, whose headquarters had been transferred to Moussoro, refused to leave the capital: they stayed on, unmolested, in N'Djamena, where they continued to receive their pay.[47] Integration into the regular forces, and more generally into the civil service, represents an access to state resources granted to certain individuals regardless of the work they provide.

Not all soldiers, however, worked on such a slack basis. One category was created to identify and reward those who had responsibilities: the '*décrétés*' (the 'decreed'). This system, set up during the term of office of President Habré, consisted in selecting some soldiers to whom a certain job or function was given. In consideration of the work they provided, they received a salary that was in addition to their pay. The 'decreed' also benefited from many advantages: a house that went with the job, free access to electricity services, and many borderline legal opportunities to make ends meet.[48]

Men in uniform were not all formally integrated into the coercive forces. Conversely, some civilians, including merchants, taxi drivers, farmers and herders, came each month to wait for their pay. 'We dress up for payday,' explained one trader in Mongo.[49] For them, being a soldier was not a profession but a way to earn some extra income. They went to the barracks only to pick up their money and did not define themselves as soldiers. But not all soldiers could start up a business and not all traders could 'dress up' to pick up their pay at the end of the month. This practice was organised by protected individuals. The soldier-trader had to belong to the clientele of a powerful military officer in order to obtain this dual status.

Other individuals who could not live from just their army income did two jobs simultaneously. Here we find another kind of 'military trader'. This practice could spread an enduring sense of confusion. In December 2005, as I was travelling with a 'market opportunity' (the nickname for Chadian transports between towns), I witnessed an unusual scene in Loumia, a small town on the highway between N'Djamena and Moundou. The shopkeeper who had just sold me a soda set off in pursuit of a visibly tipsy soldier. He hit him with a stick, shouting, 'They don't mind *who* they take in this army!' When he came back and leant against the wall of his shop, he explained, as if it were the most obvious thing in the world, that he was the superior of the 'drunkard' and had just sent him back to the camp on the edge of the main road. The military trader moved from one activity to another without even taking the trouble to 'dress up'.

Why did illegal practices and a general blurring of status became so widespread under Déby? Because these practices pervaded the whole social body. The beneficiaries of this system were the military and their relatives, and, ultimately, the regime, which put a dampener on any objections by leaving people alone and handing out sinecures and cushy jobs. This mode of army management, which consisted in following other rules than those established by laws and regulations, had many advantages. Beyond the lucrative activities it generated, it played an active part in military strategies: it allowed people to adapt to rapid reversals of alliances and ensures that loyal officers were rewarded.

The reforming power of oil money and counter-terrorism

'The demobilised went out through the door and came back in through the window'

Ever since Idriss Déby assumed power, the restructuring of the army has been presented as a priority. But how can one reform the army when any redistribution of positions of power and accumulation is not in the interests of those who hold them? The following pages present the long-standing attempt at reform. Although it belongs to the past, it will help us better understand the structural obstacles that lie in the way of attempts at reform.

In the early 1990s, an ambitious DDR programme was launched. The aim was twofold: first, to cut military spending as part of structural adjustment programmes (Chad signed the first agreement in 1987); and second, to transform the army into a professional, disciplined organisation. This programme was conducted in two phases: a first phase, lasting from 1992 to 1996, financed by French cooperation at a cost of 5 billion CFA francs (over 7.5 million euros); and a second, lasting from 1996 to 1997, funded by the World Bank to the same amount. Between July 1992 and February 1997, 27,046 people were released from the army,[50] slightly more than half of the total staff estimated at the project's launch. Of the 27,046 men demobilised, about 13,000 were retired and about 14,000 soldiers were 'deflated': that is, they were removed from staffing lists before reaching retirement age.

From a strictly numerical point of view, the programme was a success. But this ignores the significant challenges that DDR practitioners had to face at all stages of its implementation. The programme evolved into a huge and lucrative operation. According to those who closely followed the programme's implementation, Chadian officials embezzled large sums of money. Corruption, however, affected all levels: some demobilised men, especially those protected by powerful networks of patronage, turned up to be paid more than once. 'Some people were paid three or four times. They were demobilised, they got their card punched, they found another, they could move to a different town and get demobilised again,' a former head of the DDR programme told me.[51]

Finally, many demobilised men were quick to regain a place in the realm of arms. 'The demobilised went out through the door and came back in through the window,' as people say in Chad. Indeed, we need to consider the return of the demobilised soldiers through the window of the army, but also through the window of the police force, the customs office and other bodies of the security forces. If we are to believe those most closely involved, 'it is easy to return to the army. You change your name, you put your grandfather's name instead of your father's, and everything's okay!'[52] Reintegration, however, was easier for those who had good relationships with people 'in good positions' who could facilitate their recruitment. Although it is impossible to measure the proportion of demobilised men who have returned, the demobilised and the cadres of the different agencies in charge of reintegration agree that this is not a marginal phenomenon.

Other demobilised soldiers joined the politico-military movements that were recruiting in the 1990s. According to the Directorate of Demobilisation and Reintegration in the Ministry of Defence, between 3,000 and 4,000 demobilised men 'took up arms again in various forms' in the years following demobilisation.[53] Others managed to get back into the networks of road banditry, although this phenomenon is probably exaggerated.[54] One last way to put one's military expertise to good use was to sign up as a mercenary outside the borders of Chad. Thus we find demobilised men among the fighters recruited by Bozizé in Chad when he was hatching the rebellion that would enable him to overthrow Patassé in 2003 in the CAR.

In general, the DDR programme raised expectations that were not fulfilled. When the soldiers saw that the demobilised men were being given bonuses equivalent to one year's wages, the number of volunteers for demobilisation grew rapidly. Many of them spent their bonuses in a few months and found themselves in difficulties.[55] Rehabilitation programmes were planned, but only a pilot programme was actually implemented, and that not until 1999–2000,[56] several years after the launch of the first phase of demobilisation. Funded to the tune of US$3 million by the World Bank and 2 million Deutschmarks by GTZ (German Technical Cooperation Agency), this programme reached just over 2,700 demobilised soldiers (out of the 3,500 planned for) in five prefectures, i.e. 10 per cent of the total number demobilised.[57] This pilot programme encountered many problems in its implementation (including corruption) and was never extended. In the five prefectures targeted by the project, several associations of widows, orphans and civilians (the 'host communities') were created to meet the expectations of the programme. In N'Djamena, the demobilised soldiers, brought together in a dozen associations, spent a long time waiting for funding that never came. Officials of the National Rehabilitation Centre preferred to foster the illusions of the demobilised rather than face their wrath. Those let down by the DDR programmes mobilised several times – a small group of activists was jailed for several months in 1997 following a demonstration in N'Djamena.[58] In 2005, an association of demobilised men held a 'peaceful march'. The banners of the fifty or so demonstrators, mostly former soldiers, read 'Stop this hell! O Chad, think of your defenders' and '14 years of ordeal: homage to the demobilised of 1992'.[59]

The difficulties in reintegrating the demobilised hide another failure: the restructuring of the regular forces that was to accompany the downsizing of numbers. The DDR programme was meant to 'professionalise' the army by demobilising untrained ex-combatants who had been integrated or reintegrated over the years. But this ignored its political instrumentalisation. The members of the French military cooperation who followed the first phase of the process left to the Chadian general staff 'the responsibility to choose the men who will shape the future regiments, merely requiring a minimum ethnic mix'.[60] Soldiers who were allies of the MPS were kept in their jobs. Some were demobilised to be rehired immediately, the sole objective of this operation being to enable them to enjoy a very lucrative programme. Other soldiers, deemed unnecessary or undesirable, were removed from the army lists.

In the early 1990s, French soldiers drafted a project to overhaul the army. The 'Dijoud–Quesnot' plan was, according to a witness of the time, 'a comprehensive plan, a monument, a bravura piece'.[61] An order for the reorganisation of the army was issued in January 1991, but the army has never really been restructured. Only one regiment of what was to be the new army was actually formed.[62] The implementation of such a programme was obviously difficult in a context of political tensions. As has already been pointed out, in the early 1990s, the regime retrenched around those close to the presidency, while rebellions (re)formed in many parts of the country. Fighters were regularly reinstated after the peace agreements were signed.

The restructuring with which the French were to assist ran into another obstacle that was not merely a matter of circumstance. According to Chadian officers who participated in the commission for the reorganisation of the army set up in 1991, it was not possible to carry out a real census and the commission had to be satisfied with a rapid assessment.[63] Because it involved the reallocation of command posts for the best trained officers and tighter control on numbers, the reform aroused strong resistance. Also, again according to committee members, some military officials openly showed their contempt for its work, did not hesitate to interfere with it, and continued to operate parallel recruitment practices. In addition, some units refused to let themselves 'join the mix' in the new regiments. The operation to remove the lists of officers who had social capital and a reserve of weapons inversely proportional to their educational capital was a delicate matter.

The standardised DDR programmes functioned as 'anti-politics machines'[64] that reproduced local institutional logics. Several years after the end of the programmes, experts were fielded by the UNDP and the World Bank to discover that the older soldiers, who had retired with a modest bonus, were now in a difficult socio-economic situation. However, these experts did not address the most important question: namely how demobilisation and military restructuring programmes could paradoxically contribute to the militianisation of regular forces. The political exploitation of the programmes and the taking up of arms by the 'deflated' are the real failures of the DDR. In order to understand this, it is necessary to take the measure of the politicisation of the regular forces, the impunity enjoyed by those close to power, the centrality of networks of patronage, and the highly political nature of militianisation.[65]

The impossible 'professionalisation' of the army?

In the decade following this programme, the government announced new projects for the army. In April 2005, the Estates General of the Armies took place – twelve years after the Sovereign National Conference had said that it was an 'urgent' matter to hold them.[66] Five hundred people, mostly from the military, spent six days debating the restructuring of the army, under the critical eye of civil society organisations[67] and journalists who feared that the operation would serve to 'sweeten the members of a committee without any real power, to amuse the gallery'.[68] Only one significant change occurred in the wake of the Estates General: the transition to a salary scale that allows soldiers to be paid according to their rank and seniority. This measure had been proposed and discussed since the early 1990s.[69]

In 2010, twenty or so senior military officers were demobilised and received very large demobilisation bonuses.[70] A year later, a vast census was organised. Its aim was to check the payroll and to identify the 'fake soldiers'. As a result, 14,000 'fake soldiers' were dismissed from the army, the gendarmerie and the GNNT. In addition, between October 2011 and December 2012, about 5,000 soldiers, 7 per cent of them women, were demobilised.[71] However, these reforms, which allowed the government to show its good will when it came to reforming the army, had only limited effects. As Roland Marchal notes, 'a closer look over a longer period shows that financial rewards to leave the army were high and that those dismissed were also provided the means to build their own villas; furthermore many were recruited back after January 2013 when military adventures restarted'.[72]

In late 2011, command positions in the army were redistributed: officers belonging to ethnic groups that were still under-represented in the hierarchy but had been mobilised in the fighting against the rebels were appointed to key positions. This attempt to redistribute positions of power, however, did not last long. The reforms designed to demonstrate the President's good will to Chad's international partners, including France, did not have the hoped-for effect. As noted above, the key positions were held by those close to Idriss Déby. But if the army had not been 'streamlined' and 'professionalised' in the sense understood by international professionals in army reform, it was nevertheless built up into a robust body.

Oil wealth and Western security cooperation: the conditions of Chad's regional interventionism

The army, which in a few years became the regional front-line force in Mali and in the Lake Chad Basin, was not transformed by so-called 'reform' programmes but by oil money and Western support for counter-terrorism. Defence spending per capita and as a percentage of gross domestic product has grown fast over the past ten years (4.86 per cent of GDP in 2014).[73] The first oil-related income was a bonus paid by the oil consortium in 2000. At least US$4.5 billion of this signature bonus paid by Chevron was spent on weapons.[74] In the following years, Chad radically defied the World Bank, which had agreed to back the Chad–Cameroon oil project on condition that the profits went towards development and long-term poverty alleviation. The Bank invested massively – financially and politically – in the project. It had, however, underestimated the regime's capacity to skirt external pressures.[75] The original mechanism for monitoring oil revenues that was imposed in 1999 had already been dismantled by 2006. Its two principal innovations were called into question. First, the fund set up to safeguard a portion of the country's oil revenues for future generations was eliminated and the money went into the state coffers. Second, the list of the 'priority sectors', previously limited to poverty reduction areas such as health, education and basic infrastructure, grew to include energy, justice, territorial administration and, most importantly, security. Against the backdrop of an escalating politico-military crisis, an arm-wrestling contest pitted Chad against the World Bank and the European Investment Bank, the latter of which had imposed clauses prohibiting Chad from selling its oil directly on the international market, a prohibition maintained in exchange for a loan to construct the pipeline. Temporary suspension of the World Bank's aid programmes, enacted in 2006, did not stop Chad from pursuing the dismantling of the mechanism for managing petroleum resources. Chad succeeded in making its mark by denouncing the interference from international institutions and attacks on its sovereignty, by pressuring the petroleum consortium, and by playing off China's competition – the China National Petroleum Corporation (CNPC) invested in Chad in 2007. In the end, the World Bank and the European Investment Bank accepted the reimbursement of the loans contracted by the Chadian state.[76] In 2014, Chad was accepted as a member of the Extractive Industries Transparency Initiative (EITI). Transparency is only a first step, however; true accountability for the use of oil wealth remains a faraway horizon.

Idriss Déby argued that security was a *sine qua non* condition for development. Arms imports were five times higher in 2004–08 than in 1999–2003.[77] A report by CCFD-Terre solidaire puts forward one set of figures: 'Chad's military spending increased from 35.3 billion FCFA (53 million euros) in 2004 to 275.7 billion FCFA (420 million euros) in 2008, thus increasing by a factor of 7.79.'[78] Between 2006 and 2010, Chad became the third largest importer of arms in sub-Saharan Africa, appearing for the first time among the top ten: 'By far the largest supplier of arms was Ukraine, followed by a variety of other suppliers of major arms and other weapons including Belgium, Bulgaria, China, France, Israel, Libya, Russia and Singapore.'[79] By contrast, Romania and Germany refused licences for the export of military or combat equipment to the Chadian government, referring to the conflict and human rights violations in the country.[80] The army acquired warplanes, attack helicopters, tanks and missiles and became one of the best equipped on the continent. Since 2008, the military parades of 11 August (Chad's independence day) have provided an opportunity to put on displays of force.

In addition to oil wealth, the Chadian army is supported by France. The budget allocated to French structural cooperation amounts to 12 million euros per year,[81] to which must be added donations and aid initially provided by Operation Epervier and now supplied by Operation Barkhane. Many Chadian officers – starting with the current army chief, Idriss Déby, who was trained at the Ecole de guerre – were (and continue to be) trained in France. The influence of France on the training of officers is considerable, even if the former colonial power is now challenged in this area by the United States.

Following 9/11, the US launched the Pan-Sahel Initiative (PSI), a counter-terrorism programme that aimed to bolster the militaries of Chad, Mali, Niger and Mauritania. In 2005, the programme, renamed the Trans-Sahara Counterterrorism Partnership (TSCTP), expanded to include Nigeria, Senegal, Burkina Faso, Morocco, Algeria and Tunisia. Between 2009 and 2013, the United States obligated approximately US$13 million in TSCTP funds to Chad.[82] The US trained a small unit called the Special Anti-Terrorism Group (SATG), which was deployed to Mali in support of the French 'Opération Serval' in the winter and spring of 2013.[83] In the past few years, as the US has begun to consider its former Nigerian security partner no longer reliable, Chad has gained a central place in the US strategy in the Sahel under its Africa command (AFRICOM) programme. In 2015, Chad hosted the annual US-sponsored Exercise Flintlock, a regional counter-terrorism exercise for countries in the Sahel.

While experts on military issues highlight the success of the army, despite expressing alarm at the weaknesses of the regime, some issues are rarely debated. First, although using oil money to buy weapons had indeed raised a stir in 2006, Western states as well as international financial institutions seem hardly bothered by it these days. Are the risks associated with poor management of oil resources no longer relevant? Idriss Déby has eschewed saving money. Now, with the declining price of oil, public funds are evaporating. The problem of poverty remains unresolved. In 2015 and 2016, protests against rising living costs were violently repressed.[84] Second, the effectiveness of the Chadian army on the ground in Mali and against Boko Haram appears to have meant that the human rights violations by the same army in Chad and the CAR have been forgotten.[85] So can it come as any surprise that an army that has never been reformed despite twenty-five years of announcements and unfulfilled projects is attacking civilians? In a militianised army where military leaders are trained to be warriors (and not peacekeepers) and where they enjoy considerable impunity, such violations of human rights are unfortunately not mere accidents. As this chapter has attempted to show, if the various reforms implemented have never had the desired effects, this is because militianisation is neither a cultural trait nor a simple legacy of past conflicts, but a mode of government. Third, do the Chadians do the 'dirty work'? Chadian soldiers suffered heavy losses in the assault in the Ifoghas massif in February 2013[86] and were the victims of several murderous attacks thereafter. Fourth, how can we make sense of this 'shift in the security burden'?[87] Are African states finally assuming greater responsibility in resolving the continent's crises? Or do we observe the emergence of a new mode of warfare in which some units of African armies (or even local militias)[88] are specifically trained to do the job? Westerners no longer have scruples about training units that have emerged from the praetorian guard – units whose recruitment is ethnically polarised and that are known for their human rights violations. We may well wonder about the uses Idriss Déby might make of such well-equipped and well-trained units when they are not mobilised outside the country. We may worry even more about the political role they may play on the day when the question of Déby's successor arises.

CHAPTER 6

. . . .

Governing the inter-war

What is the role of the state in the reproduction of the hierarchies produced by and in war? What is the role of the state in the government of (in)security? In this final chapter, I analyse the production of inequalities and the specific positions of those powerful individuals known as 'untouchables'. I study how illegal economic activities are paradoxically shaped by the state and the role of impunity in the daily government of the inter-war. I concentrate on a militarised economic space where men in uniform coexist, collaborate or compete: namely, customs. Economic activities at customs are marked both by a gendered division of labour and by powerful political and social hierarchies. This analysis leads me to question the mainstream discourse on the state in Chad and elsewhere in the global South.

The 'untouchables': positions of accumulation and impunity

Unregulated economic activities and violent modes of appropriation in the Lake Chad Basin have been studied by Janet Roitman. In her work *Fiscal Disobedience*, she showed that such practices turn the bush and border areas into spaces for wealth creation.[1] The unregulated economy of the border, which is in no sense marginal, provides a space for new forms of social mobility for 'economic refugees' and 'military refugees'; it is a foundation for economic redistribution. The most innovative aspect in Janet Roitman's work is the way she shows how, in an environment of economic austerity, many of those who take part in such activities 'exercise claims to wealth through violent means, such as seizure and razzia, thus insisting upon the right to wealth through conquest and asserting that spoils are licit forms of wealth'.[2] Income from illegal and violent economic activities comes to be seen as a licit form of wealth. In particular, she examines the way in which seizures are problematised, and concludes that the region is marked by an 'ethics of illegality'.

Janet Roitman leaves open the question of the production of inequalities in the unregulated economy. If the unregulated economy linked to arms (or to the 'garrison *entrepôt*') is lucrative, which people are able to enrich themselves and enjoy actual social mobility? Who, at the border or in the bush, is likely to reach a position of power and accumulation? Who can engage in illegal activities unmolested? Even in a country affected by decades of conflict such as Chad, only a minority of armed men benefit from war and violent modes of accumulation. In other words, while violent modes of accumulation are ordinary, upward social mobility is exceptional.

The question of social differentiation cannot be separated from the question of the privileges and the impunity granted to those in circles close to the state. Not all men in arms enjoy access to positions of power and accumulation. It is not enough to have participated in the victory of the MPS in 1990 or to be skilled in business to rise in society. You also need to have stayed close to the MPS. However, the protection offered by closeness to power is never total, and falls from grace are common.

Impunity is one of the problems that Chadians denounce with the most virulence. They have a name for those individuals who may have been very successful financially and who are considered to enjoy total impunity: they are the 'untouchables'. Although impunity has a long history, the term 'untouchable' was popularised under Déby: it is now commonly encountered in the media and out on the street, but it was also used in more official forums, for example in texts presented to the Estates General of Justice in June 2003.

Who are these individuals who have gained positions of power and accumulation and who are described as 'untouchable' by other Chadians? How do they describe themselves? One of my interlocutors, from a powerful military family, explained what he thought was the problem of the reintegration of Goran soldiers from his village (located near Fada in north-eastern Chad) who had maintained good relations with the first circle of power:

> They got a bit of a taste of power: Goukouni, Habré, Idriss. They live for free. They have a little power, they are respected. They have a house, free electricity. If they are demobilised, they lose everything, they don't know what to do ... [The soldier] has come to town, he's respected by the beautiful women in the world. And he's told: 'You need to go home.' But where's he going to go? He doesn't want to!

My interlocutor was not officially integrated into the army. He explained his position:

> We [my parents and I] are like soldiers. I go out in my brother's car, my father's. Everyone thinks I am a soldier ... I almost am a soldier.

A friend joined in the discussion and mocked him with a wink and a nod of complicity:

> He's an untouchable! He has a gun, he goes round in a car with soldiers, he can do what he likes in town ... After all, he's a soldier!'[3]

This definition clearly illustrates the status of the so-called 'untouchables'. These soldiers and crypto-soldiers occupy positions of power in the hierarchy of the army, as well as in spaces that favour accumulation, in the margins of the state.

To be 'untouchable' means being in a privileged position in all spaces, including the most improbable, such as prison. In 2005, I conducted interviews with inmates at the prison in N'Djamena. Among the cattle rustlers, brawlers, drunks and minors, I met Bichara, a Zaghawa man whose way of talking and bodily *hexis* suggested that there were not many people he was afraid of – and certainly not the prison staff. This MPS veteran, who had taken up arms to join the *maquis* at the age of fourteen, had been integrated into the army after Déby's victory. He was one of those who fought the MDD in the early 1990s and were rewarded with a new job in customs. For over ten years, Bichara was a customs employee. He had recently been arrested following a clash between customs and traders that led to the death of a trader. Was he now in prison to await sentence? Or was he taking shelter there until his parents could negotiate *diya* with the victim's relatives? Chadian prisons regularly take in people who are at risk of reprisals and awaiting the settlement of a dispute through the traditional route. Whatever the situation, it appears that Bichara was not an ordinary prisoner. He owned several taxis and continued to conduct his business affairs from prison via his two mobile phones – which had not been confiscated, despite being banned by the regulations. During the interview, he answered his phone several times to give instructions to the taxi drivers working for him. While we talked, the superintendent of the facility came into the room to ask if the interview was over. He was quickly rebuffed by the prisoner, who replied dryly, 'No, it's not over. Leave us alone!' The superintendent promptly left. In general, the most ordinary social interactions allow you to guess the status of the individuals involved. And the representations that are based on these statuses have their own impact. Whatever fate might have in store for Bichara, he now appeared, on that January day in 2005, as an 'untouchable'. He was considered as such by the prison superintendent, by the other inmates, by the Chadian friend who had come with me, and finally by myself, as a researcher socialised in Chadian hierarchies. The phenomenon of the 'untouchables' is fostered by the impunity granted to those close to the government but also by the way they are represented. The politicisation of ethnicity has become so widespread that it is a central element in the strategies and tactics of ordinary Chadians, and it now pervades daily practices.

As I have already pointed out, those close to the regime are not all Zaghawa, and not all Zaghawa are close to the regime. Nevertheless, Zaghawa and 'untouchables' are often viewed as the same thing. The social construction of the 'untouchability' of the Zaghawa has an impact on the practical sphere: people are wary of those who are, or say they are, Zaghawa, and those who want to be feared pose as Zaghawa. In addition, identities are fluid: you can be Goran under Habré and Zaghawa under Déby. This shift is found especially among the Borogat, who, like the Bideyat, speak Beria but also Dazaga, the language of the Daza or Goran.[4]

Living by the gun in the margins of the state

A productive and organised disorder

Before the attacks by Boko Haram destabilised the whole economy of the Lake Chad Basin, the Ngueli customs station on the outskirts of N'Djamena, on the border with Cameroon, was one of the main trading places in the region. Trade between the capital of Chad and the little Cameroonian town of Kousséri, adjoining the border, was a successful and central element in the Chadian economy. Great confusion reigned in the dust of Ngueli,[5] even more than on the Cameroonian side of the border. Here you would encounter the pickups of the mobile brigade, who 'invented the highway code as they went along', in the picturesque expression often used in Chad. Turbaned men in battledress, standing in the rear of their vehicles, pursued smugglers or escorted them as far as their warehouses. A little further down, on the Logone River, which marks the border, canoes carried both smugglers and goods. On the bridge, there was always a great bustle of activity: large-scale traders and transporters rubbed shoulders with cattle dealers and women selling cloth and sugar returning from Kousséri, hiding their goods in their dresses or their lafaïs (long, colourful veils). Another group who lived off border trade were the disabled, who, under an unnumbered decree, were allowed to import goods from Cameroon without paying customs duties. On their wheelchairs you could sometimes read 'Do not touch: disabled veteran'. All the men in uniform seemed to have met up by appointment at the customs station. Indeed, here you could meet customs officers, soldiers, gendarmes, police and GNNT elements. Some, such as the ANS agents, were in civilian dress.

Only foreign travellers and novices tried to distinguish between customs officers and police. There was no point: the distinction between them was obviously blurred, and uniform was not the best indicator of their role and power. Customs officers and *bogobogos* often worked hand in hand with smugglers – when they did not practise fraud themselves. Moreover, because of the institutionalisation of illegality, traders were always smugglers as well. The activities undertaken by those working on and around the border are of many kinds, and it is difficult to classify them according to their degree of (il)legality, of (in)formality, or of (un)official status.[6]

The question remains of who, in the particular context of Chad, is in a strong position to negotiate. Not all stakeholders have the same voice. My discussion with a forwarding agent who had his 'business in the bag' – in other words, he had no legal existence but was familiar to those working in Ngueli – clearly illustrates the impact of individuals close to power on the unnumbered decrees (or laws). When talk turned to negotiating fees between traders and customs officers, he told me:

> The laws are made by the people, it's all bullshit. People have the right to change the law, if it gets in their way.
>
> *And how, concretely, is a law modified? In Ngueli, for example, how is the law changed if people think it's bullshit?*
>
> You have to go through the established people. You absolutely have to go through them![7]

In Ngueli, no legal or moral punishment is inflicted on those who circumvent the law. But you really need social capital if you are to rewrite it at will. Power relations mark the code of fraud. Interpersonal relations and political skills are key to economic success. Each participant invents tactics to live and do business in this uncertain and risky world. But while such tactics belong to a repertoire of resistance, they do not allow people to overturn power relations.

War widows: small and big profits

Let us get back to Ngueli, in the days when trade provided a living for a large number of N'Djamenois. While *bogobogos* are exclusively men, women have been numerous among traders since the 1980s.[8] Doing business in Ngueli was hard and dangerous for women. Those who did not have strong connections to 'well-seated' people or the party in power were often victims of harassment and violence. The cost of impunity granted to *bogobogos* and other men in arms is gendered.

Not all women were able to run successful businesses, nor did they all have the same flexibility when it came to circumventing or rewriting the law and the unnumbered decrees. The inequalities among women who participate in Ngueli's economy become evident when we compare the itineraries of war widows. I here compare women traders who were at either end of the social scale, but there are obviously intermediate situations.

At the bottom of the social scale we find those who illegally imported small goods from Ngueli: cloth, soap, sugar, oil, beverages and other consumer products. The activity was risky. Their knowledge of unfrequented paths and their tactics of concealing the goods under clothes and *lafaïs* did not always shelter them from sometimes violent altercations with *bogobogos*. For example, the vast majority of the widows of the Union of the Demobilised, Pensioners and Widows of Chad, one of the associations of the demobilised in N'Djamena, lived off the sugar trade.[9] Like all war widows, they were entitled to a modest pension – although it was quite inadequate. In any case, they were unable to ask for it. The cost of the administrative procedure was prohibitive, because to the administration costs were added the sums payable to officials if the procedure were to succeed – up to several hundred thousand CFA francs. Under such circumstances, the widows lived off fraud. Those I met in 2004 in N'Djamena imported three to five *koros* of sugar per day, making a daily profit of between 500 and 1,000 CFA francs (between 1 and 1.50 euros). In comparison, the rent of their small houses without water or electricity averaged 5,000 CFA francs (7.50 euros) per month, while a large bag of millet cost 15,000 CFA francs (23 euros).

The paths of the women importing sugar and other consumer products regularly crossed those of the 'Ngueli widows' who made much bigger profits. These women, who were also nicknamed 'the sisters of the President', were forwarding agents in customs who had (or claimed to have) lost their husbands in the war against Libya, the MPS rebellion or one of the wars waged under Déby. Interestingly, these successful female entrepreneurs had to justify their activities by referring to a dead husband (whom they had to replace) and to an imaginary or actual military past.

Working hand in hand with customs officers and *bogobogos*, they carried out 'legalised smuggling'[10] and did lucrative business in Ngueli. Once again, it was access to the state that made all the difference: these women were close to the presidency. This activity aroused people's greed and fed the discontent of the other traders, who accused them of selling off their goods at excessively low prices.

This state patronage does not prohibit attempts to regain control of customs by members of the government. In 2004, the Minister of Economy and Finance, Ahmat Awad Sakine, attracted attention by his efforts to limit the most criticised customs practices. In an internal ministry circular, he wrote that the 'total confusion' and 'proliferation of people taking part in customs clearance operations' seemed '*deliberately created* to allow the fraudulent export of imported goods'.[11] Ahmat Awad Sakine attempted to control the activity of the female smugglers of Ngueli. This intervention in the milieu of big smugglers angered those who were mainly involved: a hundred of them 'came down to Ngueli' to attack the customs officers – who were not all their allies.[12] Two months later, the female smugglers resumed their activities, albeit with a little more discretion: their Peugeot 504s and 505s no longer crossed the border in single file, but instead entered Chad in a disorganised way, late at night, but still escorted, as before, by men in military uniform.[13]

Bogobogos *and career customs officers*

In Ngueli's inter-war, merchants had to cope with regular customs officials as well as with demobilised soldiers who had become police officers or lived off their wits, and ex-combatants taking advantage of the economic opportunities of customs before joining the *maquis*. Regular and irregular customs officials made a living from the goods confiscated – whether or not they were imported fraudulently. But they did not all profit from them in the same way. I am here interested in two customs figures who did not have the same capital: first, the *bogobogos*, whose social capital had facilitated access to positions of accumulation; and second, career customs officers whose educational capital proved unprofitable.

Among the customs men in a position to enrich themselves were the so-called *bogobogos* or *karang-karangs*. The terms *bogobogo* and *karang-karang*, whose origins remain uncertain, are likely to have been popularised in the early 1990s.[14] These customs men, who were not officially integrated into the customs department, lived off extortion. They embodied the organised disorder and violence of the Ngueli market. Their practices were often brutal and their chases through the city were dangerous: deaths caused by stray bullets or accidents were not exceptional. The press regularly castigated this 'small group of armed illiterates who had appointed themselves customs men'.[15] They themselves had a very different view of their work. One *bogobogo* in Ngueli, an ex-soldier, told me: 'We *bogobogos* are volunteers who are not yet integrated, but we are still customs officers all the same.'[16]

What determines the position of the customs men and *bogobogos* in Ngueli and elsewhere in Chad? Sometimes, it is their status as ex-soldiers, but above all their social capital and their access to the state. This phenomenon is not new: already under Hissène Habré 'positions such as the Directorate of Customs [were] always held by relatives of the President, and they always made sure they picked up more than their fair share'.[17] Under Déby, customs remained under the 'exclusive domain of the government'.[18] Being appointed to customs, where large sums of money are in circulation, has become a way for the MPS's clients to be rewarded. At customs, maybe even more than in other bodies of law enforcement, political loyalties have taken precedence over skills. The political use of an appointment to customs was so institutionalised that the customs officers in the department of Kobé, feeling aggrieved, supported their claims by an explicit reminder of their rebellious past. In a letter sent in 2006 to the Minister of Finance, they wrote: 'We are Chadians like others, Chadians and MPS activists right from the start, so we are requesting your intervention to *give us back our rights*.'[19] The 'rights' thus claimed were leadership positions in very busy customs offices. Only six of the ninety-one signatories of the letter were appointed to positions as deputy directors, while the others continued to demand jobs.[20]

The *bogobogos*, who moved with great ease from the fight against fraud to the fight for the control and ownership of this same fraud, dominated the career customs officers. The latter were in a situation comparable to that of career soldiers who were subordinate to ex-combatants reintegrated into the army. One of my respondents, a former office manager who had been replaced by an individual he euphemistically called 'one of their relatives', defined himself as a 'customs man in the garage'.[21] He railed against the 'fake customs men' who could not 'read or write'. This observation was shared. 'We no longer have our place,' confided another career customs officer who had never gone on to positions of responsibility.[22] There is nothing surprising in the bitterness of customs officers who derive only limited profits from the border economy. However, it must be acknowledged that inequalities within customs are criticised even more in that they are embedded in an ethnicised social and political context. Indeed, while not all marginalised career customs officers are southerners, and not all southern customs officers are marginalised, both groups are often assimilated. Thus was born the figure of the 'Laoukoura'. This word, a Ngambay forename, now refers to those who are serving less educated but more powerful leaders. So, since the time of Habré, it has been said: 'Money you take to Mahamat, paper to Laoukoura.'

Figures of power

How do ordinary Chadians talk about customs and its inequalities? One afternoon, when I was with a dozen young Chadian men in a bar in Moursal, a southern district of N'Djamena, the discussion, which had been focused on romantic relationships in their crudest form, turned to customs. Three of them told of the mishap that had befallen them that day in Ngueli. At the border, a uniformed man asked Bemadjita for his identity papers.[23] He complied and showed his identity card. Another man sitting further away – who introduced himself, too, as an agent of the security forces – approached and gestured to him to remove his glasses. Bemadjita said 'But I use them to see with' and resisted. 'Can't you check my identity if I ha my glasses on? Why should I remove them?' The security office (probably from the ANS) wanted to get the young intellectual to hand over a few banknotes. Beyond petty corruption, it was the political and social hierarchies of the country and the pride of the two men that were at stake. One of the three travelling companions, Elie, who had already passed the checkpoint, turned back to intervene on his friend's behalf. While not being an 'untouchable', he had important social capital: he was married to the daughter of a respected general and ran a prosperous business in the capital. Above all, he had the 'blue, yellow and red' card: the card of an ANS agent. The confrontation ended quickly and Bemadjita was able to cross the border without losing face.

Back in N'Djamena, the incident sparked a heated debate. The dozen friends gathered in the bar agreed that such problems at customs were 'deliberate' and 'organised'. Inequalities were central to the discussion: in the same gang, some people were arrested, while others crossed the border unmolested. The debate became more heated as more and more beer was consumed. Bemadjita declared that he refused to give up. It was necessary to resist, in his view: 'I prefer to spend ten hours refusing to take off my glasses, rather than obey: they don't have any right to ask me to do that.' Djibrine did not disagree about the injustice that the situation revealed, but said that Bemadjita had become too severe on his own country ever since he had left to study in Senegal. Fabien, nicknamed 'the Beninese' because he had also studied in West Africa, seemed worried; he kept repeating in a low voice, 'We should talk about something else, we're in a bar, not in a bedroom.' When he got up to leave, the others held him back.

This anecdote shows how situations can be understood by everyone without creating a consensus. That day, everyone knew how to behave in Ngueli: the customs (or crypto-customs) man who wanted to extort money from travellers without, of course, saying so explicitly; the young intellectual reacting rebelliously; and his friend who owned a card that others did not have. Talking about the most ordinary incidents already involves entering the political sphere, as Fabien's anxiety showed. These are the 'hassles' of everyday life that privileges of those with an ANS card or those 'untouchables'. The law has not disappeared; in ..y contemporary postcolonial states, disorder and a .. of the law go together.[24] The law is the very condition of ..npunity – impunity that has meaning and political effect only if it is the privilege of a small group.

Police harassment and illegal practices are not specific to Chad: they are widespread – including outside the African continent. In Chad, the disorder that enables these illegal practices is inseparable from a particular mode of government: the *bogobogos'* activities are not only tolerated, they are also partly organised by the state. Since those close to the MPS themselves play an active part in customs, it is clear to everyone that the state does not simply condone illegalities at the border, but participates in them. Customs, like other areas where different actors encounter and confront one another, thus gives rise to questions about the (il)legitimacy of power and social hierarchies. The social ascent of *bogobogos* and of those, civilian or military, who are considered 'untouchables' is criticised more than it is admired. Because access to the state determines whether or not they can get rich from customs activities, the *bogobogos* and women who practise large-scale smuggling are more often associated with state power than with just being cunning.

Impunity and the governing of (in)security

The war of commanders in Mongo

Proposing an anthropology in the margins of the state, Venna Das and Deborah Poole underscore the importance of figures of local authority who 'represent both highly personalised forms of private power and the supposedly impersonal or neutral authority of the state'.[25] This is precisely the question raised by the unnumbered decree. This mode of government implies great room for manoeuvre for men in arms, who work both for the state and for themselves. How are such social and political orders negotiated at the local level? Let us consider a singular yet significant moment in the life of Mongo, the main city of the mountainous Guéra region, halfway between N'Djamena and Abéché.[26] In November 2005, Mongo was on the brink of war, with fighting already raging in the east; pickup trucks crisscrossed the city, going to and from the rebel-held zones. In a strained political situation, two commanders, one from the army and one from the gendarmerie, found themselves in a kind of cold war.

Ordinarily, the residents of Mongo complain little about the security forces. When I arrived in the city, the *clandos* (motorbike taxis) were negotiating with police officers over the cost of operating a taxi without the proper documentation. The president of the *clandos*' association, a member of the MPS, was optimistic: an agreement could soon be reached.[27] A few years earlier, civilians had complained about the local forces of the National and Nomadic Guard of Chad because of their racketeering and abuse. Political elites and local notables of the Guéra mobilised and were able to obtain their transfer to another region.[28] Those who stayed 'acted as customs officers at the livestock market'.[29] Despite some clouds on the horizon, relations between the regular forces and the population were relatively good by Chadian standards. A political event at N'Djamena and an incident at Mongo turned this negotiated order upside down for two weeks.

When I arrived in Mongo on 15 November 2005, the attempted *coup d'état* of two days earlier was, not surprisingly, the subject of every conversation. Among the suspects of the attack led by Djibrine Dassert were ethnic Hadjarai from the Guéra region.[30] In Mongo, civilians seemed resigned. 'For Chadians, stories of war are like music. We hear it, but we are used to it, and life continues,' one resident told me the day I arrived. Events such as coup attempts belong to the ordinariness of the inter-war. However, they have an impact on daily life. In 2005, Hadjarai were suspected of participating in the coup attempt, and, as a result, military reinforcements had been called to 'secure' the region. When the military detachment from the Guéra–Salamat military region, which was usually stationed at Am Timan (the capital of Salamat), settled in Mongo, civilians had to put up with their illegal and violent practices. A period of insecurity began: residents of Mongo stayed at home after nightfall – only men unwilling to miss a game in the European Cup football tournament ventured out.[31] People spoke of motorcycles and cars borrowed without the knowledge of their owners. They also spoke of a female shopkeeper threatened by soldiers and of girls being sexually assaulted[32] – at the time, it was difficult to get reliable information on sexual violence, which remained taboo. As far as gender-based violence and sexual violence are concerned, impunity is widespread and at all levels. But the fact that the perpetrators were 'untouchable' soldiers made it even more difficult for women to protect themselves and to challenge impunity.

This moment in the history of Mongo reveals both how regular forces have been militianised and how impunity has been institutionalised. The competition between the security forces appeared as soon as the military detachment entered the city. There were two roadblocks: one maintained by the soldiers from the detachment; the other by the gendarmes. The two groups stopped vehicles, searched for weapons and checked travellers' identities. The conflict between the two commanders broke out on 14 November, when a gendarme who had come from the neighbouring city of Bitkine to collect his pay cheque was arrested by soldiers at a roadblock. The soldiers reproached him for carrying a weapon, accused him of being a rebel, and took him to the military camp. According to the commander of the gendarmerie, the gendarme's arrest was a pretext to attack him.[33] There was not simply a rivalry between members of different units of the regular forces, but an actual opposition between two strongmen: the 'MR com' or military region commander for Guéra–Salamat, and the 'legion com' or commander of the Mongo gendarmerie legion.[34]

The regional governor, the highest-ranking representative of the state in Mongo, who was himself a former rebel and colonel in the army, intervened. He organised mediation between the two commanders with a half-dozen armed men from each side providing protection.[35] An agreement was reached: the gendarme arrested by the soldiers would be freed. However, tensions remained high. The 'legion com', also called 'the colonel', slept at the gendarmerie and spent his days under his 'hangar', a large shelter set in front of his house. He received visitors with his weapon within reach. Two mats delineated the space: the most important visitors sat on one, furnished with a rug; the colonel's social inferiors took the other. As a foreigner, I had access to the rug.[36] I was welcomed – all the more so as I had been recommended by one of the colonel's relatives. The 'legion com' explained to me that he was suspected of being complicit in the rebellion, which he denied. He seemed to be preparing for war. Men from the two camps patrolled the city and watched one another. While the attempted coup was a major concern in N'Djamena, Mongo seemed to be on the verge of another kind of war.

However, tensions relaxed before the commanders' opposition led to actual confrontations. On 1 December, two weeks after the gendarme's arrest had triggered tensions, a celebration was organised to mark the fifteenth anniversary of Idriss Déby's seizure of power. In preparation, the residents of Mongo spent several days repainting the city's walls in white and in Chad's national colours: blue, yellow and red. The celebration was the occasion for a minister, who was himself an ethnic Hadjarai native of Guéra, to recall the Hadjarai's loyalty to the regime. Moussa Kadam declared in a speech delivered in Mongo: 'Mr Governor, Mr RM com – Guéra's population aspires to peace. So, please leave people alone. No one here is complicit; no one here is a rebel.'[37] According to inhabitants of Mongo, the minister's speech tempered the zeal of and abuses by soldiers from the detachment. In addition, Guéra's political parties, trade unions and civil society organisations drafted a motion of support for President Déby in the hope of alleviating the pressure on the region. The motion's authors condemned the 'barbarous and horrible acts' perpetrated by those who attacked N'Djamena, and they saluted the 'work of democracy promoted by the President of the Republic'.[38] As for the conflict between the commander of the military detachment and the commander of the gendarmerie, it ended with the commander of the gendarmerie's departure for a neighbouring town, Ati. His transfer was not connected to the events in N'Djamena or Mongo: the decree had been published a few days before the turmoil started. The decree unknotted the situation. However, it was viewed as bad news by people in Mongo, who dreaded the arrival of a new non-Guéra commander of the gendarmerie.

During these tense two weeks, *esprit de corps* counted less than loyalty to a chief. The local popularity of the commander of the gendarmerie was rooted in his personal history. A veteran of the FAN in the 1970s, Abakar Gawi became a regular soldier after Habré took power. In 1987, he re-joined the Hadjarai dissidents of the MOSANAT, which made an alliance with the MPS in 1990. Gawi returned to N'Djamena as a liberator. In October 1991, when Maldome Bada Abbas was arrested and the Hadjarai rose up, Gawi was the 'sub-zone com' in Guéra. He re-joined his 'relatives' in the *maquis* when the army attacked the mutineers. His defection was celebrated in his home region. He was arrested, and spent several months in prison before being liberated and rehabilitated in 1992, along with other Hadjarai. He then continued his career as a regular soldier until 1996, when he was accused of, and imprisoned for, planning a *coup d'état*. He was released a few months later. Following several postings in the army and gendarmerie, he returned to his birthplace, Mongo. During our discussions he presented himself as the defender of the people against crooks, road bandits and cattle rustlers.[39] Civilians recounted that he had made enemies by arresting bandits with close relations to certain military authorities. Whatever the facts of his supposed exploits, he was able to limit abuses by gendarmes under his authority – at least when he was in his home region. His personal history and the attitude of his men made him a respected man in Guéra.

Shortly after his departure for Ati, a rumour circulated: Gawi had been the victim of an assassination attempt. Some people said that he had survived thanks to his 'bulletproof body'. It is unclear whether someone truly tried to kill Abakar Gawi; however, one thing is certain: he was not killed by bullets in Ati. He was arrested in April 2006 in N'Djamena, suspected, along with other Hadjarai officers such as Khamis Doukoun,[40] of sympathising with the rebel movement of Mahamat Nour. He is still reported missing.[41]

After the forced disappearance of Abakar Gawi, a mutiny broke out in Guéra. The Command Council of Disaffected Soldiers, which was led by a former member of the MPS, comprised a few dozen men. With no rear base or support, the insurrection failed. In September 2006, the insurgents signed a peace agreement with the government. If further proof of the fluidity of allegiances in a factional system were needed, it was another Hadjarai military figure, Colonel Daoud Soumaïn, who headed up the government column in February 2008, and who would lose his life.

Mongo residents did not interpret the conflict between the two commanders as a struggle between the gendarmerie and the army. The conflict was viewed, above all, in its personal and ethnic dimensions. A first common understanding of the situation was that the two commanders faced off because they had a personal conflict (one that no one in Mongo was able to fully explain). This reading was nonetheless inseparable from a second: the conflict was political. It opposed the military close to state power and the local gendarmes who dared defy it. The soldiers were identified with their ethnic group (people mentioned the Goran) and their access to power (people often said that they belonged to 'the people in power'). Civilians in Mongo associated the Goran with the Zaghawa, both groups being from the BET region, and assumed they were allies. Whatever the nature and the solidity of the alliance between the soldiers and the MPS, the residents of Mongo identified them with the 'untouchables' who benefit from institutionalised impunity. Moreover, they often identified the soldiers coming from Am Timan with the GNNT, with whom they had had a brush a few years before. For the people of Mongo, the distinction between the two institutions – the gendarmerie and the army – was not essential. They attached more importance to the two commanders' personal and political trajectories as well as to their regional and ethnic identities. These identities mattered because they implied access to distinct social networks and because they were linked to distinct political histories.

The conflict – or cold war – between the two commanders was not directed against the state. The disorder that seemed to reign was not the result of a failure of or a withdrawal from the state, but rather was the product of a specific mode of governing (in)security. Readers should also note that official state institutions had not disappeared either: the governor intervened to free the gendarme whose arrest launched the commanders' war, while the minister succeeded in limiting the abuses of the military detachment. Military impunity as well as interventions by state officials are all manifestations of the state. The soldiers and their commander, on the one hand, and the governor and the minister, on the other, are all authority figures. Each makes claims on the state – some with arms, others with words. Power is thus exercised through various armed and non-armed modes of operation, but the state has not withered away. Last but not least, we should note that the political and social order was negotiated but that it was exclusively negotiated by men – and for men.

'Commander Al Kanto': debating the state

State practices are the subject of lively debates. The gap between how the state is experienced and how it is idealised and envisioned lies at the centre of numerous discussions. When Chadians talk about politics, they talk about the state: the dereliction of public administration, the lack of basic public services, and the authoritarian state with which they must live. Never have I heard so much talk about the state than in Chad, where the state supposedly disappeared with the civil war, only to reappear in an amputated form just 'good enough' for international supervision.

Men in arms and their relationship to the state is a major theme of Chadian cultural productions. The soldier-bandit figure appears in numerous songs, novels, plays and radio sketches. Films with Commander Al Kanto are among the most popular cultural productions. The actor, director and producer Haikal Zakaria has built his career on military comedies, a cinematographic genre he invented. His films have been broadcast on TV Chad (the sole Chadian television channel) before being sold on VHS and DVD – the first in the series came out in 1996. With his red beret, his funny expression and his limping gait, the commander is instantly recognisable. By turns a self-proclaimed local state official, *karang-karang*, and road bandit, Al Kanto cannot be associated with any specific ethnic group. His last name is invented and his accent mixes Goran and Zaghawa tonalities.[42] Directed with modest budgets, the films are in Chadian Arabic with certain lines translated and spoken in French.[43] Walking with Haikal Zakaria in N'Djamena, I could confirm that, even out of uniform, he was known to soldiers, merchants and small-time cigarette vendors alike.

Films starring Commander Al Kanto are not only popular because they are funny and entertaining. They also ridicule the soldier-bandits and the untouchables, and they denounce the abuses of the military without ever attacking the President directly. In 'Al Kanto karang-karang', the commander assassinates a man for a *koro* of sugar before fighting with the gendarmes. He is eventually promoted to director of the mobile customs unit. In 'Al Kanto, road bandit', he throws himself into large-scale banditry after his electricity is disconnected and his car runs out of fuel. With the help of some friends, he attacks a wealthy shopkeeper. In the film, Al Kanto is an ambivalent character. He is not presented as a greedy soldier with no moral code, but as an impoverished combatant reintegrated into the army who wants to make a living and sometimes to impose justice. In 'A state within a state', the most interesting of his films, Al Kanto embodies the good, the bad, and the ugly. The commander is appointed to a position in Dar Al Kalam ('country of disorder' – a wordplay with 'Das es Salaam',[44] meaning 'country of peace'). When he arrives, a demonstration is violently suppressed by the police: twenty people are killed. Al Kanto then goes to war against the police *commissaire* and the prefect, a corrupt man booed by the residents. Al Kanto engages his enemies with the violent methods of an ex-rebel: he locks up the prefect and kills the *commissaire*, whom he deems responsible for the suppression of the demonstration. Finally arrested and brought to justice, Al Kanto pleads his case by presenting himself as a righter of wrongs who had come to Dar Al Kalam to bring order: 'You ask me to pay for the death of the *commissaire*. But who is the state? And the twenty dead students? We do nothing for them? Why do you do nothing for them? The state, it's me, the students, and the world.' A refrain from one of the film's songs is: 'Al Kanto comes from a new generation, man of truth, man of justice, man of the people.' Yet Al Kanto remains the illiterate ex-rebel who understands nothing about the law. Despite not understanding his attorney's defence argument, Al Kanto congratulates him with these words: 'You spoke well, my little brother. I'll make you a soldier, I'll give you a rank; you're going to come with us.' He is found guilty, but his brothers-in-arms free him immediately. Al Kanto is not the type of man to rot in prison!

Commander Al Kanto is thus both oppressor and defender of the oppressed. The two faces of his personality suit the actor-director. Haikal Zakaria was so closely identified with his own character that Al Kanto could not be presented as the enemy of the people. For Haikal Zakaria to be popular, Al Kanto could not be solely bad. However, this ambivalence leads to another more subtle interpretation: it allows the film 'A state within a state' to go beyond a staged confrontation between the strongmen of Dar Al Kalam. Soldier-bandits can also, in certain situations, be considered as righters of wrongs. At the core of the film lies the question of the role of men in arms in the exercise of power. Who is in a position to govern Dar Al Kalam? What is the most legitimate authority? What are the citizens' rights and who defends them? In many respects, the commander embodies the state as it is practised by men in arms in Chad. Al Kanto represents these 'untouchable' men in arms who are close to state power as he physically eliminates the *commissaire*, seizes power in Dar Al Kalam, and avoids prison thanks to his 'untouchable' friends. However, Al Kanto also promotes another political order: in court, he speaks of the state (re)claimed by the residents of Dar Al Kalam. The films point at the ambiguous role of men in arms who are simultaneously predators and protectors, and ask fundamental questions about the definitions of what is just and unjust in a violent environment.

Haikal Zakaria's political trajectory sheds light on the situation of popular people who may forget their early commitments for the sake of being co-opted.[45] On 1 May 2006, at a rally in support of the MPS candidate for President of the Republic, Idriss Déby, it was announced that the character of Al Kanto, who had remained a commander for twelve years, had been raised by President Idriss Déby to the rank of colonel. This act reflects the humour of the President as much as it does his political sense. The next day, 'Colonel' Al Kanto was welcomed warmly by the inhabitants of N'Djamena. Soldiers even came to ask him for his identity card to formalise the promotion.[46] These initiatives or jokes are part of a context in which integration into the army is a common form of reward. The case of Al Kanto's promotion assumed such importance that the actor had to organise a press conference to explain that it was actually the character Al Kanto and not the actor Haikal Zakaria who had been promoted to colonel. Four years later, Haikal Zakaria directed another film. Its subject: the 2 February 2008 attack on N'Djamena. This time, Al Kanto does not brutalise civilians; rather, he fights the rebels. In real life, Haikal Zakaria joined the MPS, and in 2011 he supported Idriss Déby in the presidential election. His activism was rewarded: he was appointed Minister for Youth and Sports before joining the many special advisers to the President. He no longer embodies this ambivalent and yet popular soldier-bandit figure.

For whom is the state 'weak' or 'fragile'?

Chad has long been considered a 'weak' or 'fragile' state. In 2015, Chad ranked sixth in the 'fragile state index' published by the Fund for Peace, a Washington-based think tank, and the influential journal *Foreign Policy*. The previous year, another think tank, the Institute of Peace Economics, ranked Chad as the country that had seen the greatest improvements in peace over the last six years in the world. What do these indexes tell us? Whether they consider Chad as still fragile or rapidly improving, they tell us very little about how the state actually functions. Nothing about how violence is produced or regulated. Contrary to the ambitions displayed, such indexes and classifications create a smokescreen that masks the concrete modes of government.

This mainstream discourse on states in the global South has already been widely criticised. Social scientists have shown that a relevant analysis cannot stop at the obvious dysfunction of state institutions. We indeed need 'to challenge the continued positioning of African societies in the role of delinquent, deviant and imperfect Other'[47] and to go beyond a normative conceptualisation that only measures the distance of existing states from the rational and legal Weberian ideal type. This move then allows us to grasp how public authority is produced in contexts of chronic violence.[48]

In addition, the 'weak' or 'fragile' state discourse rests on a major misconception: namely that violence is the result of state weakness. With such a premise, it is impossible to make sense of conflicts and violence in countries that do not suffer from a weak state but from its violent manifestations. One cannot exclude that certain states are indeed strong. The genocide of the Tutsis in Rwanda in 1994 had been carefully planned, orchestrated and implemented by the state.

I focus here on the role of the state in the reproduction of a permanent inter-war. In Chad, state power has maintained and reinforced itself even though its capacity for taxation and for providing public services has been eroded. This perspective corresponds to Chadians' own conception of the state: while they wish that there were more municipal employees, magistrates or school teachers, they view more or less regular men in arms as the agents of a brutal state. The state has been informalised, but it is neither weak nor absent, even in regions far from the capital.

There is no single model of a strong or weak state. The institutionalisation, centralisation and monopolisation of the means of violence are not the final criteria by which one can judge the strength of a state. Using 'weak' or 'fragile' is justified if applied to state bureaucracy or the public services, whose dereliction has been compounded by the imposition of neoliberal policies. For my part, I do not describe the Chadian state as weak or fragile despite the apparent dysfunction of its official institutions, in order to stress the strength of the unofficial 'shadow' state.[49] State bureaucracy and informal political networks overlap and at some points are superimposed upon one another. Thus, a colonel in the army, for example, will be more powerful if he belongs simultaneously to the official staff and to the unofficial inner circle of power. There is not a zero-sum game between the official and unofficial state: the strengthening of one does not necessarily imply the weakening of the other. Clientelism does not proliferate in the absence of strong state structures. On the contrary, it tends to develop in the context of a strong state.

During the civil war (1979–82), Chad was the archetypal collapsed state. With the spread of factional fighting throughout the entire country, very little remained of the state apparatus. New forms of government emerged as the border between the public and the private was redefined: the permanent committees, created in the south by former civil servants, took on the functions formerly assumed by the state. At the end of the civil war, Hissène Habré undertook steps to reconstruct the state by extending its control towards the south and by repelling the Libyans and their Chadian allies. In the eyes of many observers and academics (for example, William Foltz[50]), Habré was the champion of state reconstruction. Yet, the human cost of the so-called reconstruction should not be forgotten: the state was built on the repression of opposition movements as well as on the military victory against Libya celebrated by Habré in his nationalist speeches. As Foltz himself admitted, the state was organised for internal suppression and war.

Idriss Déby is not Hissène Habré. Under Habré, political killings were widespread, torture of political prisoners was systematic, and certain ethnic groups were targeted. This is not the case anymore. However, threats and the use of violence have not withered away. Under Déby, threats and violence are associated with decentralised control over the instruments of coercion. Déby's seizure of power coincided with the end of the Cold War and the acceleration of neoliberal policies. Security forces (or, rather, 'insecurity forces') have gradually gained autonomy. This process has consequences: it has led to an increase in uncertainty and insecurity. As Mirjam de Bruijn has observed, people fear being 'eaten by the state'.[51] There are two main explanations. First, some well-targeted assassinations can have as much effect as larger punitive campaigns. Second, arbitrary state practices create a sense of insecurity that is liable to discourage mobilisations and revolts. I often heard this commentary in Chad: 'When someone was arrested under Habré, we knew things would go badly for him or her, but we knew who had given the order. Today, we don't know.' Insecurity serves the MPS. By saying this, I do not mean that Chadian authorities control all the armed men who threaten or extort civilians. A large number of them work for themselves. However, if the level of control of the state over men in arms is open to question, the threat of violence with impunity and the possibility that an anonymous attack could be connected to state power have an effect. Actual and potential threats are a means of controlling populations that is every bit as effective as a bureaucratic police system. When political opponents, human rights activists or ordinary citizens are assaulted, people question the identity of the aggressors. Are they bandits who are robbing or attacking a passer-by? Or are they men well placed in the power apparatus who are executing a politically motivated order? Should one blame bad fortune or the author of the unnumbered decree? Whatever the reason for the aggression, the simple fact that one poses the question produces an effect. And any political opponent, activist or journalist who has been the victim of aggression has wondered about the potential links between this aggression and his or her activities. Uncertainties generate fear, which, in turn, discourages resistance. Contrary to a common perception, impunity is not a 'cancer',[52] a sickness that develops in remote areas where laws are no longer applied. Chad does not suffer from a security vacuum, but rather from a vacuum of accountability.

The relevant question is not whether the state is weak, but rather: how is power exercised? Who within the state is effectively strong or weak? For example, certain ministers are powerful while others are not; the President's relatives often have much more room to manoeuvre than a co-opted politician, even when the latter has been placed at the head of an important ministry. Key decisions are made within parallel cabinets. Official institutions and the government are informed of them only after the fact.[53] Another crucial question is the following: for whom is the state weak? For Chadians living in the east, who have been victims of Janjaweed attacks, the state is indeed weak. For urban dwellers who cannot appeal to the police when they have been robbed, for fear that the robbers are working hand in glove with them, the state is equally weak. For women who have been assaulted by soldiers or policemen, the state is particularly weak. But that is not an ontological characteristic of the Chadian state. The state is weak in insecure villages and urban settings but it is strong when it comes to subduing rebellions and discouraging political mobilisations. The recruitment and co-optation of armed men with fluid loyalties belong to its most efficient political strategies.

My intention is not, of course, to present this mode of government as a good one. For the large majority of people, life is hard in Chad. A more disciplined army, more respect for human rights, a better distribution of wealth and political power, and increased public services would be greatly welcomed by the population. It is nonetheless important to see uncertainty and organised disorder as powerful state resources. This is equally important in order to contest the commonly held opinion that state weakness is a major cause of armed conflicts and to consider the role played by state violence. Readers might think that I am confusing the state with power-holders or the regime. It would, however, be irrelevant to dissociate the state from its actors.[54] The state is not an empty vessel that power-holders invest in before leaving their place to others: taking power is not only taking possession of the state – it is contributing to its formation and reconfigurations, even when power-holders are not consciously or intentionally part of this process. State construction and state formation are daily travails.[55]

Erroneous analyses of modes of government are even more problematic in that they have political implications. In the case of Chad, reforms of the security sector and of the justice sector, which have been implemented during the last few years, were much needed. Such reform programmes cannot, however, meet expectations if they are based on a false understanding of the functioning of the state. In this respect, a standardised approach to security issues or institutional development is of little help. The instrumentalisation of the DDR programmes of the 1990s[56] demonstrates this quite well: international experts' propositions were astutely re-appropriated by local actors and re-routed from their objectives. Similarly, capacity-building programmes inevitably fail if they do not address the actual functioning of state administrations. The local administration, for example, is undermined not only by a lack of material and financial means, but also, and above all, by state manoeuvres. To take another example, reforms of the justice sector should rest on a correct understanding of the origins of impunity. Even if the authorities in N'Djamena do not orchestrate everything happening throughout the country, impunity is in part the result of political strategies. In order to avoid the implementation of potentially counterproductive reform programmes, informalisation and impunity should be understood for what they are: a mode of government adapted to an uncertain political environment. Programmes that do not take into account the importance of political strategies in the apparent disorder are condemned never to achieve the expected results.

CONCLUSION

· ·

Let us return to the November day in 2005 mentioned in the introduction, when a *bogobogo* stopped a recalcitrant taxi driver in dusty Ngueli. Who were the protagonists in the story? How was it that the driver could refuse to comply? As we reach the end of our book, the reader has all the clues to make sense of what happened. The protagonists' social and political identities matter. The driver knew 'well-seated' people. Without a uniform or a gun, he belonged to a group of Chadians identified as 'untouchable'. While he was not among those who had experienced the greatest social mobility (he drove a taxi that he probably did not own), he owed his position to social networks that extended to state power. The *bogobogo* acted as an unofficial customs officer, whose position was the result of an 'unnumbered decree'; his attempt to extort money from people was part of the daily routine. That day, he simply had the misfortune to stop a driver with more powerful social connections. Ganda, the demobilised soldier who accompanied me, adopted the same attitude as the passengers: he observed and awaited the dénouement. Like soldiers and demobilised soldiers with little social capital, he did not have much to say in Ngueli's militarised economy. As for the female merchants in the bus, they had to cope, on that day like any other, with a militarised and male-dominated political and economic order.

In order to explain this ordinary scene, I theorised armed violence as a *métier*, or a practical occupation, and explored the logics of war and inter-war. Comprehending what was at play that day in Ngueli requires an understanding of the protagonists' identities (the driver who was connected to powerful 'untouchables', the more or less official customs officers, and so on), and how these identities were interpreted. This book tells the story of how armed violence has become a form of political struggle as well as a rather ordinary means of making a living.

Armed violence is inscribed in a long history. But this history was not inevitable. In Chad, as elsewhere, war does not erupt suddenly when certain conditions are met, but when it is organised by political entrepreneurs who may be rebel leaders as often as they are heads of state. These political entrepreneurs are integrated into global patronage networks and benefit from foreign support. When they opt for rebellion, they do not show any particular greed or a disposition for violence. They make a tragic but quite rational choice in a context where armed struggle has remained the key to political success. As for the civilian opposition, it negotiates its survival on the political market in the grey zone between repression and co-optation.

In addition to historicising armed violence, another objective of this book has been to enquire into the rules of a milieu too often associated with disorder or chaos. Power relations and socio-economic hierarchies do not develop *despite* disorder – instead, they emerge and develop *from* that disorder. Social differentiation is strong. Savvy young men seldom experience social mobility with weapons in hand. However, their trajectories make sense if one considers that civilian life is often a daily combat. In regions where people suffer from injustice and impunity (rather than a security vacuum), where state violence coincides with massive inequalities, politico-military leaders quite easily find a cheap labour force to embark on the risky path of armed rebellions.

No need to kill anymore

Ultimately, what this book proposes is a reflection on a mode of government characterised by the recourse to arms in war and in the inter-war. This mode of government is deeply rooted in historical experience. Idriss Déby was not its inventor. The recourse to violence and the co-optation of men in arms from opposing camps date back to precolonial and colonial times. The Chadian case offers insights into a singular but not exceptional process of state formation. The state does not successfully claim a monopoly on the legitimate use of physical and symbolic violence. However, it is not the victim of a small group of unscrupulous opportunists, nor of a simple disease that a few well-intentioned ideas out of a 'good governance' toolkit could treat at a minimal cost. Not all wars make states and they certainly do not all make the same state. Wars do not necessarily generate, as in the European case, a centralisation of power, a bureaucratic rationalisation, or an increased capacity to levy taxes. In Chad, there is an economic and political rationality in giving soldiers significant room to manoeuver and to negotiate with armed men – rebels from neighbouring countries, militiamen and bandits who are liable to render services to the state. Like much of postcolonial Africa, Chad has not undergone the process of 'governmentalisation' of the state that has been experienced in Europe since the eighteenth century, when, as Foucault argued, 'it became important to manage a population'. According to Foucault, 'the managing of a population not only concerns the collective mass of phenomena, the level of its aggregate effects, it also implies the management of population in its depths and its details'.[1] By contrast, European colonisers built colonial states on weak instruments. The postcolonial state in Chad, as in many parts of postcolonial Africa, has inherited a weak grasp over the social.[2]

In Chad, the mode of government rests in part on armed men, even if no one is in a position to identify and quantify them. Disorder is a way of governing the army and the state. Men in arms who are not all fully integrated into its bureaucratic apparatus are still linked to the state. The unnumbered decrees explain this paradox. The official and legal rules, procedures and institutions (for example, the hierarchy and the army's formal chain of command) can be suspended by the simple intervention of individuals belonging to Déby's inner circle. Unnumbered decrees mark the blurring of the lines between the law (or the decree) and the event. They are issued by those who are (or who feel) authorised to issue them – and whose social position has also been decreed without a number. It is because this mode of government pervades socio-economic practices and everyday life that Chadians understand how they must react when their taxi is stopped by *bogobogos*.

Chadian unnumbered decrees recall aspects of the Tunisian *talimet*, those 'non-written instructions or orders that have the force of law'.[3] However, the mode of government in Chad differs from the 'policing state', a concept inspired by Foucault and used by Béatrice Hibou in her work on Tunisia under Ben Ali – 'a system and modes of regulation that make it possible for people's behaviour to be controlled'.[4] Admittedly, in Chad as in Tunisia, repression – actual and threatened – produces various effects, while unnumbered decrees have concrete implications for the daily life of customs officers, taxi drivers and merchants. But in Chad, the exercise of power is not about control and surveillance; nor is it about producing consensus. In the Chadian 'talkocracy', 'the best tactic consists of letting the malcontents, that is everybody, talk'[5] Critical remarks in the press and on radio and the publication of reports on human rights abuses are all possible as long as they do not inconvenience the rulers. So those who denounce the general corruption can declaim to their heart's content as long as they do not try to dismantle the mechanisms of power or point the finger at those who are responsible. Authorities rule by rewarding loyalty, sanctioning defections, and letting uncertainties play out. Concluding new alliances and consolidating old ones, with a skilful mix of repression and co-optation, is more important than the discipline of men in arms and the support of the people. The art of governing consists in managing power relations. The role of ideology is marginal.

Power is exercised through both violent and non-violent mechanisms. The most visible forms of state violence (military repression, forced disappearances) must be related to the more ordinary abuses to which people have been subjected (such as mundane harassment of civilians by the military or the police). State violence is all the more efficient in that it is combined with the distribution of positions of accumulation. The control of legal and illegal economic opportunities belongs to the art of governing: allies are momentarily granted impunity and allowed to use illegal (and sometimes violent) practices. Military-commercial networks finance clienteles and rein in the emergence of a counter-power or a counter-elite. Overt violence is the exception rather than the rule. 'Untouchables' are central figures of power: they do not need to kill (anymore) to demonstrate impunity. Even miles from a school or hospital, Chadians do not inhabit spaces independent of the state: they must come to terms with armed men whose power to extract resources and to kill depends on their access to the state as much as on their AK-47s. It matters little whether these men are soldiers integrated into the regular army, ex-rebels, freshly co-opted bandits, or even militiamen from neighbouring countries. In any case, it is difficult to know who officially appears in the ledgers of the state apparatus. Above all, this is not the right question. Rather, people ask: are they powerful? Are they 'untouchable'? Even if Chadians do not know the official status of the armed men they meet on the road, they are able to differentiate between those who have the power to threaten them and those who do not. Ending the war is not enough. The issue is to escape from the inter-war situation maintained and reproduced by the state.

Beyond the framework of stability

In Chad, armed violence is fuelled by oil rents but also by diplomatic rents. In the context of the extension of the 'global war against terrorism' in the Sahara and the Sahel, diplomatic rents have become more important as oil prices have fallen.[6] Idriss Déby has since been presented by his Western (starting with the French) backers as the man without whom the country would descend into chaos. Déby's tainted past, from his role under Habré to the enforced disappearance of Ibni Oumar Mahamat Saleh, as well as Chad's interference in the CAR, is known to all. He nevertheless remains the man without whom the West cannot manage. In many ways, Idriss Déby appears to embody the figure of the providential statesman on the cheap.

The discourse on the stability of Chad is of course disputed. Experts on Chad and Africa provide material for an important debate on the factors governing the country's stability and instability. The international press, and journals specialising in security and defence matters, echo this debate. The list of factors feeding Chad's instability is long: the conflict that erupted in Libya following the 2011 armed intervention, the regionalisation of Boko Haram, and the unresolved crises in Darfur and South Sudan. The sources of an internal crisis are also debated: experts point to a resurgence of armed movements, the risks of palace revolution, the economic crisis compounded by the fall in oil prices, or the death of the President, who is said to be seriously ill. Highlighting the fragility of the country, these analyses constitute a first critique of the discourse of international actors who granted the label 'stable' to Chad in the 2010s, a little prematurely – even if these same actors are less optimistic off the record.

The debates on the factors of stability and instability are biased, however; it is as if stability depended solely on internal and regional factors. International actors, including Western states and international organisations, consider themselves external to the 'problems'. They present themselves – and are often presented – as actors who might contribute by providing 'answers' and not as playing an active role in those very 'problems'. While not surprising, this pattern is nevertheless problematic as it is based on an assumption that there is a divide between, on the one hand, postcolonial states that need help, and, on the other, Western actors and the international community that may provide this help even when the latter are involved in the 'problems'.

It is the framework of stability itself that must be challenged. This framework makes stability the only aim, or the only possible horizon of expectation. I am obviously not saying that we should prefer war or instability to a relatively calm situation: everyday life has been less difficult in Chad since the last rebels surrendered. Instead, I want to emphasise the fact that the discourse on stability tends to ignore the violence of the mode of government and of the economy.[7] A state may be both stable for external analysts and violent for its people. Stability, in fact, is often associated with a form of status quo. Social mobilisations (strikes and demonstrations, for example) are then categorised as factors of instability. Discussing this with Western policy makers and experts, I realised that they often consider unarmed mobilisations as a threat. In their view, stability is not compatible with any challenge to the ways in which politics is carried out. However, we must now reckon with a new wave of protest leading to political change on the African continent.[8] While Chadian activists have to face not only attempts to co-opt their leaders but also the repression of street demonstrations, they also followed the mobilisations that led to the overthrow of Blaise Compaoré in Burkina Faso in late 2014 with great interest. Idriss Déby fully understood this.

In addition, wars kill less than poverty and difficult access to public health services. These are major sources of day-to-day insecurities. But because the situations of African countries – and more broadly of the global South – are perceived through the prism of stability, this fact, although known to everyone, is never placed centre stage. Drawing attention to it in a discussion among experts means adopting a position at once naive (how can she draw attention to such an obvious fact?) and irresponsible (how dare she question the goal, which is stability?). Yet, as I have attempted to show, changing the framework and not judging the situation of a country in terms of its supposed stability might, in the medium and long term, be the most reasonable and responsible of attitudes.

So a problematisation in terms of inter-war and government with arms (rather than in terms of stability and fragility) does not have merely theoretical implications. It is a way of placing issues of justice and injustice (back) at the heart of the analysis. It is an invitation to go beyond analyses that conclude, rather hastily, that what is not war is, by default, peace and stability. Moving away from the dual alternative of war or peace, fragility or stability, raises questions about human rights, the allocation of resources and the spaces of mobilisation. How can Chadian women and men challenge impunity and increase the accountability of the military and of 'well-seated' men? As the cost of impunity granted to powerful men is gendered, this question is of crucial importance for women. How can people organise unarmed social and political struggles that challenge the inequalities and hierarchies produced and reproduced in and by war? How can Chadians and their allies outside the country contest the global capital granted to Idriss Déby and, more generally, the flows of rents that fuel a violent and unjust economic and political order? Asking these questions means that we are no longer limited by the issue of how the disorder produced by conflicts is managed; instead, we can see this within the wider framework of justice and emancipation.

ABBREVIATIONS

. . . .

AEF	Afrique Equatoriale Française / French Equatorial Africa
ANR	Armée Nationale de Résistance / National Resistance Army
ANS	Agence Nationale de Sécurité / National Security Agency
ANT	Armée Nationale Tchadienne / National Army of Chad
BCSR	Bureau de Coordination et de Synthèse du Renseignement / Bureau for the Coordination and Synthesis of Intelligence
BET	Borku, Ennedi and Tibesti
CAR	Central African Republic
CCFAN	Conseil de Commandement des Forces Armées du Nord / Council of Command of the Armed Forces of the North
CDR	Conseil Démocratique Révolutionnaire / Revolutionary Democratic Council
CEFOD	Centre d'Etudes et de Formation sur le Développement / Centre for Studies and Training for Development
CNPC	China National Petroleum Corporation
CNR	Comité National de Redressement / National Recovery Committee
CNS	Conférence Nationale Souveraine / Sovereign National Conference
CNT	Concorde Nationale Tchadienne / Chadian National Concord

CRCR	Centre de Recherche et de Coordination des Renseignements / Centre for Research and Coordination of Intelligence
CSM	Conseil Supérieur Militaire / Supreme Military Council
CSNPD	Comité de Sursaut National pour la Paix et la Démocratie / National Revival Committee for Peace and Democracy
CTS	Compagnies Tchadiennes de Sécurité / Chadian Security Companies
DDR	disarmament, demobilisation and reintegration
DDS	Direction de la Documentation et de la Sécurité / Documentation and Security Directorate
DGSE	Direction Générale de la Sécurité Extérieure / General Directorate for External Security (France)
DGSSIE	Direction Générale des Services de la Sécurité des Institutions de l'Etat / General Directorate of Security Services for National Institutions
EITI	Extractive Industries Transparency Initiative
EU	European Union
EUFOR	European Union Forces
FAIDT	Front d'Action pour l'Instauration de la Démocratie au Tchad / Action Front for Establishing Democracy in Chad
FAN	Forces Armées du Nord / Armed Forces of the North
FANT	Forces Armées Nationales Tchadiennes / Chadian National Armed Forces
FAO	Forces Armées Occidentales / Western Armed Forces
FAP	Forces Armées Populaires / Popular Armed Forces
FARF	Forces Armées pour la République Fédérale / Armed Forces for a Federal Republic
FAT	Forces Armées Tchadiennes / Chadian Armed Forces

FAT–MRP	Forces Armées Tchadiennes–Mouvement Révolutionnaire du Peuple / Chadian Armed Forces–People's Revolutionary Movement
FDP	Front Démocratique Populaire / Popular Democratic Front
FEANF	Fédération des Etudiants d'Afrique Noire en France / Federation of Students from Black Africa in France
FLT	Front de Libération du Tchad / Liberation Front of Chad
FNT	Front National du Tchad / National Front of Chad
FNTR	Front National du Tchad Rénové / Renovated National Front of Chad
Frolinat	Front de Libération Nationale du Tchad / National Liberation Front of Chad
FSR	Front du Salut pour la République / Front for the Salvation of the Republic
FUC	Front Uni du Changement / United Front for Change
GDP	gross domestic product
GNNT	Garde Nationale et Nomade du Tchad / National and Nomadic Guard of Chad
GTZ	Gesellschaft für Technische Zusammenarbeit / German Technical Cooperation Agency
GUNT	Gouvernement d'Union Nationale de Transition / Transitional Government of National Unity
JEM	Justice and Equality Movement (Darfur)
MDD	Mouvement pour la Démocratie et le Développement / Movement for Democracy and Development
MDJT	Mouvement pour la Démocratie et la Justice au Tchad / Movement for Democracy and Justice in Chad
MINURCAT	United Nations Mission in the Central African Republic and Chad

MINUSCA	United Nations Multidimensional Integrated Stabilisation Mission in the Central African Republic
MINUSMA	United Nations Multidimensional Mission in Mali
MN	Mouvement National / National Movement
MNJTF	Multinational Joint Task Force
MNR	Mouvement National pour le Redressement / National Movement for Recovery
MOSANAT	Mouvement pour le Salut National du Tchad / Movement for the National Salvation of Chad
MPLT	Mouvement Populaire pour la Libération du Tchad / Popular Movement for the Liberation of Chad
MPRD	Mouvement pour la Paix, la Reconstruction et le Développement / Movement for Peace, Reconstruction and Progress
MPS	Mouvement Patriotique du Salut / Patriotic Salvation Movement
MRA	Mission de Réforme Administrative / Mission of Administrative Reform
MSA	Mouvement Socialiste Africain / African Socialist Movement
NCO	non-commissioned officer
NGO	non-governmental organisation
OCHA	United Nations Office for the Coordination of Humanitarian Aid
PDF	Popular Defence Forces (Darfur)
PPT	Parti Progressiste Tchadien / Chadian Progressive Party
PSI	Pan-Sahel Initiative
RDA	Rassemblement Démocratique Africain / African Democratic Rally
RDL	Rassemblement pour la Démocratie et les Libertés / Rally for Democracy and Freedom
RFC	Rassemblement des Forces du Changement / Rally of Forces for Change
RFI	Radio France Internationale

SATG	Special Anti-Terrorism Group
SCUD	Socle pour le Changement, l'Unité et la Démocratie / Platform for Unity, Change and Democracy
SLA	Sudan Liberation Army
TSCTP	Trans-Sahara Counterterrorism Partnership
UDT	Union Démocratique Tchadienne / Chadian Democratic Union
UFC	Union des Forces du Changement / Union of Forces for Change
UFCD	Union des Forces pour le Changement et la Démocratie/ Union of Forces for Change and Democracy
UFDD	Union des Forces pour la Démocratie et le Développement / Union of Forces for Democracy and Development
UFDD-F	Union des Forces pour la Démocratie et le Développement Fondamentale / Fundamental Union of Forces for Democracy and Development
UFDD-R	Union des Forces pour la Démocratie et le Développement Rénovée / Renewed Union of Forces for Democracy and Development
UFR	Union des Forces de la Résistance / Union of Forces of Resistance
UN	United Nations
UND	Union Nationale Démocratique / National Democratic Union
UNDP	United Nations Development Programme
UNIR	Union Nationale pour l'Indépendence et la Révolution / National Union for Independence and Revolution
UNT	Union Nationale Tchadienne / Chadian National Union
UPC	Union des Populations du Cameroun / Union of the Peoples of Cameroon

NOTES

. . . .

Foreword

1 Marielle Debos, 'Biometric voting in Chad: new technology, same old political tricks', Theconversation.com, 4 May 2016. Available at https://theconversation.com/biometric-voting-in-chad-new-technology-same-old-political-tricks-58663.

Introduction

1 'Il faut apprendre à fréquenter simultanément la guerre et la paix; se convaincre de passer de l'une à l'autre comme l'on traverse les pièces d'un château. Ainsi se donne-t-on les moyens de saisir quelle catastrophe est la boue où s'élabore notre humanité': Nimrod, *Le bal des princes*, Paris, Actes Sud, 2008, p. 153. This Chadian novelist puts these words in the mouth of Colonel Degoto, a loosely veiled stand-in for Colonel Kamougué, a figure in Chad's political life.

2 Hundreds of thousands of refugees from Darfur spilled over the border into eastern Chad. At the end of 2015, there were more than 350,000 refugees from Sudan (mainly from Darfur) in Chad.

3 Calamity Jane, 'Fraudeurs et douaniers s'entredéchirent', *L'Observateur*, 19 April 2006.

4 The *koro* is a bowl-shaped receptacle used as unit of measure. One *koro* of sugar corresponds to about 2 kilograms or 4.4 pounds.

5 David Keen, 'War and peace: what's the difference?', *International Peacekeeping*, Vol. 7, no. 4, 2000, pp. 1–22.

6 Christopher Cramer, *Civil War Is Not a Stupid Thing: Accounting for Violence in Developing Countries*, London, Hurst, 2006.

7 On the distinction between 'indiscriminate' and 'selective' violence and the reasons for the variance in the level of violence, see Stathis N. Kalyvas, *The Logic of Violence in Civil War*, Cambridge, Cambridge University Press, 2006.

8 Zachariah Mampilly, *Rebel Rulers: Insurgent Governance and Civilian Life During War*, New York, Cornell University Press, 2011.

9 Christian Geffray, *La cause des armes au Mozambique*, Paris, Karthala, 1990, p. 166.

10 Donald Crummey, 'Introduction: the "great beast"', in Donald Crummey (ed.), *Banditry, Rebellion and Social Protest in Africa*, London and Portsmouth, James Currey and Heinemann, 1986, p. 2.

11 Paul Richards, 'New war: an ethnographic approach', in Paul Richards (ed.), *No peace, No war: An Anthropology of Contemporary Armed Conflicts*, Oxford and Athens OH, James Currey and Ohio University Press, 2005, pp. 1–21.

12 Laurent Gayer, *Karachi: Ordered Disorder and the Struggle for the City*, London, Delhi, New York and Karachi, Hurst, HarperCollins and Oxford University Press, 2014, p. 11.

13 Mariane Ferme, 'The violence of numbers. Consensus, competition, and the negotiation of disputes in Sierra Leone', *Cahiers d'études africaines*, Vol. 38, no. 150–2, 1998, pp. 555–80.

14 Nancy Scheper-Hughes, *Death Without Weeping: The violence of Everyday Life in Brazil*, Berkeley and Los Angeles, University of California Press, 1992; Philippe Bourgois, 'The power of violence in war and peace: post-cold war lessons from El Salvador', *Ethnography*, Vol. 2, no. 1, 2001, pp. 5–34; Philippe Bourgois, 'Recognizing invisible violence: a thirty-year ethnographic retrospective', in Barbara Rylko-Bauer, Linda Whiteford and Paul Farmer (eds), *Global Health in Times of Violence*, Santa Fe NM, School for Advanced Research Press, 2010, pp. 18–40.

15 The Lake Chad Basin covers a vague zone including the north of Cameroon, the north of the Central African Republic, the south-east of Nigeria and the west of Chad. Janet Roitman does not seek to define its frontiers once and for all, but attempts instead 'to describe, to demarcate and to analyse the different vectors that currently comprise the Lake Chad Basin, without making any prior judgments as to their geographical situation or their origin'; 'Les recompositions du bassin du lac Tchad', *Politique africaine*, no. 94, June 2004, p. 8.

16 Janet Roitman, *Fiscal Disobedience: An Anthropology of Economic Regulation in Central Africa*, Princeton NJ, Princeton University Press, 2005.

17 Interview, N'Djamena, May 2010.

18 Stephanie Getson, 'Invisible, insecure, and inaccessible: the humanitarian crisis in Chad', *Georgetown Journal of International Affairs*, Vol. 9, no. 1, 2008, p. 138.

19 Mirjam De Bruijn and Han Van Dijk, 'The multiple experiences of civil war in the Guéra region of Chad, 1965–1990', *Sociologus*, Vol. 57, no. 1, 2007, pp. 61–98.

20 Henrik Vigh, 'Conflictual motion and political inertia: on rebellions and revolutions in Bissau and beyond', *African Studies Review*, Vol. 52, no. 2, 2009, pp. 143–64.

21 Interview, Paris, May 2008.

22 I do not elaborate here on the debate on 'old' and 'new' wars launched by the publication of the first edition of Mary Kaldor's book in 1999. As the following chapters will show, this categorisation is of no use to make sense of conflicts in Chad. Mary Kaldor, *New and Old Wars: Organised Violence in a Global Era*, Cambridge, Polity Press, 3rd edition, 2012.

23 Correspondence between the author and a woman teacher resident in N'Djamena, September 2011.

24 In 1997, the army attacked the combatants in the Armed Forces for a

Federal Republic (Forces Armées pour la République Fédérale, or FARF), a rebel group in the south that had just signed a peace agreement.

25 Carmela Garritano, 'Living precariously in the African postcolony: debt and labor relations in the films of Mahamat-Saleh Haroun', forthcoming.

26 Since the end of the proxy war between Chad and Sudan, expert reports on Chad are not as numerous as they used to be.

27 Achille Mbembe, 'Necropolitics', *Public Culture*, Vol. 15, no. 1, 2003, pp. 11–40.

28 Stephen Reyna, *Wars Without End: The Political Economy of a Precolonial African State*, Hanover, New England University Press, 1990; Roitman, *Fiscal Disobedience*, op. cit.; Issa Saïbou, *Les coupeurs de route: Histoire du banditisme rural et transfrontalier dans le bassin du lac Tchad*, Paris, Karthala, 2010.

29 Danny Hoffman, *The War Machines: Young Men and Violence in Sierra Leone and Liberia*, Durham NC, Duke University Press, 2011.

30 Louisa Lombard, 'The threat of rebellion: claiming entitled personhood in Central Africa', *Journal of the Royal Anthropological Institute*, forthcoming.

31 The question of sexual violence has long been taboo. However, at the end of 2015, women talked about such crimes during the course of witness testimony in front of the Extraordinary African Chambers in Senegal, which is trying Hissène Habré. They testified that they had been victims of sexual violence, torture and rape. One of them testified that Habré himself had raped her.

32 Jules Falquet, 'Division sexuelle du travail révolutionnaire: réflexions à partir de l'expérience salvadorienne (1970–1994)', *Cahiers d'Amérique Latine*, no. 40, 2003, pp. 109–28.

33 Laura Sjoberg and Caron E. Gentry, *Mothers, Monsters, Whores: Women's Violence in Global Politics*, London, Zed Books, 2007.

34 Henrik Vigh uses the concept of 'social navigation' to highlight 'motion within motion'. He shows how people move and manage within situations of social flux: for example, how combatants take note of the changes within their socio-political environment and seek to make the best of emergent social possibilities: *Navigating Terrains of War: Youth and Soldiering in Guinea-Bissau*, New York and Oxford: Berghahn Books, 2006; 'Motion squared: a second look at the concept of social navigation', *Anthropological Theory*, Vol. 9, no. 4, 2009, pp. 419–38. See also Mats Utas, 'Victimcy, girlfriending, soldiering: tactic agency in a young woman's social navigation of the Liberian war zone', *Anthropological Quarterly*, Vol. 78, no. 2, 2005, pp. 403–30.

35 I am here referring to the highly controversial idea that the driving force behind conflicts is the 'greed' of the belligerents rather than their 'grievance' or their political agenda. While the quest for and securing of resources are both crucial elements in armed struggle, it does not follow that the agenda of rebellions is primarily an economic one. The proponents of the economic approach to conflicts have ended up admitting that studies which seek to locate a single cause for conflicts – whether this be resources, identity or culture – do not enable us to understand why they break out, or their

differing trajectories. For the first formulations of the argument, see Paul Collier, *The Economic Causes of Civil Conflict and their Implications for Policy*, Washington DC, The World Bank, 2000; Paul Collier and Anke Hoeffler, *Greed and Grievance in Civil War*, Oxford, Centre for the Study of African Economics, 2002. For a critique of the limits of this approach by an author who has worked on economic agendas in war, see Mats Berdal, 'Beyond greed and grievance – and not too soon', *Review of International Studies*, Vol. 31, no. 4, 2005, pp. 687–98. For a critique of this approach, see, among others, Christopher Cramer, 'Homo economicus goes to war: methodological individualism, rational choice and the political economy of war', *World Development*, Vol. 30, no. 11, 2002, pp. 1845–64.

36 On the 'thirty-year struggle for Chad', see J. Millard Burr and Robert O. Collins, *Darfur: The Long Road to Disaster in Darfur*, Princeton NJ, Markus Wiener, 2006.

37 On French security policy in Africa and its links to development practices and discourses, see Bruno Charbonneau, *France and the New Imperialism: Security Policy in Sub-Saharan Africa*, Aldershot, Ashgate, 2008.

38 In 2015, Chad sat at 147 out of 168 on Transparency International's Corruption Perception Index.

39 In addition to the overall command centre in N'Djamena, there are two smaller bases in Faya-Largeau and Abéché.

40 Koen Vlassenroot, 'War and social research: the limits of empirical methodologies in war-torn environments', *Civilisations*, no. 54, 2005, pp. 191–8; Christopher Cramer, Laura Hammond and Johan Pottier (eds), *Researching Violence in Africa: Ethical and Methodological Challenges*, Leiden, Brill, 2011.

41 We should note, however, the resources available at the library of the Centre d'Etudes et de Formation sur le Développement (CEFOD) in N'Djamena, where I was able to consult the archives of the Conférence Nationale Souveraine as well as memoranda on the army produced by soldiers.

42 Géraud Magrin, *Le sud du Tchad en mutation: Des champs de coton aux sirènes de l'or noir*, Saint-Maur-des-Fossés, Cirad and Sépia, 2001, p. 18.

43 Andrea Behrends and Jan-Patrick Heiß, 'Crisis in Chad: approaching the anthropological gap', *Sociologus*, Vol. 57, no. 1, 2007, pp. 1–7.

44 Michel Taussig, *Law in a Lawless Land: Diary of a Liempieza in Colombia*, Chicago, University of Chicago Press, 2005, p. 100.

45 Cynthia Enloe, *Maneuvers: The International Politics of Militarising Women's Lives*, Berkeley, Los Angeles and London, University of California Press, 2000.

46 Michel Foucault, *The History of Sexuality*, New York, Pantheon Books, 1978, p. 59.

47 Djimet Seli, *(Dé)connexions identitaires hadjeray: Les enjeux des technologies de la communication au Tchad*, Leiden, Langaa and African Studies Centre, 2014, Chapter 2.

48 I have discussed the social marginalisation of ex-combatants in 'Quand les "libérateurs" deviennent des "bandits". Guerre et marginalisation sociale à la frontière tchado-centrafricaine', in Rémy Bazenguissa-Ganga and Sami

Makki (eds), *Sociétés en guerre: Ethnographies de mobilisations violentes*, Paris, Editions de la Maison des Sciences de l'Homme, 2012, pp. 93–110.

49 The systematic invitation to share the men's plate is not linked to the subject of my research. Marie-José Tubiana, who has worked, for example, on marriage and the transfer of property in north-east Chad and east Sudan, reports that she has never felt authorised to share the women's meal. 'Etre femme et partager la nourriture en milieu "musulman"', Conference of the International Commission on the Anthropology of Food, Lasseube, March–April 2011.

50 Howard Becker, *Writing for Social Scientists: How to Start and Finish your Thesis, Book, or Article*, Chicago, Chicago University Press, 2nd edition, 2007, p. 133.

51 Following Michel Foucault, by 'government' I mean 'structuring the possible field of action of others'. See Michel Foucault, *Dits et écrits*, Paris, Gallimard, 1994, Vol. 4, p. 237.

52 Achille Mbembe, *On the Postcolony*, Berkeley, University of California Press, 2001.

Part I: Introduction

1 Paul Veyne, *Writing History: Essay on Epistemology*, trans. Mina Moore-Rinvolucri, Middletown CT, Wesleyan University Press, 1984, p. 32 [first French edition: Paris, Le Seuil, 1971].

Chapter 1

1 Kanem appears in written history in the ninth century. The kingdom reached a peak in the twelfth century, when it controlled the wells that were essential for caravans crossing the Sahara. In the fourteenth century, the King of Kanem was forced to flee to Bornu. A century later, Bornu enjoyed a period of prosperity: the *maï* (king) Ali reconquered Kanem, which had been abandoned to the Bilala. In the sixteenth century, Bornu expanded considerably and the kingdom became Kanem-Bornu (Kanem being a dependency of Bornu). On the states of Central Sudan, see Barkindo Bawuro, 'Early states of the Central Sudan: Kanem, Borno and some of their neighbours to *c.* 1500 A.D.', in J. F. A. Ajayi and Michael Crowder (eds), *History of West Africa*, Vol. 1, New York, Longman, 1985, pp. 225–54.

2 On Dar Sila, see René-Joseph Bret, *Vie du Sultan Mohamed Bakhit 1856–1916: la penetration française au Dar Sila*, Paris, Editions du CNRS, 1987.

3 Issa Hassan Khayar, *Tchad: Regards sur les élites ouaddaïennes*, Paris, Editions du CNRS, 1984, p. 50.

4 Denis D. Cordell, *Dar al-Kuti and the Last Years of Trans-Saharan Slave Trade*, Madison WI, University of Wisconsin Press, 1985.

5 Jacques Le Cornec, *Histoire politique du Tchad de 1900 à 1962*, Paris, LGDJ, 1963, pp. 14ff.

6 Mario J. Azevedo, *Roots of Violence: A History of War in Chad*, London and New York, Routledge, 1998, p. 18.

7 Charles Tilly, *Coercion, Capital and European States: AD 990–1992*, Oxford, Blackwell, 1990.

8 Reyna, *Wars Without End*, op. cit., p. 39.

9 Azevedo, *Roots of Violence*, op. cit., p. 24.

10 Reyna takes this expression from the explorer Gustav Nachtigal: see Reyna, *Wars Without End*, op. cit., p. 166.

11 Ibid.

12 Ibid., pp. 138–41.

13 Ibid., pp. 47–64. On the impact of the introduction of firearms in the region of Central Sudan, see Joseph P. Smaldone, 'Firearms in Central Sudan: a reevaluation', *Journal of African History*, no. 13, 1972, pp. 591–607.

14 Le Cornec, *Histoire politique du Tchad*, op. cit., p. 18.

15 Mohammed Ibn Omar El-Tounsy, *Voyage au Ouadây*, trans. from the Arabic by Dr Perron, Paris, 1851.

16 Extracts from a song of praise apparently addressed to Sultan Hummay (eleventh century), quoted in John Iliffe, *Honour in African History*, Cambridge, Cambridge University Press, 2005, pp. 12–13.

17 Janet Roitman, 'The Garrison-Entrepôt', *Cahiers d'études africaines*, Vol. 38, nos. 150–2, 1998, pp. 307–8.

18 Mario J. Azevedo, 'Power and slavery in Central Africa: Chad (1890–1925)', *Journal of Negro History*, Vol. 67, no. 3, 1982, pp. 198–211.

19 The term 'Sara' refers to different groups. According to Jean-Pierre Magnant, 'for the Ngambay, "Sara" designates what the French call "sara madjingay"; for the inhabitants of May-Kebbi and Tandjilé, "sara" includes the populations of the two Logone regions and Moyen-Chari, and for the people in the zones under Islamic influence, all animists apart from the Hadjarai of Guéra were "Sara"'. Jean-Pierre Magnant, 'La conscience ethnique chez les populations sara', in Jean-Pierre Chrétien and Gérard Prunier (eds), *Les ethnies ont une histoire*, Paris, Karthala-ACCT, 1989, p. 334.

20 Denis D. Cordell, 'The Awlad Sulayman of Libya and Chad: power and adaptation in the Sahara and Sahel', *Canadian Journal of African Studies*, Vol. 19, no. 2, 1985, p. 330.

21 Edward Evans-Pritchard, *The Sanussi of Cyrenaika*, Oxford, Oxford University Press, 1949.

22 The 'tirailleurs sénégalais' were a corps of colonial infantry in the French army. They were initially recruited from Senegal.

23 In the words of Pierre Hugot: *Le Tchad*, Paris, Nouvelles éditions latines, 1965.

24 Jean Ferrandi, 'Un chevalier noir', *L'illustration*, no. 3599, 17 February 1912, p. 121.

25 Marielle Debos, 'Chad (1900–1960)', in *Online Encyclopedia of Mass Violence*, Paris, Presses de Sciences Po, 2008.

26 Jean-Louis Triaud, *La légende noire de la Sanûsiyya: une confrérie musulmane saharienne sous le regard français (1840–1930)*, Paris, Maison des sciences de l'homme, 1995, pp. 778–9.

27 They were suspected of hatching a plot against the French – something contradicted by the historical source. Bernard Lanne, 'Résistances et mouvements anticoloniaux au Tchad (1914–1940)', *Revue d'histoire d'Outre-mer*, Vol. 80, no. 300, 1993, pp. 425–42.

28 Samuel Decalo, *Historical Dictionary of Chad*, African Historical Dictionaries no. 13, Metuchen NJ and London, The Scarecrow Press, 1977, pp. 8–9.

29 Claude Arditi, 'Du "prix de la kola" au détournement de l'aide internationale: clientélisme et corruption au Tchad (1900–1998)', in Giorgio Blundo (ed.), *Monnayer les pouvoirs: Espaces, mécanismes et représentations de la corruption*, Paris and Geneva, Presses universitaires de France (PUF) and Graduate Institute of Development Studies, 2000, p. 265.

30 Triaud, *La légende noire de la Sanûsiyya*, op. cit., pp. 617–18.

31 Georges Joubert, 'Le faki Naïm', *Bulletin de la société des recherches congolaises*, no. 24, 1937, pp. 5–64.

32 Khayar, *Tchad: Regards*, op. cit., pp. 72–3.

33 Joubert, 'Le faki Naïm', op. cit. p. 31.

34 Ibid., p. 45.

35 Letter from Colonel Ducarre to the commander of the district, dated 1920, reproduced in Joubert, 'Le faki Naïm', op. cit., p. 48.

36 Ibid., p. 49.

37 Report of the administrator (G.), acting as the temporary replacement of M. Lavit, fourth quarter of 1922, reproduced in Joubert, 'Le faki Naïm', op. cit., p. 52.

38 Ibid., p. 63.

39 Mario J. Azevedo, 'The human price of development: the Brazzaville railroad and the Sara of Chad', *African Studies Review*, Vol. 14, no. 1, 1981, p. 1.

40 Mbembe, *On the Postcolony*, op. cit., p. 26.

41 To begin with, it was grown in only the fertile zones of the south; it was later extended as far as the latitude of Fort-Lamy in the 1950s and 1960s. See Magrin, *Le sud du Tchad*, op. cit.

42 Claude Arditi, 'Des paysans plus professionnels que les développeurs? L'exemple du coton au Tchad (1930–2002)', *Revue tiers monde*, no. 180, 2004, pp. 841–65.

43 René Lemarchand, 'The politics of Sara ethnicity: a note on the origins of the civil war in Chad', *Cahiers d'études africaines*, Vol. 20, no. 80, 1980, p. 469.

44 Roitman, 'The Garrison-Entrepôt', op. cit. p. 308.

45 Roitman, *Fiscal Disobedience*, op. cit.

46 Azevedo, 'The human price of development', op. cit., p. 12.

47 André Gide, *Voyage au Congo, suivi de Le Retour du Tchad*, Paris, Folio, 2004 [1929], p. 223.

48 Bernard Lanne, 'La politique française à l'égard de l'islam au Tchad (1900–1958)', in Jean-Pierre Magnant (ed.), *L'islam au Tchad*, Bordeaux, Centre d'Etude de l'Afrique Noire, 1992, p. 107.

49 Félix Eboué's memory is honoured both in Chad and in France (his body is interned in the Pantheon in Paris).

50 Eric Jennings, *Free French Africa in World War II: The African Resistance*, Cambridge, Cambridge University Press, 2015.

51 Azevedo, *Roots of Violence*, op. cit. pp. 75–6.

52 Gregory Mann, *Native Sons: West African Veterans and France in the Twentieth Century*, Durham NC and London, Duke University Press, 2006.

53 F. Aerts, 'Les Tchadiens et le service militaire', *Tropiques: Revue des troupes coloniales*, no. 632, 1954, pp. 60–1.

54 The appropriation of the name of de Gaulle was not an isolated case in Central Africa. See Georges Balandier, *The Sociology of Black Africa: Social Dynamics in Central Africa*, London, Andre Deutsch, 1970.

55 Arnaud Dingammadji, 'La glorieuse épopée des tirailleurs sénégalais du Tchad (1940–1945)', in *Tchad: Page d'histoire*, N'Djamena, Centre Al Mouna, pp. 61–72.

56 The level of education was not very high in the country as a whole, but it was even more marginal in Muslim areas. See Issa Hassan Khayar, *Le Refus de l'école: Contribution à l'étude des problèmes de l'éducation chez les Musulmans du Ouaddaï (Tchad)*, Paris, Librairie d'Amérique et d'Orient, 1976; Claude Arditi, 'Les conséquences du refus de l'école chez les populations musulmanes du Tchad au XXe siècle', *Journal des africanistes*, Vol. 73, no. 1, 2003, pp. 7–22.

57 With the creation of the French Union in 1946, 'colonies' were renamed 'overseas territories'. 'Subjects' in the French empire became citizens, even if all 'citizens' were not equal. On changes in notions of citizenship, nationality and sovereignty between the end of the Second World War and the independence of French Africa, see Frederick Cooper, *Citizenship between Empire and Nation: Remaking France and French Africa, 1945–1960*, Princeton NJ, Princeton University Press, 2014.

58 Lemarchand, 'The politics of Sara ethnicity', op. cit., pp. 457–8.

59 In 1958, General de Gaulle returned to power to preserve *Algérie française*. However, he would preside over the independence of Algeria in 1962, while reconfiguring the French empire in Africa.

60 While representing Chad at an international conference, Gabriel Lisette learned that he would be arrested if he returned to Chad. He stayed in exile.

61 Bernard Lanne, 'La coopération française: un témoignage', *Afrique Contemporaine*, no. 188, 1998, pp. 119–26.

62 Mahmood Mamdani, *Citizenship and Subject: Contemporary Africa and the Legacy of Colonialism*, Princeton NJ, Princeton University Press, 1996.

Chapter 2

1 Max Weber, 'The profession and vocation of politics', in Peter Lassman and Ronald Speirs (eds), *Weber: Political Writings*, Cambridge, Cambridge University Press, 1994, pp. 309–69.

2 It is difficult to date the appearance of the original French term '*politico-militaire*' with any precision. It can be found in a speech given by Hissène Habré on 18 June 1982 (quoted by Robert Buijtenhuijs in *Le Frolinat et les guerres civiles du Tchad, 1977–1984. La révolution introuvable*, Leiden and Paris, Afrika-Studiecentrum and Karthala, 1987, p. 340) but it probably appeared long before then. Robert Buijtenhuijs uses it to refer to the first Frolinat cadres in his work *Le Frolinat et les révoltes populaires du Tchad, 1965–1976*, Paris and New York, La Haye and Mouton, 1978, p. 331.

3 Between 1956 and 1971, the French army fought a counter-insurgency

against the Union des Populations du Cameroun (UPC) and its supporters among the civilian population. This was led by the French and the local militias they trained and armed, although this has long been denied by French officials. The publication of *Kamerun*, a detailed study of this war, led the government to finally recognise France's involvement in these bloody colonial and postcolonial repressions. See Thomas Deltombe, Manuel Domergue and Jacob Tatsitsa, *Kamerun! Une guerre cachée aux origines de la Françafrique*, Paris, La Découverte, 2011.

4 Thierno Bah, 'Soldiers and "combatants": the conquest of political power in Chad 1965–1990', in Eboe Hutchful and Abdoulaye Bathily (eds), *The Military and Militarism in Africa*, Dakar, CODESRIA, 1998, p. 438.

5 See Introduction.

6 Interview, N'Djamena, November 2004.

7 Bah, 'Soldiers and "combatants"', op. cit., p. 440; Mahamat Saleh Yacoub, *Des Rebelles aux seigneurs de guerre: La désagrégation de l'armée nationale*, N'Djamena, Editions Al Mouna, 2005, p. 35.

8 John Lonsdale, 'Moral ethnicity and political tribalism', in Preben Kaarsholm and Jan Hultin (eds), *Inventions and Boundaries: Historical and Anthropological Approaches to the Study of Ethnicity and Nationalism*, Roskilde, Denmark, Institute for Development Studies, 1994, pp. 131–50.

9 For the events of this day, see the testimony of Kayar Oumar Deffalah, 'Le lundi 16 septembre 1963', in *Tchad: Page d'histoire*, N'Djamena, Centre Al Mouna, pp. 45–52.

10 Jean-Pierre Bat, *Le Syndrome Foccart: La politique française en Afrique de 1959 à nos jours*, Paris, Folio Histoire, 2012, p. 206.

11 Y. B. Oulatar, 'L'armée: à quoi sert-elle?', *N'Djamena Hebdo*, 15 October 1992.

12 Vincent Nouzille, *Les tueurs de la république: Assassinats et opérations spéciales des services secrets*, Paris, Fayard, 2015, p. 58.

13 Bat, *Le Syndrome Foccart*, op. cit., pp. 205ff.

14 Golbert, 'Déclaration de l'armée nationale tchadienne à la Conférence nationale souveraine'. Document from the CEFOD archives.

15 Oulatar, 'L'armée', op. cit.

16 Buijtenhuijs, *Le Frolinat et les guerres civiles du Tchad*, op. cit., p. 52.

17 Netcho Abbo, *Mangalmé, 1965: La révolte des Moubi*, Saint-Maur-des-Fossés, Editions Sépia, 1996.

18 Buijtenhuijs, *Le Frolinat et les révoltes populaires*, op. cit., p. 109.

19 As Catherine Baroin points out, the *derdé* had only a very limited role before colonisation. See her *Anarchie et cohésion sociale chez les Toubou: Les Daza Kéšerda (Niger)*, Cambridge and Paris, Cambridge University Press and Editions de la Maison des Sciences de l'Homme, 1985, pp. 75–6.

20 Raymond Depardon, *Tchad 1: l'embuscade* (1970), *Tchad 2* (1975), *Tchad 3* (1976) and *Les rebelles du Tibesti* (1976).

21 Marie-Laure De Decker and Ornella Tondini, *Pour le Tchad*, Paris, Le Sycomore, 1978.

22 In 1979, the third army assumed the name Mouvement Populaire pour la Libération du Tchad (MPLT or Popular Movement for the Liberation of Chad).

23 Bat, *Le Syndrome Foccart*, op. cit., p. 231.

24 The aim of the fires was to drive out the combatants and deprive them of their supply of dates for eating. See Laurent Correau and Goukouni Oueddeï, *Goukouni Weddeye: Témoignage pour l'histoire du Tchad*, Paris, Radio France Internationale, 2008.

25 Michel Goya, 'L'intervention militaire française au Tchad (1969–1972)', *Lettre du RETEX-Recherche*, 2013.

26 Buijtenhuijs, *Le Frolinat et les guerres civiles du Tchad*, op. cit., p. 108.

27 For a description of the 1960s underground movement in the first army, see Buijtenhuijs, *Le Frolinat et les révoltes populaires*, op. cit., pp. 133–9.

28 Gilles Dorronsoro, *Revolution Unending: Afghanistan, 1979 to the Present*, trans. John King, New York, Columbia University Press, 2005.

29 Acheikh Ibn Oumar, 'Quelques réflexions sur l'échec du Frolinat', paper presented at the conference organised by the Forum de la juste voie, Paris, 28 November 2008.

30 Christian Seignobos, who was a lecturer at the University of N'Djamena, recalls that women encouraged his Guran and Arab students to leave the university and to join the rebellion. See his 'Review of *Le métier des armes*', *Afrique contemporaine*, no. 246, 2013, pp. 151–3.

31 Paul Doornbos, 'La révolution dérapée. La violence dans l'est du Tchad (1978–1981)', *Politique africaine*, no. 7, 1982, p. 9.

32 Buijtenhuijs, *Le Frolinat et les guerres civiles du Tchad*, op. cit., p. 416.

33 Baba Moustapha, *Le souffle de l'harmattan*, Saint-Maur-des-Fossés, Editions Sépia, PMCT, 2000, p. 254.

34 Karl Mannheim, 'The problem of generations', in Karl Mannheim, *Essays on the Sociology of Knowledge*, New York, Oxford University Press, 1952, pp. 276–320.

35 Interview, N'Djamena, October 2005.

36 Interview with Gali Ngothé Gatta, N'Djamena, September 2005.

37 Buijtenhuijs, *Le Frolinat et les révoltes populaires*, op. cit., p. 128.

38 Gali Ngothé Gatta and Mahamat Saleh Yacoub (eds), *Frolinat: Chronique d'une déchirure*, N'Djamena, Editions Al Mouna, 2005.

39 Enoch Djondang, 'Pour quelle paix prétendent-ils lutter?', 7 August 2007, Tchadactuel. Available at http://www.tchadactuel.com/?p=100.

40 Ahmed Lyadish, 'L'égoïsme des petits dieux', paper presented at the conference 'Héritage et expérimentation en politique dans les pays d'Afrique francophone' organised by the network Démocratie Effective, Orleans, 31 January 2009. Available at http://www.tchadoscopie.com/article-27646077.html.

41 Robert Buijtenhuijs, 'Les potentialités révolutionnaires de l'Afrique noire: les élites dissidentes', *Cahiers d'études africaines*, Vol. 18, no. 69, 1978, p. 84.

42 Quoted in Ahmat Saleh Bodoumi, *La victoire des révoltés*, N'Djamena, Yagabi, 2013, p. 127. The author, who grew up in Tibesti, was educated in a school created by Frolinat combatants and became a combatant himself.

43 Interview with Gali Ngothé Gatta, N'Djamena, September 2005.

44 Field notes, N'Djamena, November 2005.

45 Interview, N'Djamena, 23 November 2004. Translated from Chadian Arabic.

46 Interview, N'Djamena, September 2005.

47 In 1979, at the Lagos conference, the Frolinat was divided into nine tendencies: the Forces Armées du Nord (FAN) of Hissène Habré, the Forces Armées Populaires (FAP) of Goukouni Oueddeï, the Mouvement Populaire pour la Libération du Tchad (MPLT) of Aboubakar Abderhamane, the Forces Armées Occidentales (FAO) of Moussa Medela, the first army of Mahamat Abba Seïd, the Frolinat originel of Abba Siddick, the Frolinat fondamental of Hadjéro Senoussi, the Armée Volcan of Adoum Dana, and the Conseil Démocratique Révolutionnaire (CDR) of Ahmat Acyl. As well as the tendencies of the Frolinat, there was a political party close to it, namely the Union Nationale Démocratique (UND) of Facho Balam. The Forces Armées Tchadiennes (FAT), led by Wadal Abdelkader Kamougué, constituted the eleventh group to participate in the conference.

48 Jean-Pierre Magnant, 'La guerre tchadienne: une mise au point', *Politique africaine*, no. 35, 1989, pp. 138–41.

49 Peter Fuchs, *La religion des Hadjeray*, Paris, L'Harmattan, PMCT, 1997.

50 This subterranean prison was created by covering with a layer of concrete a swimming pool that had been the preserve of the families of French soldiers during the colonial period.

51 See the documentary film *Talking About Rose* about the opponent Rose Lokissim, who was arrested, tortured and assassinated under Habré. The film, directed by Isabel Coixet, came out in 2015.

52 Marie-José Tubiana, *Parcours de femmes: Les nouvelles élites*, Paris, Editions Sépia, PMCT, 2004.

53 Commission d'enquête nationale du ministère tchadien de la Justice, *Les crimes et détournements de l'ex-Président Habré et de ses complices*, Paris, L'Harmattan, 1993. After years of mobilisation on the part of Chadian and international human rights organisations, Habré was eventually charged by a Senegalese special tribunal (a special jurisdiction created by an agreement between Senegal and the African Union) for war crimes and torture, and crimes against humanity. He was imprisoned in Senegal, where he had fled into exile. The Habré affair is a matter of some delicacy. Idriss Déby himself was a pillar of the Habré regime. He had been Habré's Commander in Chief during the period of violent repression known as 'Black September'. In tandem with the proceedings under way in Senegal, the criminal court in N'Djamena tried Habré's presumed accomplices. They were accused of murder, torture, kidnapping, arbitrary detention, and assault and battery. In March 2015, the criminal court upheld the sentence of forced labour for twenty defendants, acquitted four, and withdrew the charges against four persons presumed dead.

54 Human Rights Watch, *Chad: The Victims of Hissène Habré Still Awaiting Justice*, Vol. 17, no. 10 (A), New York, Human Rights Watch, July 2005; Michael Bronner, 'Our man in Africa', *Foreign Policy*, January–February 2014.

55 The name 'log-tan' refers to two regions in the south of Chad: Logone and Tandjilé.

56 Interviews with women who had lived with codos, N'Djamena and Moundou, 2005 and 2006.

57 The conflict with Libya came to an end with the victory of Chad in 1987. The judicial disagreement was settled in 1994 when the International Court of Justice ruled that the Aouzou Strip was Chadian. However, Operation Epervier continued until August 2014, when it was replaced by Operation Barkhane.

58 See 'Tchad, l'engagement à reculons', in *Libération*, 12 August 1983.

59 Guy Hocquenghem, *Lettre ouverte à ceux qui sont passés du col Mao au Rotary*, Paris, Agone, 2003.

60 Garondé Djarma, *Témoignage d'un militant du Frolinat*, Paris, L'Harmattan, 2003, pp. 221–5, 260–8.

61 'Beri' is the term used by the members of the group when talking about themselves with other Beri. The Beri are better known by the Arab names *Zaghawa* and *Bideyat*, which are used by other groups in Chad as well as by the Beri themselves when they are talking to non-Beri. In Chad, the term *Zaghawa* is often used to refer both to the Zaghawa and the Bideyat.

62 For an eye-witness account, see Zakaria Fadoul Khidir, *Les moments difficiles dans les prisons d'Hissène Habré en 1989*, Paris, Editions Sépia, 1998.

63 Robert Buijtenhuijs, *Transition et élections au Tchad 1993–1997: Restauration autoritaire et recomposition politique*, Leiden and Paris, Afrika-Studiecentrum and Karthala, 1998. Buijtenhuijs is here taking up a notion coined by Jean-François Bayart.

64 On the working conditions of the Commission of Inquiry and the impact of its recommendations, see the account by the Chadian magistrate who presided over it: Mahamat Hassan Abakar, *Chronique d'une enquête criminelle nationale: Le cas du régime de Hissein Habré, 1982–1990*, Paris, L'Harmattan, PMCT, 2006.

65 This was held between 15 January and 7 April 1993. On the CNS, see the work by Robert Buijtenhuijs published shortly after he attended the debates: *La conférence nationale souveraine du Tchad: Un essai d'histoire immédiate*, Paris, Karthala, 1993. See also his 'revised and corrected' reading in Chapter 1 of *Transition et élections*, op. cit.

66 Bichara Idriss Haggar, *Tchad: Les partis politiques et les mouvements d'opposition armés de 1990 à 2012*, Paris, L'Harmattan, PMCT, 2015.

67 Chadian rebellions rarely vanished from the politico-military sphere: when rebel leaders joined the party in power, one faction generally dissented and took up the torch of struggle. It is therefore difficult to give dates for beginnings and endings: the dates indicated here refer to the periods of military activities of these movements.

68 The accord signed in 1992 was broken in 1994.

69 In 1998, the ANR's politico-military activities decreased. In 2003, Mahamat Garfa signed an accord with the government, while most of his elements stayed in the *maquis*.

70 Despite the boycott, a French minister, Xavier Darcos, visited N'Djamena to congratulate Idriss Déby.

71 On the rebel coalitions of 2005–09, see Chapter 3.

72 General Benoît Puga supervised the operations in Chad. He was later appointed the French President's Military Chief of Staff (i.e. military adviser to the President) under Nicolas Sarkozy. He remained in this position after François Hollande was elected. Roland Marchal, 'Military (mis)adventures in Mali', *African Affairs*, Vol. 112, no. 448, 2013, pp. 486–97.

73 Roland Marchal, 'Understanding French policy toward Chad/Sudan? A difficult task', African Arguments, 2009. Available at http://africanarguments.org/2009/06/04/understanding-french-policy-toward-chadsudan-a-difficult-task-1/.

74 Bruno Charbonneau, 'Dreams of empire: France, Europe and the new interventionism in Africa', *Modern and Contemporary France*, Vol. 16, no. 3, 2008, pp. 279–95.

75 Jérôme Tubiana, *Renouncing the Rebels: Local and Regional Dimensions of Chad–Sudan Rapprochement*, Geneva, Small Arms Survey, 2011.

76 Ketil Fred Hansen, 'A democratic dictator's success: how Chad's President Déby defeated the military opposition in three years (2008–2011)', *Journal of Contemporary African Studies*, Vol. 31, no. 4, 2013, pp. 583–99.

77 CSAPR, *Les partis politiques tchadiens: Quelle démocratie pour quelle paix?*, N'Djamena, Comité de Suivi de l'Appel à la Paix et à la Réconciliation (CSAPR), 2013. Available at http://www.acordinternational.org/silo/files/rapport-sur-les-partis-politiques-tchad.pdf. The CSAPR is a civil society network working for peace and reconciliation.

78 Ibni Oumar Mahamat Saleh was arrested when the rebel coalition launched an attack on N'Djamena. Two other politicians, former President Lol Mahamat Choua and the federalist member of parliament Ngarledji Yorongar, were arrested the same day in similar circumstances. They were, however, released a few weeks later. The *Report of the Commission of Inquiry into the events of 28 January to 8 February 2008 and its consequences*, published in N'Djamena in September 2008, concluded that the Chadian government and its army were responsible for the enforced disappearance of Ibni Oumar Mahamat Saleh. After four years of investigation, in July 2013 the justice system in Chad dismissed the case, as the examining magistrate considered that he had not received compelling evidence on those who had ordered, carried out and assisted with this kidnapping and killing. In 2012, the family of Ibni Oumar Mahamat Saleh filed a complaint with the High Court in Paris.

79 Roné Beyem, *Tchad: L'ambivalence culturelle et l'intégration nationale*, Paris, L'Harmattan, 2000.

80 The use of the lexicon of democracy does not exclude bellicose allusions and bad puns: the 2005 mutineers who followed the young rebel Yaya Dillo Djerou named their movement SCUD, an acronym of *Socle pour le Changement, l'Unité et la Démocratie* (Platform for Unity, Change and Democracy).

81 Interview given by Déby to the newspaper *Le Monde*: 'We respond to a military attack by organising democracy right on schedule', *Le Monde*, 19 April 2006. After the February 2008 attack launched by the new rebel coalition, his speeches gave out the same message, witness the one granted to the television channel France 24 on 7 March 2008.

82 Johanne Favre, 'Insécurités: Une interprétation environnementale de la violence au Ouaddaï (Tchad oriental)', PhD thesis in geography, University of Paris 1 Panthéon-Sorbonne, 2008, p. 194.

83 'There was one dead and three wounded among the demonstrators. Arrests ensued. Soldiers indulged in pillaging' (ibid., p. 195).

84 'There were some forty dead, and 179 wounded, of which thirty-one later died from their wounds. Two hundred people were arrested' (ibid., p. 195). According to official figures, there were forty-one dead and 152 wounded: Buijtenhuijs, *La conference nationale souveraine*, op. cit., p. 204.

85 Favre, 'Insécurités', op. cit., p. 195.

86 Ibid., p. 196.

87 Babett Jánszky and Grit Jungstand, 'State, conflict and pastoralism in contemporary eastern Chad: the case of Zaghawa–Tama relationships', in Michael Bollig, Michael Schnegg and Hans-Peter Wotzka (eds), *Pastoralism in Africa: Past, Present, and Future*, London and New York, Berghahn, 2013, pp. 363–86.

88 The value of the *diya* also varies with the age and sex of the victim: the amount paid is usually less for a woman than for a man.

89 Interview, Moundou, 2005.

90 Interviews with ex-combatants of the FUC, Guéréda, May 2010.

91 Not all the FUC rebels were Tama and not all the Tama recruited in the FUC lived in Chad. According to Jérôme Tubiana, nearly 60 per cent of rebels captured by government forces following the failed offensive of April 2006 were Sudanese, usually of Chadian origin: *The Chad–Sudan Proxy War and the 'Darfurization' of Chad: Myths and Reality*, HSBA Working Paper no. 12, Geneva, Small Arms Survey, Geneva, 2008, p. 34.

92 Human Rights Watch, *Early to War: Child Soldiers in Chad Conflict*, Vol. 19, no. 4(A), New York, Human Rights Watch, July 2007.

93 According to Amnesty International, around a quarter of the FUC combatants were minors of between twelve and eighteen years of age. See *A Compromised Future: Children Recruitment by Armed Forces and Groups in Eastern Chad*, London, Amnesty International, 2011, p. 23. According to the educators in charge of rehabilitating former child soldiers of the FUC, most of them volunteered to join the rebels as taking up arms was a way of protecting themselves in a context of insecurity, but some were paid to join up. Interviews, Guéréda, May 2010.

94 Tubiana, *The Chad–Sudan Proxy War*, op. cit., p. 42.

95 In *Daratt* (*Dry Season*), the young Atim's grandfather asks him to avenge his father. Atim is then torn between the duty to obey and the friendship that he eventually feels for his father's killer. The film came out in 2006 and won the Special Jury Prize at the Venice International Film Festival that same year.

96 Interview, France, 2008.

97 Louisa Lombard, 'The autonomous zone conundrum. Armed conservation and rebellion in North-Eastern CAR', in Louisa Lombard and Tatiana Carayannis (eds), *Making Sense of the Central African Republic*, London, Zed Books, 2015, p. 143.

Part II: Introduction

1 Interview, N'Djamena, December 2005.

Chapter 3

1 Janet M. Bujra, 'The dynamics of political action: a new look at factionalism', *American Anthropologist, New Series*, Vol. 75, no 1, 1973, pp. 132–52.
2 Writing about Chadian rebellions, Roger Charlton and Roy May used this notion: 'Warlords and militarism in Chad', *Review of African Political Economy*, no. 45–6, 1989, pp. 12–25. For a typology of African rebellions, see Christopher Clapham, 'Analysing African insurgencies', in Christopher Clapham (ed.), *African Guerrillas*, London, James Currey, 1998, pp. 1–18. Clapham himself discussed the typology he offered in '*African Guerrillas* revisited', in Morten Bøås and Kevin C. Dunn (eds), *African Guerrillas: Raging Against the Machine*, Boulder CO, Lynne Rienner, 2007, pp. 221–33. William Reno offered another typology that comprises five categories of rebels, including the warlord rebels: William Reno, *Warfare in Independent Africa*, Cambridge, Cambridge University Press, 2011. For his first definition of the warlord, see William Reno: *Warlord Politics and African States*, Boulder CO, Lynne Rienner, 1998.
3 René Lemarchand, 'Chad: the misadventures of the North–South dialectic', *African Studies Review*, Vol. 29, no 3, 1986, pp. 27–41.
4 Sam C. Nolutshungu, *Limits of Anarchy: Intervention and State Formation in Chad*, Charlottesville VA and London, University Press of Virginia, 1996, p. 19.
5 Ibid., p. 263.
6 Mats Utas defines 'bigmanity' in 'Bigmanity and network governance in African conflicts', in Mats Utas (ed.), *African Conflicts and Informal Power: Big Men and Networks*, London, Zed Books, 2012, pp. 1–34.
7 Quoted by Bichara Idriss Haggar in *Tchad: Témoignage et combat politique d'un exilé*, Paris, L'Harmattan, 2003, p. 182.
8 Pierre Bourdieu warns against the 'biographical illusion': 'The suggested coherence and directedness of a biography is an artifact'. See 'The biographical illusion', in Paul du Gay, Jessica Evans and Peter Redman (eds), *Identity: A Reader*, London, Thousand Oaks CA and New Delhi, Sage, 2000, pp. 297–303.
9 Buijtenhuijs, *Le Frolinat et les guerres civiles du Tchad*, op. cit., p. 351.
10 Ibid., p. 354.
11 Julie Flint and Alex de Waal, *Darfur: A Short History of a Long War*, London and New York, Zed Books, 2005, pp. 54–5.
12 Buijtenhuijs, *Le Frolinat et les guerres civiles du Tchad*, op. cit., p. 277.
13 Acheikh Ibn Oumar, 'If, by some quirk of fate, the regime were to hold out its hand to me, I think I would not reply with a definitive "no", but I would set out conditions' ('Si, par extraordinaire …'), interview by Lyadish Ahmed, 12 February 2009, Tchadactuel. Available at http://www.tchadactuel.com/?p=3654.
14 Ibid.

15 Interview with Acheikh Ibn Oumar, Paris, March 2006.

16 UFDD-F, 'L'UFDD/F précise au sujet de M. Acheikh Ibn Oumar' ('The UFDD-F gives details about M. Acheikh Ibn-Oumar'), press release, Massaguet, 5 February 2008.

17 Acheikh Ibn Oumar, 'Si, par extraordinaire ...', op. cit.

18 On Soubiane's political trajectory, see Chapter 4.

19 Interview with a member of the CNR, France, 2006.

20 Nour's trajectory is based on interviews with ex-rebels that I conducted in N'Djamena and Guéréda in 2010 as well as on a report: Tubiana, *The Chad–Sudan Proxy War*, op. cit.

21 ICG, *Tchad: Vers le retour de la guerre?*, Africa Report no. 11, Brussels, International Crisis Group (ICG), 2006.

22 The Sudan of the 2000s did not have the expansionist aims of the Libya of the 1970s and 1980s.

23 A.B., 'Les assaillants viennent de Sarh et Bousso', *Le Progrès*, N'Djamena, 21 November 2005.

24 Field notes, November 2005.

25 'Sudan targets Central Africa', *Africa Confidential*, Vol. 47, no 24, 1 December 2006, p. 5.

26 Manalo, 'Arrestations dans le milieu sudiste de la grande muette', *Le Temps*, N'Djamena, 21–27 June 2006.

27 Dassert's trajectory is based on interviews with one of his followers based in France as well as on press articles. See in particular Jean-Claude Nékim, 'Dassert avait intronisé Déby', *N'Djamena Bi-Hebdo*, 17–20 November 2005.

28 Nder Gata, 'Que reste-t-il du serment de Bamina?', *N'Djamena Hebdo*, 22 October 1992.

29 Dassert Djibrine, Gam Ousmane and Bendjo, 'Non à la dérive', *N'Djamena Hebdo*, 3 December 1992.

30 Interview with one of Moïse Ketté's ex-followers, South of Chad, September 2006.

31 Strategies of extraversion were defined by Jean-François Bayart as the leading actors' strategies to mobilise resources derived from their (possibly unequal) relationship with the external environment. See Jean-François Bayart, *The State in Africa: The Politics of the Belly*, London, Longman, 1993; Jean-François Bayart, 'Africa in the world: a history of extraversion', *African Affairs*, no. 99, 2000, pp. 217–67.

32 Interview with a former politico-military leader, Paris, May 2008.

33 Interview, France, 2008.

34 Jeremy M. Weinstein, *Inside Rebellion: The Politics of Insurgent Violence*, New York, Cambridge University Press, 2006. For a critique, see, Yvan Guichaoua, 'Circumstantial alliances and loose loyalties in rebellion making: the case of Tuareg insurgency in Northern Niger (2007–2009)' in Yvan Guichaoua (ed.), *Understanding Collective Political Violence*, Basingstoke, Palgrave Macmillan, 2011, pp. 244–66.

35 Roland Marchal, 'The roots of the Darfur conflict and the Chadian civil war', *Public Culture*, Vol. 20, no. 3, 2008, pp. 429–36; Roland Marchal, 'The unseen regional implications of the crisis in Darfur', in Alex de Waal

(ed.), *War in Darfur and the Search for Peace*, Harvard MA and London, Harvard University Press and Justice Africa, 2007, pp. 177–98.

36 On the history of alliances on the Chad–Sudan border, see Andrea Behrends, 'The Darfur conflict and the Chad/Sudan border: regional context and local re-configurations', *Sociologus*, Vol. 57, no. 1, 2007, pp. 99–131; Babett Jánszky and Tim Jánszky, 'Tchad/Soudan: des alliances changeantes', *Outre-Terre*, no. 20, 2007, pp. 289–300.

37 On clans among the Zaghawa, see Marie-José Tubiana, *Des troupeaux et des femmes. Mariage et transferts de biens chez les Beri (Zaghawa et Bideyat) du Tchad et du Soudan*, Paris, L'Harmattan, 1985, pp. 195–200. The author explains that there are clans, lineages and tribes. The clan brings together the agnatic descendants of a single ancestor, lineage corresponds to a segmentation of the clan that occurs when its members are too numerous, and the tribe brings together clans that share the same territory. The clan is the most important group politically speaking.

38 The Erdimi brothers are the cousins of Idriss Déby, even if they are generally presented as his nephews.

39 Interview, Paris, 11 May 2008.

40 Khalil Ibrahim was expelled from Chad in April 2011. He was then considered a barrier to the rapprochement between N'Djamena and Khartoum. A few months later, he was killed by the Sudanese armed forces.

Chapter 4

1 Field notes, France, November 2012.

2 Alex de Waal, *The Real Politics of the Horn of Africa: Money, War and the Business of Power*, London, Polity, 2015, p. 16.

3 Ibid., p. 57.

4 Interview, N'Djamena, September 2006.

5 Alex de Waal, 'When kleptocracy becomes insolvent: brute causes of the civil war in South Sudan,' *African Affairs*, no. 113/452, 2014, p. 361.

6 Interview, Paris, December 2008.

7 Tubiana, *The Chad–Sudan Proxy War*, op. cit., pp. 36–8.

8 Buijtenhuijs, *Le Frolinat et les guerres civiles du Tchad*, op. cit., p. 427.

9 Sonia Rolley, 'A la croisée des couloirs d'hôtel', Radio France Internationale, 29 April 2007.

10 Andreas Mehler, 'Peace and power sharing in Africa: a not so obvious relationship', *African Affairs*, Vol. 108, no. 432, 2009, pp. 453–73.

11 Alex de Waal, 'I will not sign', *London Review of Books*, Vol. 28, no. 23, 30 November 2006; Victor Tanner and Jérôme Tubiana, *Divided they Fall: The Fragmentation of Darfur's Rebel Groups*, Geneva, Small Arms Survey, Graduate Institute of International Studies, 2007.

12 Buijtenhuijs, *Le Frolinat et les guerres civiles du Tchad*, op. cit., p. 435.

13 The following politico-military leaders were present: Mahamat Garfa, Acheikh Ibn Oumar, Mahamat Ali Hassballah, Hissène Koty, Hissène Lamine, Laokein Bardé, Dr Al-Harris Bachar, Goukouni Oueddeï, Moussa Medela, Brahim Mallah, Moussa Batran and Adoum Yacoub. The latter represented the ANR, which, deserted by its founders, found in him the

leader they needed for the conference. Two leaders refused to take part: Djidi Hissein-Mi and Mahamat Abba Seid.

14 On this topic, see the highly instructive account given by Bichara Idriss Haggar, a political cadre from the CNR (a movement led by Abbas Koty until his death): *Tchad: Témoignage*, op. cit., especially Chapter 5.

15 Stathis N. Kalyvas, 'Ethnic defections in civil war', *Comparative Political Studies*, Vol. 41, no 8, 2008, p. 1063.

16 See Chapter 2.

17 'Tchad: Déby entre rébellion et élections', *La lettre du continent*, 3 February 1994.

18 Laokein Bardé was at the time staying with one of those who had facilitated the accord, Julien Beassemda, whose house was attacked and pillaged. Interview with Julien Beassemda, Moundou, 7 September 2006.

19 Bardé is also said to have demanded the departure of Hassaballah Soubiane, the then prefect of Moundou, and refused the ministerial post that was offered to him. Interviews with five participants in the negotiations, N'Djamena and Moundou, September 2006.

20 Interview, Moundou, September 2006.

21 Interview with a Chadian politico-military cadre, Paris, February 2009; interview with a former member of the FSR, N'Djamena, May 2010. The communiqués of the Chadian rebel movements enable us to follow the complex history of the alliances of Captain Ismaïl. See, for example, FSR, 'Communiqué no 10: fusion des forces', 19 February 2008, available at http://makaila.over-blog.com/article-16909394.html.

22 Human Rights Watch, 'Briefing to the UN Security Council on the situation in Chad and the Central African Republic', New York, 4 December 2008. According to accounts gathered in the Dar Sila, the CNT participated in attacks against the villages of Tierno and Marena: Jérôme Tubiana and Victor Tanner, 'Au Tchad, un second Darfour?' *Outre-Terre*, no. 20, 2007, p. 309.

23 Interview, N'Djamena, September 2006.

24 Interview, N'Djamena, May 2010.

25 Béatrice Hibou, *Anatomie politique de la domination*, Paris, La Découverte, 2011, p. 37. [An English translation, *Political Anatomy of Domination*, is due to be published in 2017.]

26 Ismaël Idriss Ismaël, Vice-President of the FUC, was made Secretary of State for Foreign Relations in charge of African integration, and Raoul Laona Gong became Secretary of State, Secretary General to the Government, in charge of relations with the National Assembly.

27 Interview, Guéréda, May 2010.

28 He was killed in February 2013 on the border between Chad and the CAR by Central African rebels. According to a government communiqué published in the press, he had become a highway robber.

29 Until they were freed in 2011 as part of an amnesty granted by the President to former rebels, the inhabitants of the Dar Tama did not know whether the prisoners were dead or alive.

30 Elections were organised only in the towns considered to be important. Guéréda was excluded from the process. By contrast, elections were held in

Iriba, even though this town, located in the President's home region, has a smaller population than Guéréda.

31 Interview, Guéréda, May 2010.
32 Giorgio Blundo, 'Dealing with the local state: the informal privatization of street-level bureaucracies in Senegal', *Development and Change*, Vol. 7, no. 4, 2006, pp. 799–819; Thomas Bierschenk and Jean-Pierre Olivier de Sardan (eds), *States at Work: Dynamics of African Bureaucracies*, Leiden, Brill, 2014.
33 The MN itself was a coalition of several factions: the FSR led by Soubiane, the Union des Forces pour la Démocratie et le Développement Rénovée (UFDD-R) led by Issa Moussa Tamboulet and the Mouvement National pour le Redressement (MNR) led by Mahamat Ahmat Hamid.
34 Interview with Soubiane, N'Djamena, April 2010.
35 Interviews with ex-combatants, N'Djamena, April 2010.
36 Interview, N'Djamena, May 2010.
37 In April and May 2010, I spent several days with Nahor and his supporters and carried out detailed interviews with two of them. I had already interviewed Nahor several times during his exile in France. I also interviewed Michel Mbaïlemal during his short stay in N'Djamena in May 2010 when he met the authorities to negotiate his rapprochement with the government.
38 Interview, N'Djamena, April 2010.

Chapter 5

1 The MINUSMA is composed of 8,576 male soldiers and only 125 female soldiers; the Chadian contingent is composed of 1,074 male soldiers and 13 female soldiers. Réseau de recherche sur les opérations de paix, 'MINUSMA', last update on 31 January 2015. Available at http://www.operationspaix.net/182-operation-minusma.html.
2 Boko Haram adopted the name Islamic State's West Africa Province after swearing allegiance to Islamic State.
3 The MNJTF is a multinational formation of troops from Benin, Cameroon, Chad, Niger and Nigeria. Its headquarters are in N'Djamena. The African Union Peace and Security Council authorised the deployment of the MNJTF in January 2015.
4 National Assembly (France), 'Engagement et diplomatie: quelle doctrine pour nos interventions militaires?', white paper of the Foreign Affairs Committee of the French National Assembly, 20 May 2015.
5 Such violence is all too common during peacekeeping operations. French peacekeepers in the CAR face questioning over accusations of raping children. These cases have raised questions about how international peacekeeping forces handle suspected abuses by their soldiers. For a gender perspective on peacekeeping operations, see Sarah Whitworth, *Men, Militarism and UN Peacekeeping: A Gendered Analysis*, Boulder CO, Lynne Rienner, 2004; Annica Kronsell, *Gender, Sex and the Postnational Defense: Militarism and Peacekeeping*, New York, Oxford University Press, 2012.
6 Audit report on the armed forces of the Chadian army, 19 February–5 March 2005, p. 26.

7 Republic of Chad, 'Rapport des travaux de la commission défense et sécurité à la Conférence Nationale Souveraine', N'Djamena, 1993, p. 9.

8 Kamougué Waldal Abdelkader, 'J'ai la caution du chef de l'Etat pour réorganiser l'armée nationale', *Tchad et Culture*, no. 67, July 2008.

9 These figures were given on the website on the presidency: available at https://www.presidence.td/fr-news-119.html. On the 2011 census and the subsequent reform, see the end of the chapter.

10 National Assembly (France), 'L'évolution du dispositif militaire français en Afrique et le suivi des opérations en cours', Report of the Commission for National Defence and the Armed Forces, Paris, National Assembly, 2014.

11 Amnesty International, *A Compromised Future*, op. cit.

12 Sonia Rolley, *Retour du Tchad: Carnet d'une correspondante*, Paris, Actes Sud, 2010.

13 National Assembly (France), 'L'évolution du dispositif militaire français', op. cit.

14 Roland Marchal, 'An emerging military power in Central Africa? Chad under Idriss Déby', forthcoming.

15 At this time he was taking orders from General Oumar Bikomo, but he was the de facto leader of the *Fatim*. See Christophe Boisbouvier, 'Armée tchadienne: Mahamat Idriss Déby Itno, un monsieur très discret', *Jeune Afrique*, 14 February 2013.

16 The GNNT was created at independence by the merger of two bodies: the Native Guard of French Equatorial Africa, set up in 1910 as the first police force in Chad, and the Nomadic Guard, set up in 1951, which was a police force adapted to the country's desert regions.

17 According to the 1996 constitution, this *Méhariste* paramilitary body is meant to carry out homeland security tasks: the protection of political and administrative authorities and public buildings, the maintenance of order in rural and nomadic areas, and the surveillance of prisons. However, its real tasks are much wider.

18 Colonel Nadjimdoumgar et al., 'Mémorandum sur l'armée', 1992. See also the 'Fiche à l'attention du ministre de la Défense nationale, des anciens combattants et victimes de guerre pour la sous-commission de restructuration de l'armée nationale tchadienne' ('Memo to the Minister of National Defence, ex-combatants and victims of war, for the sub-commission for restructuring the Chadian national army'), 22 August 1992.

19 Interview with one of the authors of the memorandum, N'Djamena, December 2004.

20 Caporal D. Boïndé (pseudonym), 'Une Grande Muette qui ne peut plus se taire', *N'Djamena Hebdo*, 25 March 1993. See also Mbaïngommal, 'Danyo, le faire-valoir de l'ANT?', *Le Temps*, N'Djamena, 10–16 November 1999. 'Mbaïngommal' means 'the boss does not lie' in Ngambaye, the language spoken in the region of Moundou.

21 ICG, *Tchad: Vers le retour de la guerre?*, Africa Report no. 111, Brussels, International Crisis Group (ICG), 2006, p. 2.

22 Jérôme Tubiana, 'Land and power: the case of the pouvoir Zaghawa', contribution to the blog 'African Arguments', 28 May 2008. Available at

http://africanarguments.org/2008/05/28/land-and-power-the-case-of-the-zaghawa/.

23 The first exception was the appointment of Moussa Faki, the President's nephew, in 2003, at a time when the country was entering the oil period. Indeed, this appointment caused a great stir among the political class, who interpreted it as an attempt to extend presidential control. The second exception was the appointment of Youssouf Saleh Abbas in 2008; he was a Ouaddian who had just returned to N'Djamena after a period of exile in France.

24 Favre, 'Insécurités. Une interprétation environnementale', op. cit., p. 191.

25 Speech by the MP Adoum Mahamat Konto at the National Assembly, 18 November 2005. Remarks were reported in the press: see Sylvain Darma, 'Routouang devant les députés', *Notre Temps*, 22–28 November 2005, p. 5.

26 Interviews with military instructors, N'Djamena, 2005.

27 Interview with female high school pupils in the same class as colonels, N'Djamena, December 2005.

28 Interview in Chad, 2005.

29 Flint and de Waal, *Darfur*, op. cit., p. 24.

30 Interview, N'Djamena, December 2005.

31 Yacoub, *Des rebelles*, op. cit., p. 141.

32 Séby Aguid, a relative of Idriss Déby, had occupied several strategic posts before defecting. In April 2006, he joined the SCUD rebellion and died during the fighting in December 2006.

33 French National Assembly, Rapport d'information no. 2114, p. 229.

34 Adoum Antoine Goulgué, 'Après l'attaque du 13 avril, arrestations et exécutions sont monnaies courantes', *Le Temps*, 17–23 May 2006.

35 Samory Ngaradoumbé, 'Le raid manqué du FUCD', *L'Observateur*, 19 April 2006.

36 On the fear of the Zaghawa, see the article by Issa Mohamed Dargali published on 16 April 2006 on the website http://www.tchadactuel.com (a supporter of the rebel movement of Timan Erdimi) and then reprinted in the press: 'Les leçons de la bataille de N'Djamena: la communauté zaghawa est-elle en danger de disparition?', *Le Temps*, 26 April–2 May 2005.

37 Interviews with political and military cadres, France, 2008 and 2009.

38 Yacoub, *Des rebelles*, op. cit., p. 125.

39 If we are to believe the French soldiers writing in the review *Assaut*, they fired 'like total idiots'; see Yves Debay, 'Le rezzou', *Assaut*, no. 28, 2008, p. 37.

40 Christine Pawlitzky and Babett Jánszky, 'Sources of violence, conflict mediation and reconciliation: a socio-anthropological study on Dar Sila', New York, United Nations Office for the Coordination of Humanitarian Aid (OCHA), 2008.

41 Tubiana and Tanner, 'Au Tchad', op. cit.

42 Tubiana, *The Chad–Sudan Proxy War*, op. cit., pp. 38, 52.

43 Interview, Abéché, October 2005.

44 Interview with a former army supply officer, N'Djamena, January 2005.

45 800 million CFA francs (1.2 million euros) were subsequently found during a search at the home of the paymaster general of the armies. See Daniel

Ralongar N'Diékhor, 'Les déboires du clan au pouvoir', *N'Djamena Bi-Hebdo*, 24–26 May 2004.

46 Interview with a soldier who had become a *bogobogo*, N'Djamena, December 2004.

47 Audit report, op. cit.

48 Interview with 'decreed' officers, N'Djamena, November 2004.

49 Interview with a soldier-trader, Mongo, November 2005.

50 Republic of Chad, National Committee for Reintegration (Comité national de réinsertion), 'Document de cadrage macro-économique et stratégique de démobilisation et de réinsertion en république du Tchad', N'Djamena, February 2004.

51 Interview with a former official of DDR programmes, N'Djamena, January 2005.

52 Interview with an ex-combatant of the MDD who re-joined the army after the peace accord and was then demobilised, N'Djamena, December 2005.

53 Jean-Paul Bel, Sandre Vitali and Youssouf Hunwanou, 'Programme de démobilisation et de réinsertion des ex-soldats en République du Tchad', report for Mission T&B Consult/Channel Research, 2004.

54 The demobilised, who have had a bad press, are often accused of being road bandits. While some of them have indeed become bandits, it has never been proven that there are more of them than there are active soldiers or civilians within these networks.

55 In the first phase of demobilisation (from July 1992 to December 1996), which involved 19,773 soldiers, officers received a bonus of 320,000 CFA francs (around 480 euros), NCOs 270,000 CFA francs (around 410 euros) and privates 200,000 CFA francs (around 300 euros). During the second phase, which concerned 7,270 soldiers, officers received 765,000 CFA francs (around 1,170 euros), NCOs 660,000 CFA francs (around 1,000 euros) and privates 510,000 CFA francs (around 780 euros): CERDO, 'Enquête sur la situation socio-économique des ex-combattants démobilisés', N'Djamena, Centre d'Etudes et de Recherches pour la Dynamique des Organisations (CERDO), August 2004.

56 The process was launched in July 1977, but the pilot project kicked off only in January 1999.

57 The five prefectures concerned were BET, Ouaddai, Mayo-Kebbi, Moyen-Chari and Chari-Baguirmi.

58 Interview with a former official of the CNR, N'Djamena, December 2004.

59 Scene witnessed on the avenue Mobutu in N'Djamena, 3 October 2005.

60 Géraldine Faes, quoted by Buijtenhuijs, *Transition et élections*, op. cit., p. 95.

61 Interview with a senior officer in the French army, Paris, March 2006.

62 Interviews with officers given the task of reorganising the army, and consultation of their archives, N'Djamena, December 2004 and January 2005.

63 Interviews, N'Djamena, January 2005.

64 James Ferguson, *The Anti-politics Machine: 'Development', Depoliticization and Bureaucratic Power in Lesotho*, London and Minneapolis, University of Minnesota Press, 1994.

65 On the discrepancies between the language of official donor documents and the local experiences, see Andreas Mehler, 'Why security forces do not deliver security: evidence from Liberia and the Central African Republic', *Armed Forces & Society*, Vol. 38, no. 1, 2012, pp. 49–69; Marielle Debos and Joël Glasman (eds), 'Corps habillés: Politique des métiers de l'ordre', special issue of *Politique africaine*, no. 128, 2012.

66 Republic of Chad, 'Rapport des travaux', p. 13.

67 Coalition of human rights associations (Collectif des associations de défense des droits de l'Homme), 'Mémorandum sur les Etats généraux des armées: Etats généraux des armées ou réunion des états majors?', N'Djamena, 15 April 2005.

68 Alladoum Nadingar, 'Les Etats généraux des armées se dessinent', *N'Djamena bi-Hebdo*, February 2005.

69 Personal archives of officers of the army consulted by the author.

70 The generals concerned received a flat-rate bonus of 15 million CFA francs (around 22,900 euros) and a vehicle. They also received a flat rate of 4.8 million CFA francs (around 7,320 euros) per annum, over a period of three years.

71 INSEED, 'Recensement et profilage des militaires démobilisés: rapport final', Institut National de la Statistique, des Etudes Economiques et Démographiques du Tchad (INSEED), N'Djamena, August 2013.

72 Marchal, 'An emerging military power', op. cit.

73 David Chuter and Florence Gaub, *Understanding African Armies*, ISS report no. 27, Paris, EU Institute for Security Studies (ISS), 2016.

74 Celeste Hicks, *Africa's New Oil: Power, Pipelines and Future Fortunes*, London, Zed Books, 2015, p. 32.

75 Scott Pegg, 'Chronicle of a death foretold: the collapse of the Chad–Cameroon pipeline project', *African Affairs*, Vol. 108, no. 431, 2009, pp. 311–20.

76 Thierry Vircoulon, 'Oil in Chad: the fragile state's easy victory over international institutions', *On the African Peacebuilding Agenda*, Brussels, International Crisis Group (ICG), September 2010.

77 Pieter Wezeman, *Arms Flows to the Conflict in Chad*, SIPRI Background Paper, Solna, Sweden, Stockholm International Peace Research Institute (SIPRI), 2009.

78 CCFD-Terre Solidaire, *Le Développement piégé: les transferts d'armes et le développement au Tchad (2005–2010)*, Paris, CCFD-Terre Solidaire, 2012. Available at http://ccfd-terresolidaire.org/IMG/pdf/rapport_tchad_ccfd-ts.pdf.

79 Pieter D. Wezeman, Siemon T. Wezeman and Lucie Béraud-Sudreau, *Arms Flow to Sub-Saharan Africa*, SIPRI Policy Paper no. 30, Solna, Sweden, Stockholm International Peace Research Institute (SIPRI), 2009.

80 Ibid.

81 French National Assembly, Rapport d'information no. 2114, p. 149.

82 Benjamin Nickels and Margot Shorey, 'Chad: a precarious counterterrorism partner', *CTC Sentinel*, Vol. 8, no. 4, 2015.

83 Lesley Anne Warner, 'The Trans Sahara Counter Terrorism Partnership: building partner capacity to counter terrorism and violent extremism', Alexandria VA, Centre for Naval Analyses, March 2014, p. 77. The author

notes that, 'prior to deployment, the SATG was highly capable, but as President Idriss Déby feared a coup, they were not given logistics support capability'.

84 The police force killed four people, but the official authorities denied these killings. As Ketil Hansen argues, 'Chad is renowned for both a brutal police force and for a significant discrepancy between what people report happening, and what the official Chad recognises as facts': 'Petrol, price protests and police brutality in Chad', *Insight on Conflict*, 21 April 2015. Available at http://www.insightonconflict.org/2015/04/petrol-price-protests-police-brutality-chad/.

85 The violence perpetrated by the Nigerian army in the north-east of the country is well known. Conversely, little is known about the behaviour of the other armies intervening against Boko Haram. Some eye-witness reports suggest that civilian populations have not been spared in these zones, to which journalists can gain access only if they are embedded with armies.

86 During this assault, led by the Chadian and French armies, there were twenty-seven deaths on the Chadian side and three on the French. The rules of engagement of the two armies are not the same, and the Chadians take more risks. See Christophe Boisbouvier, *Hollande l'Africain*, Paris, La Découverte, 2015, p. 222.

87 Celeste Hicks, 'Chad and the West: shifting the security burden?', Egmont Institute Africa Policy Brief, no. 12, July 2015.

88 This hypothesis was put forward by Danny Hoffman in the conclusion of his book: *The War Machines*, op. cit.

Chapter 6

1 Roitman, *Fiscal Disobedience*, op. cit.

2 Ibid., p. 13.

3 Interview, N'Djamena, December 2005.

4 Correspondence between the author and Marie-José Tubiana, 8 August 2009.

5 For a description of the atmosphere at Ngueli, see the beginning of the novel by Ali Abdel-Rhamane Haggar, *Le prix du rêve*, N'Djamena, Editions Al Mouna, 2002.

6 Karine Bennafla, *Le commerce frontalier en Afrique centrale: Acteurs, espaces, pratiques*, Paris, Karthala, 2002.

7 Interview, N'Djamena, November 2004.

8 Adam Mahamat, 'Activités transfrontalières des femmes sur le pont de Nguéli (Tchad-Cameroun)', *Locus: Revista de História*, Vol. 18, no. 2, 2013, pp. 41–57

9 Interview with members of the association, N'Djamena, 2004 and 2005.

10 The expression is used by the *N'Djamena Bi-Hebdo* editorial board: 'Awad contre la fraude', 11–14 November 2004.

11 'Circular no. 022/MEF/SG/014/DGDDI/DRDCCS/04, for the attention of District heads, Customs offices, and official Customs commissioners', N'Djamena, 5 November 2004 (my emphasis).

12 Hubert Bénadji, 'Awad réussira-t-il son pari?', *N'Djamena Hebdo*, 15–17 November 2004.

13 Ahmat Zeidane and R.S., 'Des contrebandières reprennent services', *Le Progrès*, 28 January 2005.

14 A song by the artist David Warpalé on '*bogobogo*' and '*karang-karang*' contributed to the popularisation of these terms.

15 'Editorial: Bogobogo ou désordre?', *Le Temps*, 21–27 September 2005.

16 Interview with a *bogobogo*, N'Djamena, December 2004.

17 Oulatar YB, 'Les raisons d'un collapsus', *N'Djamena Hebdo*, 1991.

18 Interview with a senior official of the Ministry of Economy and Finance, November 2004.

19 Letter written by customs officials from the Kobé department and addressed to the Minister of Economy and Finance, 28 February 2006. Quoted in Phil de Fer, 'Les douaniers de Kobé manifestent leur mécontentement', *L'Observateur*, 21 June 2006 (my emphasis).

20 Phil de Fer, 'Quand les douaniers rouspètent', *L'Observateur*, 2 August 2006.

21 Interview, N'Djamena, November 2005.

22 Interview, N'Djamena, November 2004.

23 I am not using their real names here.

24 Jean Comaroff and John Comaroff (eds), *Law and Disorder in the Postcolony*, Chicago and London, University of Chicago Press, 2006.

25 Veena Das and Deborah Poole, 'The state and its margins. Comparative ethnographies', in Veena Das and Deborah Poole (eds), *Anthropology in the Margins of the State*, Santa Fe NM and Oxford, School of American Research Press and James Currey, 2004, p. 14.

26 On the history of Guéra and the impact of past wars on the region, see de Bruijn and Van Dijk, 'The multiple experience', op. cit.

27 Interview with the president and members of the *clandos*' association, Mongo, November 2005.

28 My informants referred to an informal committee of Hadjarai notables and the Guéra departmental council of the MPS. Several dates were given.

29 Interview with a shopkeeper, Mongo, 16 November 2005.

30 On the attempted *coup d'état* by Djibrine Dassert, see Chapter 3.

31 The city's cultural centre possessed a television that worked thanks to a generator. Of the fifty people attending the football match, there were two women: a female friend and me.

32 The Chadian press only reported these facts three weeks later. Adoum Tchéré, 'Les militaires traumatisent Mongo', *Le Progrès*, 5 December 2006; Calamity Jane, 'Mongo sous la coupe réglée du com RM', *L'Observateur*, 7 December 2005.

33 Interview with the commander of the gendarme legion, November 2005.

34 In 2005, there were twelve military regions and twenty gendarme legions.

35 Interview with a witness to the mediation, Mongo, November 2005.

36 I was the sole woman under the hangar. Chadian women were inside the house.

37 Speech by Moussa Kadam given on 1 December 2005 and reported in the press.

38 Adopted on 18 November 2005 in Mongo, the motion was signed by MPS militants and allied parties, as well as by opposition parties and civil society organisations.

39 Interview with Colonel Abakar Gawi, Mongo, 18, 21 and 23 November 2005.

40 Abakar Gawi and Khamis Doukoun were relatives. Khamis Doukoun also took part in several insurgencies. He was a colonel in the army when he was arrested. I explain Khamis Doukoun's political trajectory in 'Living by the gun in Chad: armed violence as a practical occupation', *Journal of Modern African Studies*, Vol. 49, no. 3, 2011, pp. 409–28.

41 Amnesty International, *Double Misfortune: Deepening Human Rights Crisis in Chad*, London, Amnesty International, 2008.

42 I interviewed Haikal Zakaria several times in 2004, 2005, 2006 and 2010.

43 Subtitles are not an option since the film must be understood by people who cannot read.

44 Haikal Zakaria has the leading role in Issa Serge Coelo's film *Daresalam*. The film, which was released in France and Chad in 2000, brings to the screen village peasant revolts and the beginnings of the Frolinat rebellion.

45 Jérôme Tubiana and Clotilde Warin, 'This punchline has been approved for all audiences', *Foreign Policy*, 30 June 2016. Available at http://foreignpolicy. com/2016/06/30/this-punchline-has-been-approved-for-all-audiences/.

46 Interview with Haikal Zakaria, September 2006.

47 Jonathan Hill, 'Beyond the other? A postcolonial critique of the failed state thesis', *African Identities*, no. 3, 2005, pp. 139–54.

48 There is now an important body of literature on this issue. For a critical review, see Kasper Hoffman and Tom Kirk, 'Public authority and the provision of public goods in conflict-affected and transitioning regions', Justice and Security Research Programme Paper no. 7, London, London School of Economics and Political Science, 2013. For case studies, see, among others, Tobias Hagmann and Didier Péclard (eds), *Negotiating Statehood: Dynamics of Power and Domination in Africa*, Malden MA, Wiley-Blackwell, 2011; Kristof Titeca and Tom de Herdt, 'Real governance beyond the "failed state": negotiating the education sector in the Democratic Republic of Congo', *African Affairs*, Vol. 110, no. 439, 2011, pp. 213–31; Koen Vlassenroot and Timothy Raeymaekers (eds), 'Governance without government in African crises', special issue of *Afrika Focus*, Vol. 21, no. 2, 2008; Klaus Schlichte (ed.), *The Dynamics of States: The Formation and Crises of State Domination Outside the OECD*, Aldershot, Ashgate, 2005.

49 Reno, *Warlord Politics*, op. cit., p. 2. On the concept of the 'shadow state', see also his *Corruption and State Politics in Sierra Leone*, Cambridge, Cambridge University Press, 1995.

50 William Foltz, 'Reconstructing the state of Chad', in William Zartman (ed.), *Collapsed States*, Boulder CO, Lynne Rienner, 1995, pp. 13–31.

51 Mirjam de Bruijn, 'The impossibility of civil organizations in post-war Chad', in Alice Bellagamba and George Klute (eds), *Beside the State: Emergent Powers in Contemporary Africa*, Cologne, Rüdiger Köppe Verlag, 2008, p. 90.

52 Angelique Chrisafis, 'Impunity and lawlessness the cancer of Chad', *The Guardian*, 16 March 2009.

53 ICG, *Chad: Powder Keg in the East*, Africa Report no. 149, Brussels, International Crisis Group (ICG), 2009, p. 3.

54 Béatrice Hibou, 'The "privatization" of the state: north Africa in comparative perspective', in Schlichte, *The Dynamics of States*, op. cit., pp. 74–5.

55 On the distinction between the 'construction' and the 'formation' of the state, see John Lonsdale, 'The conquest state of Kenya 1895–1905', in Bruce Berman and John Lonsdale (eds), *Unhappy Valley: Conflict in Kenya and Africa. Vol. 1: State and Class*, London, Nairobi and Athens OH, James Currey, Heinemann Kenya and Ohio University Press, 1992, pp. 13–44.

56 See Chapter 5.

Conclusion

1 Michel Foucault, 'Governmentality', in Graham Burchell, Colin Gordon and Peter Miller (eds), *The Foucault Effect: Studies in Governmentality*, Chicago, University of Chicago Press, 1991, p. 102.

2 Jeffrey Herbst, *States and Power in Africa: Comparative Lessons in Authority and Control*, Princeton NJ, Princeton University Press, 2000.

3 Béatrice Hibou, *The Force of Obedience: The Political Economy of Repression in Tunisia*, trans. Andrew Brown, Cambridge, Polity, 2011, p. 284.

4 Ibid., p. 279. Béatrice Hibou uses Michel Foucault's concept of the policing state.

5 Nimrod, 'La poudrière (voyage au Tchad)', *Afrique et Histoire* no. 3, 2005, p. 292. In the article, Nimrod recalls Idriss Déby's response to criticisms lodged against him: 'the dog barks, the caravan passes'. The Chadian press regularly uses the proverb in its caricatures of Déby.

6 In the case of Chad, as in the case of post-war Angola, the renegotiation of the regional and international status is based not on a transformation of the country's insertion in the world economy but on an enabling international context. The recent plunging price of oil may threaten these countries' regional and international status: Ricardo Soares de Oliveira, *Magnificent and Beggar Land: Angola Since the Civil War*, London, Hurst, 2015, p. 199.

7 Séverine Autesserre shows that international actors labeled the DRC as 'post-conflict' despite the continued violence and, more generally, that they tend to consider that certain levels of violence are innate and acceptable in African countries that have been affected by protracted crises. See *The Trouble With the Congo: Local Violence and the Failure of International Peacebuilding*, Cambridge, Cambridge University Press, 2010.

8 Zacharia Mampilly and Adam Branch, *Africa Uprising: Popular Protest and Political Change*, London, Zed Books, 2015.

BIBLIOGRAPHY

· ·

Abakar, Mahamat Hassan, *Chronique d'une enquête criminelle nationale: le cas du régime de Hissein Habré, 1982–1990*, Paris, L'Harmattan, PMCT, 2006.

Abbo, Netcho, *Mangalmé, 1965: La révolte des Moubi*, Saint-Maur-des-Fossés, Editions Sépia, 1996.

Aerts, F., 'Les Tchadiens et le service militaire', *Tropiques: Revue des troupes coloniales*, no. 632, 1954, pp. 55–61.

Ajayi, J. F. A. and Michael Crowder (eds), *History of West Africa*, Vol. 1, New York, Longman, 1985.

Amnesty International, *Double Misfortune: Deepening Human Rights Crisis in Chad*, London, Amnesty International, 2008.

Amnesty International, *A Compromised Future: Children Recruitment by Armed Forces and Groups in Eastern Chad*, London, Amnesty International, 2011.

Arditi, Claude, 'Du "prix de la kola" au détournement de l'aide internationale: clientélisme et corruption au Tchad (1900–1998)', in Giorgio Blundo (ed.), *Monnayer les pouvoirs: Espaces, mécanismes et représentations de la corruption*, Paris and Geneva, Presses Universitaire de France and Institut Universitaire d'Etudes du Développement, 2000.

Arditi, Claude, 'Les conséquences du refus de l'école chez les populations musulmanes du Tchad au XXe siècle', *Journal des africanistes*, Vol. 73, no. 1, 2003, pp. 7–22.

Arditi, Claude, 'Des paysans plus professionnels que les développeurs? L'exemple du coton au Tchad (1930–2002)', *Revue tiers monde*, no. 180, 2004, pp. 841–65.

Autesserre, Séverine, *The Trouble With the Congo: Local Violence and the Failure of International Peacebuilding*, Cambridge, Cambridge University Press, 2010.

Azevedo, Mario J., 'The human price of development: the Brazzaville railroad and the Sara of Chad', *African Studies Review*, Vol. 14, no. 1, 1981, pp. 1–18.

Azevedo, Mario J., 'Power and slavery in Central Africa: Chad (1890–1925)', *Journal of Negro History*, Vol. 67, no. 3, 1982, pp. 198–211.

Azevedo Mario J., *Roots of Violence: A History of War in Chad*, London and New York, Routledge, 1998.

Bah, Thierno, 'Soldiers and "combatants": the conquest of political power in Chad 1965–1990', in Eboe Hutchful and Abdoulaye Bathily (eds), *The Military and Militarism in Africa*, Dakar, CODESRIA, 1998, pp. 430–70.

Balandier, Georges, *The Sociology of Black Africa: Social Dynamics in Central Africa*, London, Andre Deutsch, 1970.

Baroin, Catherine, *Anarchie et cohésion sociale chez les Toubou: Les Daza Késerda (Niger)*, Cambridge and Paris, Cambridge University Press and Editions de la Maison des Sciences de l'Homme, 1985.

Bat, Jean-Pierre, *Le Syndrome Foccart: La politique française en Afrique de 1959 à nos jours*, Paris, Folio Histoire, 2012.

Bawuro, Barkindo, 'Early states of the Central Sudan: Kanem, Borno and some of their neighbours to c. 1500 A.D.', in J. F. A. Ajayi and Michael Crowder (eds), *History of West Africa*, Vol. 1, New York, Longman, 1985, pp. 225–54.

Bayart, Jean-François, *The State in Africa: The Politics of the Belly*, London, Longman, 1993.

Bayart, Jean-François, 'Africa in the world: a history of extraversion', *African Affairs*, no. 99, 2000, pp. 217–67.

Becker, Howard, *Writing for Social Scientists: How to Start and Finish Your Thesis, Book, or Article*, Chicago, Chicago University Press, 2nd edition, 2007.

Behrends, Andrea, 'The Darfur conflict and the Chad/Sudan border: regional context and local re-configurations', *Sociologus*, Vol. 57, no. 1, 2007, pp. 99–131.

Behrends, Andrea and Jan-Patrick Heiß, 'Crisis in Chad: approaching the anthropological gap', *Sociologus*, Vol. 57, no. 1, 2007, pp. 1–7.

Bel, Jean-Paul, Sandre Vitali and Youssouf Hunwanou, 'Programme de démobilisation et de réinsertion des ex-soldats en République du Tchad', Mission T&B Consult and Channel Research, 2004.

Bellagamba, Alice and George Klute (eds), *Beside the State: Emergent Powers in Contemporary Africa*, Cologne, Rüdiger Köppe Verlag, 2008.

Bennafla, Karine, *Le commerce frontalier en Afrique centrale: Acteurs, espaces, pratiques*, Paris, Karthala, 2002.

Berdal, Mats, 'Beyond greed and grievance – and not too soon', *Review of International Studies*, Vol. 31, no. 4, 2005, pp. 687–98.

Berman, Bruce and John Lonsdale, *Unhappy Valley: Conflict in Kenya and Africa. Vol. 1: State and Class*, London, Nairobi and Athens OH, James Currey, Heinemann Kenya and Ohio University Press, 1992.

Beyem, Roné, *Tchad: L'ambivalence culturelle et l'intégration nationale*, Paris, L'Harmattan, 2000.

Bierschenk, Thomas and Jean-Pierre Olivier de Sardan (eds), *States at Work: Dynamics of African Bureaucracies*, Leiden, Brill, 2014.

Blundo, Giorgio, 'Dealing with the local state: the informal privatization of street-level bureaucracies in Senegal', *Development and Change*, Vol. 7, no. 4, 2006, pp. 799–819.

Bøås, Morten and Kevin C. Dunn (eds), *African Guerrillas: Raging against the Machine*, Boulder CO, Lynne Rienner, 2007.

Bodoumi, Ahmat Saleh, *La victoire des révoltés*, N'Djamena, Yagabi, 2013.

Boisbouvier, Christophe, *Hollande l'Africain*, Paris, La Découverte, 2015.

Bollig, Michael, Michael Schnegg and Hans-Peter Wotzka (eds), *Pastoralism in Africa: Past, Present, and Future*, London and New York, Berghahn, 2013.

Bourdieu, Pierre, 'The biographical illusion', in Paul du Gay, Jessica Evans and Peter Redman (eds), *Identity: A Reader*, London, Thousand Oaks CA and New Delhi, Sage, 2000, pp. 297–303.

Bourgois, Philippe, 'The power of violence in war and peace: post-cold war lessons from El Salvador', *Ethnography*, Vol. 2, no. 1, 2001, pp. 5–34

Bourgois, Philippe, 'Recognizing invisible violence: a thirty-year ethnographic retrospective', in Barbara Rylko-Bauer, Linda Whiteford and Paul Farmer (eds), *Global Health in Times of Violence*, Santa Fe NM, School for Advanced Research Press, 2010, pp. 18–40.

Bret, René-Joseph, *Vie du Sultan Mohamed Bakhit 1856–1916: la penetration française au Dar Sila*, Paris, Editions du CNRS, 1987.

Bronner, Michael, 'Our man in Africa', *Foreign Policy*, January–February 2014.

Buijtenhuijs, Robert, 'Les potentialités révolutionnaires de l'Afrique noire: les élites dissidentes', *Cahiers d'études africaines*, Vol. 18, no. 69, 1978, pp. 79–92.

Buijtenhuijs, Robert, *Le Frolinat et les révoltes populaires du Tchad, 1965–1976*, Paris and New York, La Haye and Mouton, 1978.

Buijtenhuijs, Robert, *Le Frolinat et les guerres civiles du Tchad, 1977–1984. La révolution introuvable*, Leiden and Paris, Afrika-Studiecentrum and Karthala, 1987.

Buijtenhuijs, Robert, *La conférence nationale souveraine du Tchad: Un essai d'histoire immédiate*, Paris, Karthala, 1993.

Buijtenhuijs, Robert, *Transition et élections au Tchad 1993–1997. Restauration autoritaire et recomposition politique*, Leiden and Paris, Afrika-Studiecentrum and Karthala, 1998.

Bujra, Janet M., 'The dynamics of political action: a new look at factionalism', *American Anthropologist: New Series*, Vol. 75, no. 1, 1973, pp. 132–52.

Burchell, Graham, Colin Gordon and Peter Miller (eds), *The Foucault Effect: Studies in Governmentality*, Chicago, University of Chicago Press, 1991.

Burr, J. Millard and Robert O. Collins, *Darfur: The Long Road to Disaster in Darfur*, Princeton NJ, Markus Wiener, 2006.

CCFD-Terre Solidaire, *Le Développement piégé: les transferts d'armes et le développement au Tchad (2005–2010)*, Paris, Comité Catholique contre la Faim et pour le Développement (CCFD)-Terre Solidaire, 2012. Available at http://ccfd-terresolidaire.org/IMG/pdf/rapport_tchad_ccfd-ts.pdf.

CERDO, 'Enquête sur la situation socio-économique des ex-combattants démobilisés', Centre d'Etudes et de Recherches pour la Dynamique des Organisations (CERDO), N'Djamena, August 2004.

Charbonneau, Bruno, 'Dreams of empire: France, Europe and the new interventionism in Africa', *Modern and Contemporary France*, Vol. 16, no. 3, 2008, pp. 279–95.

Charbonneau, Bruno, *France and the New Imperialism: Security Policy in Sub-Saharan Africa*, Aldershot, Ashgate, 2008.

Charlton, Roger and Roy May, 'Warlords and militarism in Chad', *Review of African Political Economy*, no. 45–46, 1989, pp. 12–25.

Chrétien, Jean-Pierre and Gérard Prunier (eds), *Les ethnies ont une histoire*, Paris, Karthala-ACCT, 1989.

Chuter, David and Florence Gaub, *Understanding African Armies*, ISS report no. 27, Paris, EU Institute for Security Studies (ISS), 2016.

Clapham, Christopher (ed.), *African Guerrillas*, London, James Currey, 1998.

Clapham, Christopher, 'African Guerrillas revisited', in Morten Bøås and Kevin C. Dunn (eds), *African Guerrillas: Raging against the Machine*, Boulder CO, Lynne Rienner, 2007, pp. 221–33.

Coalition of Human Rights Associations, 'Mémorandum sur les Etats généraux des armées: Etats généraux des armées ou réunion des états majors?', Coalition of Human Rights Associations (Collectif des Associations de Défense des Droits de l'Homme), N'Djamena, 15 April 2005.

Collier, Paul, *The Economic Causes of Civil Conflict and their Implications for Policy*, Washington DC, World Bank, 2000.

Collier, Paul and Anke Hoeffler, *Greed and Grievance in Civil War*, Oxford, Centre for the Study of African Economics, 2002.

Comaroff, Jean and John Comaroff (eds), *Law and Disorder in the Postcolony*, Chicago and London, University of Chicago Press, 2006.

Commission d'enquête nationale du ministère tchadien de la Justice, *Les crimes et détournements de l'ex-Président Habré et de ses complices*, Paris, L'Harmattan, 1993.

Cooper, Frederick, *Citizenship between Empire and Nation: Remaking France and French Africa, 1945–1960*, Princeton NJ, Princeton University Press, 2014.

Cordell, Denis D., 'The Awlad Sulayman of Libya and Chad: power and adaptation in the Sahara and Sahel', *Canadian Journal of African Studies*, Vol. 19, no. 2, 1985, pp. 319–43.

Cordell, Denis D., *Dar al-Kuti and the Last Years of trans-Saharan Slave Trade*, Madison WI, University of Wisconsin Press, 1985.

Correau, Laurent and Goukouni Oueddeï, *Goukouni Weddeye: Témoignage pour l'histoire du Tchad*, Paris, Radio France Internationale, 2008.

Cramer, Christopher, 'Homo economicus goes to war: methodological individualism, rational choice and the political economy of war', *World Development*, Vol. 30, no. 11, 2002, pp. 1845–64.

Cramer, Christopher, *Civil War Is Not a Stupid Thing: Accounting for Violence in Developing Countries*, London, Hurst, 2006.

Cramer, Christopher, Laura Hammond and Johan Pottier (eds), *Researching Violence in Africa: Ethical and Methodological Challenges*, Leiden, Brill, 2011.

Crummey, Donald, *Banditry, Rebellion and Social Protest in Africa*, London and Portsmouth NH, James Currey and Heinemann, 1986.

CSAPR, *Les partis politiques tchadiens: Quelle démocratie pour quelle paix?*, N'Djamena, Comité de Suivi de l'Appel à la Paix et à la Réconciliation (CSAPR), 2013. Available at http://www.acordinternational.org/silo/files/rapport-sur-les-partis-politiques-tchad.pdf.

Das, Veena and Deborah Poole (eds), *Anthropology in the Margins of the State*, Santa Fe NM and Oxford, School of American Research Press and James Currey, 2004.

de Bruijn, Mirjam, 'The impossibility of civil organizations in post-war Chad', in Alice Bellagamba and George Klute (eds), *Beside the State: Emergent Powers in Contemporary Africa*, Cologne, Rüdiger Köppe Verlag, 2008, pp. 89–105.

de Bruijn, Mirjam and Han Van Dijk, 'The multiple experiences of civil war in the Guéra Region of Chad, 1965–1990', Sociologus, Vol. 57, no. 1, 2007, pp. 61–98.

De Decker, Marie-Laure and Ornella Tondini, Pour le Tchad, Paris, Le Sycomore, 1978.

de Waal, Alex, 'I will not sign', London Review of Books, Vol. 28, no. 23, 30 November 2006.

de Waal, Alex (ed.), War in Darfur and the Search for Peace, Harvard MA and London, Harvard University Press and Justice Africa, 2007.

de Waal, Alex, 'When kleptocracy becomes insolvent: brute causes of the civil war in South Sudan,' African Affairs, no. 113/452, 2014, pp. 347–69.

de Waal, Alex, The Real Politics of the Horn of Africa: Money, War and the Business of Power, London, Polity, 2015.

Debos, Marielle, 'Chad (1900–1960)', Online Encyclopedia of Mass Violence, Paris, Presses de Sciences Po, 2008.

Debos, Marielle, 'Living by the gun in Chad: armed violence as a practical occupation', Journal of Modern African Studies, Vol. 49, no. 3, 2011, pp. 409–28.

Debos, Marielle, 'Quand les "libérateurs" deviennent des "bandits". Guerre et marginalisation sociale à la frontière tchado-centrafricaine', in Rémy Bazenguissa-Ganga and Sami Makki (eds), Sociétés en guerre: Ethnographies de mobilisations violentes, Paris, Editions de la Maison des Sciences de l'Homme, 2012, pp. 93–110.

Debos, Marielle, 'Biometric voting in Chad: new technology, same old political tricks', Theconversation.com, 4 May 2016. Available at https://theconversation.com/biometric-voting-in-chad-new-technology-same-old-political-tricks-58663.

Debos, Marielle and Joël Glasman (eds), 'Corps habillés: Politique des métiers de l'ordre', special issue of Politique africaine, no. 128, 2012.

Decalo, Samuel, Historical Dictionary of Chad, African Historical Dictionaries no. 13, Metuchen NJ and London, Scarecrow Press, 1977.

Deffalah, Kayar Oumar, 'Le lundi 16 septembre 1963', in Tchad. Page d'histoire, N'Djamena, Centre Al Mouna, pp. 45–52.

Deltombe, Thomas, Manuel Domergue and Jacob Tatsitsa, Kamerun! Une guerre cachée aux origines de la Françafrique, Paris, La Découverte, 2011.

Dingammadji, Arnaud, 'La glorieuse épopée des tirailleurs sénégalais du Tchad (1940–1945)', in Tchad: Page d'histoire, N'Djamena, Centre Al Mouna, pp. 61–72.

Djarma, Garondé, Témoignage d'un militant du Frolinat, Paris, L'Harmattan, 2003.

Doornbos, Paul, 'La révolution dérapée. La violence dans l'est du Tchad (1978–1981)', Politique africaine, no. 7, 1982, pp. 5–13.

Dorronsoro, Gilles, Revolution Unending: Afghanistan, 1979 to the Present, trans. John King, New York, Columbia University Press, 2005.

du Gay, Paul, Jessica Evans and Peter Redman (eds), Identity: A Reader, London, Thousand Oaks CA and New Delhi, Sage, 2000.

El-Tounsy, Mohammed Ibn Omar, Voyage au Ouadây, trans. from the Arabic by Dr Perron, Paris, 1851.

Enloe, Cynthia, *Maneuvers: The International Politics Of Militarising Women's Lives*, Berkeley, Los Angeles and London, University of California Press, 2000.

Evans-Pritchard, Edward, *The Sanussi of Cyrenaika*, Oxford, Oxford University Press, 1949.

Falquet, Jules, 'Division sexuelle du travail révolutionnaire: réflexions à partir de l'expérience salvadorienne (1970–1994)', *Cahiers d'Amérique Latine*, no. 40, 2003, pp. 109–28.

Favre, Johanne, 'Insécurités: Une interprétation environnementale de la violence au Ouaddaï (Tchad oriental)', PhD thesis, University of Paris 1 Panthéon-Sorbonne, 2008.

Ferguson, James, *The Anti-politics Machine: 'Development', Depoliticization and Bureaucratic Power in Lesotho*, London and Minneapolis, University of Minnesota Press, 1990 and 1994.

Ferme, Mariane, 'The violence of numbers: consensus, competition, and the negotiation of disputes in Sierra Leone', *Cahiers d'études africaines*, Vol. 38, no. 150–152, 1998, pp. 555–80.

Ferrandi, Jean, 'Un chevalier noir', *L'illustration*, no. 3599, 17 February 1912, p. 121.

Flint, Julie and Alex de Waal, *Darfur: A Short History of a Long War*, London and New York, Zed Books, 2005.

Foltz, William, 'Reconstructing the state of Chad', in William Zartman (ed.), *Collapsed States*, Boulder CO, Lynne Rienner, 1995, pp. 13–31.

Foucault, Michel, *The History of Sexuality*, New York, Pantheon Books, 1978.

Foucault, Michel, 'Governmentality', in Graham Burchell, Colin Gordon and Peter Miller (eds), *The Foucault Effect: Studies in Governmentality*, Chicago, University of Chicago Press, 1991, pp. 87–104.

Foucault, Michel, *Dits et écrits*, Vol. 4, Paris, Gallimard, 1994.

Fuchs, Peter, *La religion des Hadjeray*, Paris, L'Harmattan, PMCT, 1997.

Garritano, Carmela, 'Living precariously in the African postcolony: debt and labor relations in the films of Mahamat-Saleh Haroun', forthcoming.

Gatta, Gali Ngothé and Mahamat Saleh Yacoub (eds), *Frolinat: Chronique d'une déchirure*, N'Djamena, Editions Al Mouna, 2005.

Gayer, Laurent, *Karachi: Ordered Disorder and the Struggle for the City*, London, Delhi, New York and Karachi, Hurst, HarperCollins and Oxford University Press, 2014.

Geffray, Christian, *La cause des armes au Mozambique*, Paris, Karthala, 1990.

Getson, Stephanie, 'Invisible, insecure, and inaccessible: the humanitarian crisis in Chad', *Georgetown Journal of International Affairs*, Vol. 9, no. 1, 2008, pp. 137–43.

Gide, André, *Voyage au Congo, suivi de Le Retour du Tchad*, Paris, Folio, 2004 [1st edition 1929].

Girogio, Blundo (ed.), *Monnayer les pouvoirs: Espaces, mécanismes et représentations de la corruption*, Paris and Geneva, Presses Universitaire de France and Institut Universitaire d'Etudes du Développement, 2000.

Goya, Michel, 'L'intervention militaire française au Tchad (1969–1972)', *Lettre du RETEX-Recherche*, 2013.

Guichaoua, Yvan (ed.), *Understanding Collective Political Violence*, Basingstoke, Palgrave Macmillan, 2011.

Guichaoua, Yvan, 'Circumstantial alliances and loose loyalties in rebellion making: the case of Tuareg insurgency in northern Niger (2007–2009)', in Yvan Guichaoua (ed.), *Understanding Collective Political Violence*, Basingstoke, Palgrave Macmillan, 2011, pp. 244–66.

Haggar, Ali Abdel-Rhamane, *Le prix du rêve*, N'Djamena, Editions Al Mouna, 2002.

Haggar, Bichara Idriss, *Tchad: Témoignage et combat politique d'un exilé*, Paris, L'Harmattan, 2003.

Haggar, Bichara Idriss, *Tchad: Les partis politiques et les mouvements d'opposition armés de 1990 à 2012*, Paris, L'Harmattan, PMCT, 2015.

Hagmann, Tobias and Didier Péclard (eds), *Negotiating Statehood: Dynamics of Power and Domination in Africa*, Malden MA, Wiley-Blackwell, 2011.

Hansen, Ketil Fred, 'A democratic dictator's success: how Chad's President Deby defeated the military opposition in three years (2008–2011)', *Journal of Contemporary African Studies*, Vol. 31, no. 4, 2013, pp. 583–99.

Hansen, Ketil Fred, 'Petrol, price protests and police brutality in Chad', *Insight on Conflict*, 21 April 2015. Available at http://www.insightonconflict.org/2015/04/petrol-price-protests-police-brutality-chad/.

Herbst, Jeffrey, *States and Power in Africa: Comparative Lessons in Authority and Control*, Princeton NJ, Princeton University Press, 2000.

Hibou, Béatrice (ed.), *Privatizing the State,* New York, Columbia University Press, 2004.

Hibou, Béatrice, 'The "privatization" of the state: north Africa in comparative perspective', in Klaus Schlichte (ed.), *The Dynamics of States: The Formation and Crises of State Domination outside the OECD*, Aldershot, Ashgate, 2005, pp. 74–5.

Hibou, Béatrice, *The Force of Obedience: The Political Economy of Repression in Tunisia*, trans. Andrew Brown, Cambridge, Polity, 2011.

Hibou, Béatrice, *Anatomie politique de la domination*, Paris, La Découverte, 2011. [English translation, *Political Anatomy of Domination*, to be published in 2017.]

Hicks, Celeste, 'Chad and the West: shifting the security burden?', Egmont Institute Africa Policy Brief, no.12, July 2015.

Hicks, Celeste, *Africa's New Oil: Power, Pipelines and Future Fortunes*, London, Zed Books, 2015.

Hill, Jonathan, 'Beyond the other? A postcolonial critique of the failed state thesis', *African Identities*, no. 3, 2005, pp.139–54.

Hocquenghem, Guy, *Lettre ouverte à ceux qui sont passés du col Mao au Rotary*, Paris, Agone, 2003.

Hoffman, Danny, *The War Machines: Young Men and Violence in Sierra Leone and Liberia*, Durham NC, Duke University Press, 2011.

Hoffman, Kasper and Tom Kirk, 'Public authority and the provision of public goods in conflict-affected and transitioning regions', Justice and Security Research Programme Paper no. 7, London, London School of Economics and Political Science, 2013.

Hugot, Pierre, *Le Tchad*, Paris, Nouvelles éditions latines, 1965.

Human Rights Watch, *Chad: The Victims of Hissène Habré Still Awaiting Justice*, New York, Human Rights Watch, Vol. 17, no. 10(A), July 2005.

Human Rights Watch, *Early to War: Child Soldiers in Chad Conflict*, New York, Human Rights Watch, Vol. 19, no. 4(A), July 2007.

Human Rights Watch, 'Briefing to the UN Security Council on the situation in Chad and the Central African Republic', New York, Human Rights Watch, 4 December 2008.

Hutchful, Eboe and Abdoulaye Bathily (eds), *The Military and Militarism in Africa*, Dakar, CODESRIA, 1998.

Ibn Oumar, Acheikh, 'Quelques réflexions sur l'échec du Frolinat', paper presented at the conference organised by the Forum de la juste voie, Paris, 28 November 2008.

ICG, *Tchad: Vers le retour de la guerre?*, Africa Report no. 11, Brussels, International Crisis Group (ICG), June 2006.

ICG, *Chad: Powder Keg in the East*, Africa report no. 149, Brussels, International Crisis Group (ICG), 2009.

Iliffe, John, *Honour in African History*, Cambridge, Cambridge University Press, 2005.

INSEED, 'Recensement et profilage des militaires démobilisés: rapport final', N'Djamena, Institut National de la Statistique, des Etudes Economiques et Démographiques du Tchad (INSEED), August 2013.

Jánszky, Babett and Tim Jánszky, 'Tchad/Soudan: des alliances changeantes', *Outre-Terre*, no. 20, 2007, pp. 289–300.

Jánszky, Babett and Grit Jungstand, 'State, conflict and pastoralism in contemporary eastern Chad: the case of Zaghawa–Tama relationships', in Michael Bollig, Michael Schnegg and Hans-Peter Wotzka (eds), *Pastoralism in Africa: Past, Present, and Future*, London and New York, Berghahn, 2013, pp. 363–86.

Jennings, Eric, *Free French Africa in World War II: The African Resistance*, Cambridge, Cambridge University Press, 2015.

Joubert, Georges, 'Le faki Naïm', *Bulletin de la société des recherches congolaises*, no. 24, 1937, pp. 5–64.

Kaarsholm, Preben and Jan Hultin (eds), *Inventions and Boundaries: Historical and Anthropological Approaches to the Study of Ethnicity and Nationalism*, Roskilde, Denmark, Institute for Development Studies, 1994.

Kaldor, Mary, *New and Old Wars: Organised Violence in a Global Era*, Cambridge, Polity Press, 3rd edition, 2012.

Kalyvas, Stathis N., *The Logic of Violence in Civil War*, Cambridge, Cambridge University Press, 2006.

Kalyvas, Stathis N., 'Ethnic defections in civil war', *Comparative Political Studies*, Vol. 41, no. 8, 2008, pp. 1043–68.

Keen, David, 'War and peace: what's the difference?', *International Peacekeeping*, Vol. 7, no. 4, 2000, pp. 1–22.

Khayar, Issa Hassan, *Le Refus de l'école: Contribution à l'étude des problèmes de l'éducation chez les Musulmans du Ouaddaï (Tchad)*, Paris, Librairie d'Amérique et d'Orient, 1976.

Khayar, Issa Hassan, *Tchad: Regards sur les élites ouaddaïennes*, Paris, Editions du CNRS, 1984.

Khidir, Zakaria Fadoul, *Les moments difficiles dans les prisons d'Hissène Habré en 1989*, Paris, Editions Sépia, 1998.

Kronsell, Annica, *Gender, Sex and the Postnational Defense: Militarism and Peacekeeping*, New York, Oxford University Press, 2012.

Lanne Bernard, 'La politique française à l'égard de l'islam au Tchad (1900–1958)', in Jean-Pierre Magnant (ed.), *L'islam au Tchad*, Bordeaux, Centre d'Etude de l'Afrique Noire, 1992, pp. 99–126.

Lanne, Bernard, 'Résistances et mouvements anticoloniaux au Tchad (1914–1940)', *Revue d'histoire d'Outre-mer*, Vol. 80, no. 300, 1993, pp. 425–42.

Lanne, Bernard, 'La coopération française: un témoignage', *Afrique Contemporaine*, no. 188, 1998, pp. 119–26.

Lassman, Peter and Ronald Speirs (eds), *Weber: Political Writings*, Cambridge, Cambridge University Press, 1994, pp. 309–69.

Le Cornec, Jacques, *Histoire politique du Tchad de 1900 à 1962*, Paris, LGDJ, 1963.

Lemarchand, René, 'The politics of Sara ethnicity: a note on the origins of the civil war in Chad', *Cahiers d'études africaines*, Vol. 20, no. 80, 1980, pp. 449–71.

Lemarchand, René, 'Chad: the misadventures of the North–South dialectic', *African Studies Review*, Vol. 29, no. 3, September 1986, pp. 27–41.

Lombard, Louisa, 'The autonomous zone conundrum: armed conservation and rebellion in North-Eastern CAR', in Louisa Lombard and Tatiana Carayannis (eds), *Making Sense of the Central African Republic*, London, Zed Books, 2015, pp. 142–65.

Lombard, Louisa, 'The threat of rebellion: claiming entitled personhood in Central Africa', *Journal of the Royal Anthropological Institute*, forthcoming.

Lombard, Louisa and Tatiana Carayannis (eds), *Making Sense of the Central African Republic*, London, Zed Books, 2015.

Lonsdale, John, 'The conquest state of Kenya 1895–1905', in Bruce Berman and John Lonsdale (eds), *Unhappy Valley: Conflict in Kenya and Africa. Vol. 1: State and Class*, London, Nairobi and Athens OH, James Currey, Heinemann Kenya and Ohio University Press, 1992, pp. 13–44.

Lonsdale, John, 'Moral ethnicity and political tribalism', in Preben Kaarsholm and Jan Hultin (eds), *Inventions and Boundaries: Historical and Anthropological Approaches to the Study of Ethnicity and Nationalism*, Roskilde, Denmark, Institute for Development Studies, 1994, pp. 131–50.

Lyadish, Ahmed, 'L'égoïsme des petits dieux', paper presented at the conference 'Héritage et expérimentation en politique dans les pays d'Afrique francophone', organised by the network Démocratie Effective, Orleans, 31 January 2009. Available at http://www.tchadoscopie.com/article-27646077.html.

Magnant, Jean-Pierre, 'La conscience ethnique chez les populations sara', in Jean-Pierre Chrétien and Gérard Prunier (eds), *Les ethnies ont une histoire*, Paris, Karthala-ACCT, 1989, pp. 329–36.

Magnant, Jean-Pierre, 'La guerre tchadienne: une mise au point', *Politique africaine*, no. 35, October 1989, pp. 138–41.

Magnant, Jean-Pierre (ed.), *L'islam au Tchad*, Bordeaux, Centre d'Etude de l'Afrique Noire, 1992.

Magrin, Géraud, *Le sud du Tchad en mutation: Des champs de coton aux sirènes de l'or noir*, Saint-Maur-des-Fossés, Cirad and Editions Sépia, 2001.

Mahamat, Adam, 'Activités transfrontalières des femmes sur le pont de Nguéli (Tchad-Cameroun)', *Locus: Revista de Históória*, Vol. 18, no. 2, 2013, pp. 41–57.

Mamdani, Mahmood, *Citizenship and Subject: Contemporary Africa and the Legacy of Colonialism*, Princeton NJ, Princeton University Press, 1996.

Mampilly, Zachariah, *Rebel Rulers: Insurgent Governance and Civilian Life During War*, New York: Cornell University Press, 2011.

Mampilly, Zacharia and Adam Branch, *Africa Uprising: Popular Protest and Political Change*, London, Zed Books, 2015.

Mann, Gregory, *Native Sons: West African Veterans and France in the Twentieth Century*, Durham NC and London, Duke University Press, 2006.

Mannheim, Karl, *Essays on the Sociology of Knowledge*, New York, Oxford University Press, 1952.

Marchal, Roland, 'The unseen regional implications of the crisis in Darfur', in Alex de Waal (ed.), *War in Darfur and the Search for Peace*, Harvard MA and London, Harvard University Press and Justice Africa, 2007, pp. 177–98.

Marchal, Roland, 'The roots of the Darfur conflict and the Chadian civil war', *Public Culture*, Vol. 20, no. 3, 2008, pp. 429–36.

Marchal, Roland, 'Understanding French policy toward Chad/Sudan? A difficult task', contribution to the blog African Arguments, 2009. Available at http://africanarguments.org/2009/06/04/understanding-french-policy-toward-chadsudan-a-difficult-task-1/.

Marchal, Roland, 'Military (mis)adventures in Mali', *African Affairs*, Vol. 112, no. 448, 2013, pp. 486–97.

Marchal, Roland, 'An emerging military power in Central Africa? Chad under Idriss Déby', forthcoming.

Mbembe, Achille, *On the Postcolony*, Berkeley, University of California Press, 2001.

Mbembe, Achille, 'Necropolitics', *Public Culture*, Vol. 15, no. 1, 2003, pp. 11–40.

Mehler, Andreas, 'Peace and power sharing in Africa: a not so obvious relationship', *African Affairs*, Vol. 108, no. 432, 2009, pp. 453–73.

Mehler, Andreas, 'Why security forces do not deliver security: evidence from Liberia and the Central African Republic', *Armed Forces & Society*, Vol. 38, no. 1, 2012, pp. 49–69.

Moustapha, Baba, *Le souffle de l'harmattan*, Saint-Maur-des-Fossés, Editions Sépia, PMCT, 2000.

National Assembly (France), 'L'évolution du dispositif militaire français en Afrique et le suivi des opérations en cours', Paris, Commission for National Defence and the Armed Forces, 2014.

National Assembly (France), 'Engagement et diplomatie: quelle doctrine pour nos interventions militaires?', white paper, Paris, Foreign Affairs Committee of the French National Assembly, 20 May 2015.

Nickels, Benjamin and Margot Shorey, 'Chad: a precarious counterterrorism partner', *CTC Sentinel*, Vol. 8, no. 4, 2015.

Nimrod, 'La poudrière (voyage au Tchad)', *Afrique et Histoire*, no. 3, 2005, pp. 289–95.

Nimrod, *Le bal des princes*, Paris, Actes Sud, 2008.

Nolutshungu, Sam C., *Limits of Anarchy: Intervention and State Formation in Chad*, Charlottesville and London, University Press of Virginia, 1996.

Nouzille, Vincent, *Les tueurs de la république: Assassinats et opérations spéciales des services secrets*, Paris, Fayard, 2015.

Pawlitzky, Christine and Babett Jnszky, 'Sources of violence, conflict mediation and reconciliation: a socio-anthropological study on Dar Sila', New York, United Nations Office for the Coordination of Humanitarian Aid (OCHA), 2008.

Pegg, Scott, 'Chronicle of a death foretold: the collapse of the Chad–Cameroon pipeline project', *African Affairs*, Vol. 108, no. 431, 2009, pp. 311–20.

Reno, William, *Corruption and State Politics in Sierra Leone*, Cambridge, Cambridge University Press, 1995.

Reno, William, *Warlord Politics and African States*, Boulder CO, Lynne Rienner, 1998.

Reno, William, *Warfare in Independent Africa*, Cambridge, Cambridge University Press, 2011.

Republic of Chad, 'Fiche à l'attention du ministre de la Défense nationale, des anciens combattants et victimes de guerre pour la sous-commission de restructuration de l'armée nationale tchadienne' ('Memo to the Minister of National Defence, ex-combattants and victims of war, for the subcommission for restucturing the Chadian national army'), N'Djamena, Republic of Chad, 22 August 1992.

Republic of Chad, *Rapport des travaux de la commission défense et sécurité à la Conférence Nationale Souveraine*, N'Djamena, Republic of Chad, 1993.

Republic of Chad, 'Document de cadrage macro-économique et stratégique de démobilisation et de réinsertion en république du Tchad', N'Djamena, National Committee for Reintegration (Comité national de réinsertion (CNR)), February 2004.

Republic of Chad, 'Circular no. 022/MEF/SG/014/DGDDI/DRDCCS/04, for the attention of district heads, customs offices, and official customs commissioners', N'Djamena, Republic of Chad, 5 November 2004.

Republic of Chad, *Audit Report on the Armed Forces of the Chadian Army*, N'Djamena, Republic of Chad, 19 February–5 March 2005.

Réseau de recherche sur les opérations de paix, 'MINUSMA', last update on 31 January 2015. Available at http://www.operationspaix.net/182-operation-minusma.html.

Reyna, Stephen, *Wars Without End: The Political Economy of a Precolonial African state*, Hanover NH, University Press of New England, 1990.

Richards, Paul, (ed.), *No Peace, No War: An Anthropology of Contemporary Armed Conflicts*, Oxford and Athens OH, James Currey and Ohio University Press, 2005.

Roitman, Janet, 'The garrison-entrepôt', *Cahiers d'études africaines*, Vol. 38, no. 150–152, 1998, pp. 297–329.

Roitman, Janet, 'Les recompositions du bassin du lac Tchad', *Politique africaine*, no. 94, June 2004, pp.7–22.

Roitman, Janet, *Fiscal Disobedience: An Anthropology of Economic Regulation in Central Africa*, Princeton NJ, Princeton University Press, 2005.

Rolley, Sonia, *Retour du Tchad: Carnet d'une correspondante*, Paris, Actes Sud, 2010.

Rylko-Bauer, Barbara, Linda Whiteford and Paul Farmer (eds), *Global Health in Times of Violence*, Santa Fe NM, School for Advanced Research Press, 2010.

Saïbou, Issa, *Les coupeurs de route: Histoire du banditisme rural et transfrontalier dans le bassin du lac Tchad*, Paris, Karthala, 2010.

Scheper-Hughes, Nancy, *Death Without Weeping: The Violence of Everyday Life in Brazil*, Berkeley and Los Angeles, University of California Press, 1992.

Schlichte, Klaus (ed.), *The Dynamics of States: The Formation and Crises of State Domination outside the OECD*, Aldershot, Ashgate, 2005.

Seignobos, Christian, 'Review of *Le métier des armes au Tchad* by Marielle Debos', *Afrique contemporaine*, no. 246, 2013, pp. 151–3.

Seli, Djimet, *(Dé)connexions identitaires hadjeray: Les enjeux des technologies de la communication au Tchad*, Leiden, Langaa and African Studies Centre, 2014.

Sjoberg, Laura and Caron E. Gentry, *Mothers, Monsters, Whores: Women's Violence in Global Politics*, London, Zed Books, 2007.

Smaldone, Joseph P., 'Firearms in Central Sudan: a reevaluation', *Journal of African History*, no. 13, 1972, pp. 591–607.

Soares de Oliveira, Ricardo, *Magnificent and Beggar Land: Angola since the Civil War*, London, Hurst, 2015.

Tanner, Victor and Jérôme Tubiana, *Divided They Fall: The Fragmentation of Darfur's Rebel Groups*, Geneva, Small Arms Survey, Graduate Institute of International Studies, 2007.

Taussig, Michel, *Law in a Lawless Land: Diary of a* liempieza *in Colombia*, Chicago, University of Chicago Press, 2005.

Tilly, Charles, *Coercion, Capital and European States: AD 990–1992*, Oxford, Blackwell, 1990.

Titeca, Kristof and Tom de Herdt, 'Real governance beyond the "failed state": negotiating the education sector in the Democratic Republic of Congo', *African Affairs*, Vol. 110, no. 439, 2011, pp. 213–31.

Triaud, Jean-Louis, *La légende noire de la Sanûsiyya: une confrérie musulmane saharienne sous le regard français (1840–1930)*, Paris, Editions de la Maison des Sciences de l'Homme, 1995.

Tubiana, Jérôme, *The Chad–Sudan Proxy War and the 'Darfurization' of Chad: Myths and Reality*, HSBA Working Paper, no. 12, Geneva, Small Arms Survey, 2008.

Tubiana, Jérôme, 'Land and power: the case of the pouvoir Zaghawa', contribution to the blog 'African Arguments', 28 May 2008. Available at http://africanarguments.org/2008/05/28/land-and-power-the-case-of-the-zaghawa/.

Tubiana, Jérôme, *Renouncing the Rebels: Local and Regional Dimensions of Chad–Sudan Rapprochement*, Geneva, Small Arms Survey, 2011.

Tubiana, Jérôme and Victor Tanner, 'Au Tchad, un second Darfour?' *Outre-Terre*, no. 20, 2007, pp. 301–15.

Tubiana, Jérôme and Clotilde Warin, 'This punchline has been approved for all audiences', *Foreign Policy*, 30 June 2016. Available at http://foreignpolicy. com/2016/06/30/this-punchline-has-been-approved-for-all-audiences/.

Tubiana, Marie-José, *Des troupeaux et des femmes: Mariage et transferts de biens chez les Beri (Zaghawa et Bideyat) du Tchad et du Soudan*, Paris, L'Harmattan, 1985.

Tubiana, Marie-José, *Parcours de femmes: Les nouvelles élites,* Paris, Editions Sépia, PMCT, 2004.

Tubiana, Marie-José, 'Etre femme et partager la nourriture en milieu "musulman"', conference of the International Commission on the Anthropology of Food, Lasseube, March–April 2011.

Utas, Mats, 'Victimcy, girlfriending, soldiering: tactic agency in a young woman's social navigation of the Liberian war zone', *Anthropological Quarterly*, Vol. 78, no. 2, 2005, pp. 403–30.

Utas, Mats (ed.), *African Conflicts and Informal Power: Big Men and Networks*, London, Zed Books, 2012.

Utas, Mats, 'Bigmanity and network governance in African conflicts', in Mats Utas (ed.), *African Conflicts and Informal Power: Big Men and Networks*, London, Zed Books, 2012, pp. 1–34.

Veyne, Paul, *Writing History: Essay on Epistemology*, trans. Mina Moore-Rinvolucri, Middletown CT, Wesleyan University Press, 1984 [1st French edition: Paris, Le Seuil, 1971].

Vigh, Henrik, *Navigating Terrains of War: Youth and Soldiering in Guinea-Bissau*, New York and Oxford, Berghahn, 2006.

Vigh, Henrik 'Motion squared: a second look at the concept of social navigation', *Anthropological Theory*, Vol. 9, no. 4, 2009, pp. 419–38.

Vigh, Henrik, 'Conflictual motion and political inertia: on rebellions and revolutions in Bissau and beyond', *African Studies Review*, Vol. 52, no. 2, 2009, pp. 143–64.

Vircoulon, Thierry, 'Oil in Chad: the fragile state's easy victory over international institutions', in *On the African Peacebuilding Agenda*, Brussels, International Crisis Group (ICG), 9 September 2010.

Vlassenroot, Koen, 'War and social research: the limits of empirical methodologies in war-torn environments', *Civilisations*, no. 54, 2005, pp. 191–8.

Vlassenroot, Koen and Timothy Raeymaekers (eds), 'Governance without government in African crises', special issue of *Afrika Focus*, Vol. 21, no. 2, 2008.

Warner, Lesley Anne, 'The Trans Sahara Counter Terrorism Partnership: Building Partner Capacity to Counter Terrorism and Violent Extremism', Alexandria VA, Centre for Naval Analyses, March 2014.

Weber, Max, 'The profession and vocation of politics', in Peter Lassman and Ronald Speirs (eds), *Weber: Political Writings*, Cambridge, Cambridge University Press, 1994, pp. 309–69.

Weinstein, Jeremy M., *Inside Rebellion: The Politics of Insurgent Violence*, New York, Cambridge University Press, 2006.

Wezeman, Pieter D., *Arms Flows to the Conflict in Chad*, SIPRI Background Paper, Solna, Sweden, Stockholm International Peace Research Institute (SIPRI), 2009.

Wezeman, Pieter D., Siemon T. Wezeman and Lucie Béraud-Sudreau, *Arms Flow to Sub-Saharan Africa*, SIPRI Policy Paper no. 30, Solna, Sweden, Stockholm International Peace Research Institute (SIPRI), 2009.

Whitworth, Sarah, *Men, Militarism and UN Peacekeeping: A Gendered Analysis*, Boulder CO, Lynne Rienner, 2004.

Yacoub, Mahamat Saleh, *Des Rebelles aux seigneurs de guerre: La désagrégation de l'armée nationale*, N'Djamena, Editions Al Mouna, 2005.

Films

Coelo, Serge Issa, *Daresalam*, Tchad and France, 2000, 105 minutes.

Coixet, Isabel, *Parler de Rose (Talking About Rose)*, Miss Wasabi Films, 2016, 30 minutes.

Depardon, Raymond, *Tchad 1: l'embuscade*, 1970, 12 minutes.

Depardon, Raymond, *Tchad 2*, 1975.

Depardon, Raymond, *Tchad 3*, 1976.

Depardon, Raymond, *Les rebelles du Tibesti*, Agence Gamma, 1976, 56 minutes.

Haroun, Mahamat Saleh, *Un homme qui crie (A Screaming Man)*, Pili Films and Goï Goï Productions, 92 minutes.

Zakaria, Haikal, *Al Kanto, la formation*, N'Djamena, Al Kanto Production, 1993.

Zakaria, Haikal, *Al Kanto, l'administrateur*, N'Djamena, Al Kanto Production, 1995.

Zakaria, Haikal, *Al Kanto et les coupeurs de route*, N'Djamena, Al Kanto Production, 1997.

Zakaria, Haikal, *Al Kanto, karang-karang*, N'Djamena, Al Kanto Production, 1999.

Zakaria, Haikal, *Un Etat dans un Etat*, N'Djamena, Al Kanto Production, 2000.

Zakaria, Haikal, *Sida, prévention sans Frontière*, N'Djamena, Al Kanto Production, 2005, 75 minutes.

Zakaria, Haikal, *2 Février*, N'Djamena, Al Kanto Production, 2010, 45 minutes.

INDEX

. . . .

family members of political figures, problem of, 88, 96
Fatim armed forces, 124
Faya-Largeau, taking of, 50, 51
federalism, 70, 103
Fédération des Etudiants d'Afrique Noire en France (FEANF), 53
fictional soldiers, paid wages, 134
fictitious jobs, incomes from, 134–5
field, relationship of, 5
fieldwork, 18–22
Fontbonne, Paul, 63, 93
forced disappearances of people, 9, 69, 162, 176–8
forced labour, 36–40
Forces Armées du Nord (FAN), 48, 58, 60, 62, 122
Forces Armées Nationales Tchadiennes (FANT), 60
Forces Armées Occidentales (FAO), 49, 57
Forces Armées Populaires (FAP), 51, 55, 56
Forces Armées pour la République Fédérale (FARF), 65, 103–4, 115
Forces Armées Tchadiennes (FAT), 46, 57
Forces Armées Tchadiennes–Mouvement Révolutionnaire du Peuple (FAT-MRP), 63, 90
foreign capital in Chad, 92
Foucault, Michel, 175–6
fragile state index, 167
fragmentation of armed groups, 102
France, 16, 17–18, 23, 26, 30, 42, 46, 49–50, 53, 58, 60, 61, 63, 64, 66, 79, 81, 83, 92, 93, 98, 110, 115, 141, 143, 177; as coloniser, 32–42; bad reputation of, 22; funding

of DDR programme, 138; influence on training of officers, 145; intervention in Mali, xi, 121; opts for policy of indirect government, 34; support for army of Chad, 144; resistance to, 32
Franceville conference, 102, 104
fraternisation by combatants, 7
Free French forces, 38–9
French Cameroon, 38
French Equatorial Africa, 27, 33, 38
Front d'Action pour l'Instauration de la Démocratie au Tchad (FAIDT), 65, 71
Front Démocratique Populaire (FDP), 115
Front de Libération du Tchad (FLT), 47
Front de Libération Nationale du Tchad (Frolinat), 12, 45, 46, 47, 50, 52, 53, 58, 80–5 *passim*; cadres of, 54; creation of, 47; generations of, 52–7; leadership of, 54–5; represents breakpoint, 53; rivalries within, 78; split in, 54
Frolinat Volcan, 48
Front du Salut pour la République (FSR), 105–6
Front National du Tchad (FNT), 65, 72, 103
Front National du Tchad Rénové (FNTR), 65, 72
Front Populaire pour le Redressement (FPR), 117
Front Uni du Changement (FUC), 13, 83, 85, 86–7, 108–9, 131; 3rd Brigade, 73

Gaddafi, Muammar, 50, 60, 81, 88; *Green Book*, 7